HAUNTING
the Korean Diaspora

HAUNTING the Korean Diaspora

Shame, Secrecy, and the Forgotten War

Grace M. Cho

UNIVERSITY OF MINNESOTA PRESS
Minneapolis • London

The University of Minnesota Press gratefully acknowledges the financial assistance provided for the publication of this book from the Office of the Dean of Humanities and Social Sciences at College of Staten Island–City University of New York.

A portion of chapter 4 was published as "Prostituted and Vulnerable Bodies," in *Gendered Bodies: Feminist Perspectives,* ed. Judith Lorber and Lisa Jean Moore (Cary, N.C.: Roxbury Publishing, 2007), 210–14; reprinted by permission of Oxford University Press, Inc. Portions of chapters 4 and 5 have been previously published as "Diaspora of Camptown: The Forgotten War's Monstrous Family," *Women's Studies Quarterly* 34, nos. 1–2 (2006): 309–31. A shorter version of chapter 6 was published as "Voices from the *Teum:* Synesthetic Trauma and the Ghosts of Korean Diaspora," in *The Affective Turn: Theorizing the Social,* ed. Patricia Clough with Jean Halley (Durham, N.C.: Duke University Press, 2007), 151–69. Portions of chapter 6 were published by Sage Publications as Grace M. Cho and Hosu Kim, "Dreaming in Tongues," *Qualitative Inquiry* 11, no. 3 (2005): 445–57, and as Grace M. Cho, "Murmurs in the Storytelling Machine," *Cultural Studies—Critical Methodologies* 4, no. 4 (2004): 426–32. Portions of chapter 6 have been performed in "6.25 History beneath the Skin," a performance art piece in *Still Present Pasts: Korean Americans and the "Forgotten War."*

In chapter 2, the poem "Cheju Do" by Yong Yuk appears courtesy of the author.

Unless otherwise credited, photographs are from U.S. National Archives and Records Administration.

Published by the University of Minnesota Press
111 Third Avenue South, Suite 290
Minneapolis, MN 55401-2520
http://www.upress.umn.edu

Library of Congress Cataloging-in-Publication Data

Cho, Grace M.
Haunting the Korean diaspora : shame, secrecy, and the forgotten war / Grace M. Cho.
p. cm.
Includes bibliographical references and index.
ISBN 978-0-8166-5274-7 (hardcover : alk. paper) — ISBN 978-0-8166-5275-4 (pbk. : alk. paper)
1. Korean Americans—Psychology. 2. Korean American women—Psychology. 3. Immigrants—United States—Psychology. 4. Prostitutes—Korea (South)—History—20th century. 5. War brides—United States—History—20th century. 6. Psychic trauma—Korea (South). 7. Shame—United States. 8. Secrecy—United States. 9. Korean War, 1950–1953—Psychological aspects. 10. Korean War, 1950–1953—Women. I. Title.
E184.K6C473 2008
951.904'2082—dc22 2008018143

Printed in the United States of America on acid-free paper

The University of Minnesota is an equal-opportunity educator and employer.

15 14 13 12 11 10 09 08 10 9 8 7 6 5 4 3 2 1

For my mother

1941–2008

Contents

A Note on Transliteration

All Korean words are spelled according to the Revised Romanization system, with the exception of words directly quoted from previously published texts and proper names whose orthography is publicly known. Although the Revised Romanization system was adopted as the official system of South Korea in 2000, its use has not yet become widespread in the United States. Therefore, many of the works cited in this text use the older McCune-Reischauer system (or variations of it). In a few instances, words are spelled in nonstandard Korean to reflect either a regional dialect or North Korean spelling variations, but these words are transliterated according to the Revised Romanization system. As is consistent with standard practice, I retain the spellings of Korean names as they appear in English-language publications. I follow the Korean naming convention of surname followed by given name whenever the person referenced is Korean, and the Western convention of given name followed by surname in reference to Korean Americans.

Acknowledgments

As befits a writing project about unconscious entanglements, it is both a challenge and a pleasure to try to name all the minds and bodies that have made this book possible. Before this book's becoming, Patricia Clough created an affective-pedagogical space in which thought could unfold, and her commitment to this project has been unfaltering ever since. I am blessed to have found a home in her space. Thank you.

Jeffrey Bussolini, Mitchell Duneier, Hester Eisenstein, Michelle Fine, Jean Halley, Grace Hong, David Kazanjian, Daniel Kim, Rose Kim, Carla Marcantonio, Lisa Jean Moore, Ananya Mukherjea, Ron Nerio, Jackie Orr, Rosalind Petchesky, Salvador Vidal-Ortiz, Jonathan Wynn, Sunghee Yook, and "the book group"—the contributing authors of *The Affective Turn*—have all read pieces of this work at various stages, listened to me talk through them, or watched me perform them. They have challenged me to think in different directions while also encouraging my intellectual choices. Special thanks go to Rafael de la Dehesa and Hosu Kim for providing all manner of support, while also reading drafts of these chapters, at every step of the way. In particular, I am grateful to Rafael for his limitless generosity of time and spirit and for absorbing much of the excess energy that was produced while writing this book so that I could maintain enough coherence to finish it.

I thank Hosu for being my intellectual partner of many years, for providing the translation of Korean source materials into English, and for giving me the courage to look for my Korean tongue. Both of them have taught me the meaning of shared experience. I also give thanks to Allen Shelton and Nayan Shah for their invitations to speak and perform pieces of this work, from which I was able to open myself to new networks of thought, and to bell hooks for introducing me to Theresa Hak Kyung Cha. April Burns, Gillian Chi, and Emiliano Valerio, as members of my New York family, have made long-term investments of their emotional resources in my work and life. I am grateful to be part of this community in which risk taking is enabled by love and compassion.

I am indebted to the collectives that inevitably informed "my" project. Thanks to all the artists and coordinators of *Still Present Pasts: Korean Americans and the "Forgotten War"* for recognizing my creative potential and for sharing theirs with me. I give thanks to Ramsay Liem and Deann Borshay Liem for responding to my countless queries as I crafted this book; to Yul-san Liem, Injoo Whang, and Ji Young Yoo for granting me permission to reproduce their visual artworks; and to the oral history participants on whom the project was based for having the courage to bring private grief into public discourse. I am grateful to the Korea Education and Exposure Program for offering me a wealth of information and inspiration that shaped my process of revision and to the Park Slope Foundation Program for providing refuge and reminding me of the importance of gratitude.

Without my blood family, I would have had no motivation to write. My deepest gratitude goes to my mother for leading the way, to her sister for being my living link to the peninsula, and to my father for taking responsibility. In ways that I have yet to fully comprehend, my mother and her kin created this book with me. To those who would have preferred that I keep quiet, my wish is that you will read with compassionate eyes.

Finally, I acknowledge the various sources of institutional support I have received. I am grateful to the Professional Staff Congress of the City University of New York awards program for funding parts of this research and to Amal Othman, my research assistant at the College of Staten Island, for fact checking portions of the text. At the University of Minnesota Press, Jason Weidemann was extremely generous in his editorial feedback; perhaps more important, he has demonstrated an unwavering enthusiasm about my project. Adam Brunner gave me the most prompt, patient, and reassuring help I could have hoped for. In the final stages, Marilyn Martin and Nancy Sauro did a meticulous job of copyediting. To all the staff behind the scenes at the Press, thank you. I could not have made a better choice.

Introduction
The Fabric of Erasure

What haunts are not the dead, but the gaps left within us by the secrets of others . . . the burial of an unspeakable fact . . . like a ventriloquist, like a stranger within.

—Nicolas Abraham and Maria Torok, *The Shell and the Kernel*

My life seemed a lot like the lives of other kids around me, but there always seemed to be this tension and anxiety, which was sort of going through my family like an unhappy wind; there were silences which became part of the fabric of our daily lives.

—Kevin Ryu, *Still Present Pasts*

An Uncertain Beginning

I want to tell you a story, not of anything in particular that happened in my family, but of how silence came to define my daily fabric.[1] I'm uncertain as to when or where this story begins, but one version of it begins in a small rural town in the United States.

Most nights, when my father wasn't stationed somewhere far and away, we ate dinners together, "as a family." He always made it a point to say grace before every meal, to give thanks for the abundance of food on our plates, because this was an abundance that had been unavailable during his own childhood. In many ways, we were among the fortunate. My father had worked his way out of poverty to become one of the wealthy in a poor community. He enjoyed relatively little of the fruits of his own labor, but instead worked for the benefit of the next generation. And there I was, poised to become upwardly mobile, Ivy League educated, and well assimilated into my parents' American dream. So my father said grace before every family dinner, and then we sat together silently, eating the meals my mother cooked. Although I know she was there at the table, I have some vague memory

that she was, at the same time, not there but somewhere in the background.

It would take time to flesh out the fullness of my mother's seeming absence from our silent family dinners. Over time, I would come to know that this was not the norm everywhere, and my curiosity would mount about what could have produced such a dynamic. The abnormalities in my family life were barely perceived silences that blew through our house from time to time before settling into the background. But there was also a special quality to our wind, which I now know was somehow related to that sense of my mother's being both there and not there. Eventually, my ear would become attuned to background noise. And even, or perhaps especially, when you are explicitly taught to keep quiet and not ask too many questions, you can't resist pulling on that thread of familiar silence once the edges of the fabric have begun to fray.

In 1973, Oakville was a lot like it is now. It was a community of hardworking white families, many of whom had lived there for generations, passing down homes and businesses and farms from fathers to sons.

There were no Koreans in Oakville in 1973, when we arrived. Adults spoke in hushed voices, speculating about what circumstances might have led to our landing in their town. But the children were blunt. They asked if my mother was a war bride and if my father was in fact my real father. My mother taught me to ignore such questions about where we had come from and why we were there. She taught me this by her own example of not answering, even when it was her own child asking the questions. If I wanted to know about her life in Korea, she would stare silently at some spot on the wall until the intensity of her gaze compelled me to be quiet, too. It was as if not speaking might make us seem less strange. My father was the only one in our family who was not a stranger in Oakville. His roots in that town had been laid down long before.

Over the course of years, there was a slow trickle of other families like ours settling in. American men with their Korean wives and children, Korean wives who led lives of isolation and were the subject of neighborhood gossip. My mother's life was lonely, too, until, one by one, other members of her family started to come. What I remember now was that my father was very tolerant of having our house so full of Koreans. Despite the presence of my mother's family during much of my childhood, there was still an absence of a story about my mother's family and her life in Korea and the circumstances under which we had moved to the United States.

And there were words that remained unspoken in my house, words that I would not come to know until years into my adulthood, words about which my mother only recently asked, "Who taught you the meaning of that?"

Yanggongju. Yankee whore. Western princess. GI bride. *Yanggalbo. Yangssaekshi.* GI's plaything. UN lady. Bar girl. Entertainment hostess. *Wianbu.* Fallen woman. Formerly a comfort woman. Formerly called a comfort woman. Daughter of a comfort woman. Camptown prostitute. Military bride.

According to Nicolas Abraham and Maria Torok, "These are often the very words that rule an entire family's history," unmentionable words that "give sustenance to the phantom."[2] *Yanggongju,* literally meaning "Western princess," broadly refers to a Korean woman who has sexual relations with Americans; it is most often used pejoratively to refer to a woman who is a prostitute for the U.S. military. It is a term that has been translated in various ways and whose meanings have shifted according to specific historical and political contexts.[3] This word that is so full of meaning is at the same time an unspeakable and "phantomogenic" word for the Korean diaspora.[4] The process of nurturing a ghost through shame and secrecy has made *yanggongju* both central and subjugated in the story that I want to tell.

The woman who provides sexual labor for the U.S. military is at once a hypervisible object of loathing and desire for Koreans on the peninsula and a shadowy figure hidden in the collective psyche of the Korean diaspora. She is the Westernized woman working in the bars around U.S. military camptowns who is officially condemned by both the Korean and U.S. governments but unofficially praised for providing R&R to the American soldiers and dollars to the Korean economy. She is both the patriot who serves her country by keeping U.S. interests engaged and the tragic victim of U.S. imperialism who fans the flames of anti-American politics. She is the woman who simultaneously provokes her compatriots' hatred because of her complicity with Korea's subordination and inspires their envy because she is within arm's reach of the American dream. She is the dutiful daughter who works to support the very same family that shuns her, the serviceman's wife who becomes her family's hope for the future, the protective mother who hides her past from her children. She is a representation of over a million Korean women who have worked in prostitution for the U.S. military and of over 100,000 who have married American GIs. She is a representation of these real Korean women, and yet still a figure built out of layers of collective trauma and fantasy. The Korean woman who provides her sexual labor to Americans, whether through marriage or prostitution, paradoxically emerges as the ghostly figure of all that has been erased.

I want to tell you a story about this figure, although I am uncertain about where the story begins or whether a logical beginning even exists. There is a certain chronology, some would say starting with the Korean War, which was fought from 1950 to 1953, but some would argue that her story started in 1945 with the arrival of U.S. troops on the Korean peninsula, while others would locate her beginning earlier still, with the conscription of comfort women for the Japanese military. There is a chronology that is useful to keep in mind, but the story I want to tell is about the ways in which the figure of the yanggongju gets its very life from the effects of trauma, and the temporality of trauma is never faithful to linear timelines.

Entry Points

> Somewhere, sometime, something was lost, but no story can be told about it; no memory can retrieve it.
>
> —Judith Butler, "After Loss, What Then?"

As an embodiment of the losses of Korea's colonial and post-colonial history—the deracination from indigenous language and culture under Japanese imperialism, the loss of autonomy under U.S. military dominance since 1945, the decimation of the peninsula and its people during the Korean War, and the deferral of the war's resolution—the yanggongju is the embodiment of the accumulation of often unacknowledged grief from these events. Beneath each of these instances of trauma, there are stories to be told, yet the yanggongju does not lend herself to an easy narrative. How does one tell a story about the figure of a woman who has been both very present and often hidden in the history of U.S.–Korea relations, particularly when that figure embodies a trauma that forecloses memory? And what might such an uncertain telling yield? If, in the words of David Eng and David Kazanjian, "what is lost is only known by what remains of it, by how these remains are produced, read, and sustained," the study of such a figure presents an opportunity to engage in and develop new reading and writing practices.[5] There are multiple points of entry into this project of excavating the remnants of trauma so that they can be pieced together to tell a story about the yanggongju as a figure of loss and creativity, but I offer three. Throughout the remainder of this text I will be returning to these three incipient moments rather than building a progressive narrative.

The most recent introduction to this story began in the early 1990s, when the abuses of Korean women's sexual labor gained unprecedented visibility, and this is the beginning that is perhaps most revealing about the past, particularly about how the past is brought to bear on the present. In December 1991, Ha Koon Ja was one of three elderly women to come out as a former comfort woman for the Japanese Imperial Army, publicly shaming her nation, her colonizers, and herself.[6] Although the secret that broke from her lips was her own, it had haunted those around her, including activists who had persuaded Ha Koon Ja and the other women to "travel . . . from fifty years in the past to awaken the world from a collective amnesia about Imperial Japan's massive enslavement of Asian women," and file a lawsuit against the Japanese government for the systematic recruitment and abduction of Korean women for military sex work.[7] This was the first occasion on which these women's experiences were openly recognized. The public nature of their speaking triggered others to come out as former comfort women, and the international media further exposed these women's stories. What is more interesting than their speaking is the fact of their silence for the fifty years prior to December 1991. What appeared to be a trauma of the past made itself present in Korean national consciousness. Although the women who took legal action against the Japanese government managed to expose the atrocities of a hidden chapter of Korean history, the official Japanese position has ranged from refusal to make a formal apology to outright denial that such abuses occurred, thus further enforcing these women's silence and demonstrating how this trauma has yet to be resolved after so many years of bringing it to the surface.[8]

The group of women who were brave enough to speak out are only a small fraction of the women who were conscripted into sexual labor for the Japanese. The others remain silent, and those who have died probably believed that their secrets would be laid to rest with them. Cho'e Myŏngsun's testimony expresses this desire for secrecy, even among those who have gone public: "I have lived looking forward only to death, and without telling anybody my story. My tribulation has remained buried deep in my heart. . . . My story, as hidden as it is from those around me, will follow me to my grave."[9]

As Abraham and Torok's work on "transgenerational haunting" suggests, an unspeakable trauma does not die out with the person who first experienced it. Rather, it takes on a life of its own, emerging from the spaces where secrets are concealed: "*The phantom which returns to haunt bears witness to the existence of the dead buried within the other.*"[10] During those fifty years when the Korean comfort women tried to maintain silence about their sexual enslavement, their secrets were already being transmitted to the next generations of women, some of whom would follow (or be led into) the same path of sexual servitude. Some research suggests that early generations of camptown sex workers were the daughters of former comfort women who had inherited the secrets of their family's history of forced sexual labor. The comfort woman, or *wianbu,* is the yanggongju's ghost.

On the heels of this "breaking silence" by the surviving wianbu comes the haunting presence of the dead yanggongju, who would become a spectral force that made visible the continuing traumas of U.S. military domination. In October 1992, a Korean sex worker named Yun Geum-i was murdered by a U.S. serviceman who had been one of her clients, and this particular killing of a camptown sex worker renewed anti–U.S. activism both on the peninsula and among transnational activist groups. What distinguished this incident was that Yun's body did not rest beneath the shame of what Koreans preferred to keep quiet about, nor did she submit to the U.S. military's power to disappear women like her. Yun's murder sparked massive anti–U.S. protests across the southern half of the peninsula, to the extent that her murderer became the first U.S. serviceman to be tried in Korean courts. October 1992 was certainly not the first time a camptown sex worker had been killed, but it was the first time the general public rallied around the figure of the yanggongju. The dead yanggongju set into motion not only a surge of political protests but also a proliferation of writing about Yun in particular, and the yanggongju more generally, among Korean and Korean American scholars.[11] The exposure of Korean women's sexual labor in the 1990s did not simply reveal some sordid secret; it unleashed the traumatic effects of colonization and war that had been accumulating in the Korean diasporic unconscious for fifty years. The surfacing of ghosts yielded an intensification of haunting in which the yanggongju became overinvested with conflicting feelings of grief, hope, shame, and rage. While many surviving comfort women and their supporters wished to dissociate themselves from the yanggongju, both figures emerged from historical and political contexts that were similarly haunted by militarized sexual violence and imperial domination. The next entry point speaks further to the continuity between wianbu and yanggongju.

The second version of the story begins in 1945. The end of World War II marked a critical juncture in the history of the United States' ascent to global power through the development of technologies of militarism and capitalism, as well as an instance of incipient loss of that very power, because the West's metanarratives would begin to unravel in the post-1945 era. The Korean peninsula would serve both as a living laboratory for technologies of domination and as a site of contestation over the United States' fantasy of itself as a nation of saviors. On September 8, 1945,

U.S. troops began an occupation of Korea that would officially last until the inception of the South Korean state in 1948, but troops have remained there ever since. For Koreans, September 1945 was a moment of liberation just days after the end of a thirty-five-year period of brutal colonization by Japan, but it also heralded the beginning of an era of U.S. military domination on the southern half of the peninsula that continues to this day. It was a psychic space between two wars, one of which would be forgotten. In the context of the making of the yanggongju, September 1945 signaled the transition between the system of sexual slavery set up for the Japanese Imperial Army (the comfort stations) and the system of camptown prostitution set up for the U.S. military *(gijichon)*.[12] It was a moment in which the traumas from the past encountered the traumas from the future. For the Koreans who had been forced into laboring abroad for the Japanese, September 1945 was a moment of return to an alienated homeland that was already divided and soon to be devastated again. The yanggongju bears the traces of this devastation as a haunted and haunting figure that transmits her trauma across boundaries of time and space. September 1945 and its aftermath, the Korean War and its aftermath, are in the past, but they are not over. There are endless ways in which to enter this story, but I will tell you just one more beginning.

On June 25, 1950, my father celebrated his thirty-first birthday. He was a man who valued thrift and hard work and had hopes of raising a family. He spent most of his life in the rural community of Oakville. He began farming as soon as he was old enough to walk, and by the age of thirty-one had opened a small butcher shop.[13] He had rarely traveled outside his home state, so on this day he was probably not thinking about the battles that were being waged in a country most people in his town had never heard of. Most Americans, if they knew where Korea was, thought it was part of Japan or China.[14] My father had already served in the U.S. Navy during World War II and had no aspirations of a career in the military, so he put foreign affairs out of mind once he returned

from duty. After the war, he concerned himself only with small-town life—raising his pigs, running his shop, and planning for the day when a child would bear his name. My father's thirty-first birthday was probably unremarkable. Most likely, he did his day's work as usual and later enjoyed a dinner at home in the company of his wife. He could not have imagined the importance of the events that took place on this particular birthday that appeared to be like any other—that the war that had erupted half a world away would start the slow motor of desire and necessity that would pull him there to that unknown country and to a woman who was not his wife.

June 25, 1950, was officially the first day of the Korean War, although combatants from the north and south had been exchanging fire across the thirty-eighth parallel for nearly two years prior to that. June 25, 1950, was the day that the Korean War escalated beyond a civil war fought by guerrilla armies to a conflict taken up by Cold War superpowers, and for the United States, this would be an important moment in its long-term commitment to war. U.S. and U.N. forces began bombing north of the thirty-eighth parallel, but in a matter of weeks both the North Korean Army and the Allied forces were targeting cities and towns in the south as well. The Korean War set into motion a massive migration in which millions of people fled in search of safety. They retreated to small villages that were not yet targets or hid in tunnels or basements of abandoned houses.

I'm not sure at what point my mother and her family were forced to leave their home and belongings and the very record of their existence. Their family photographs were burned up along with everything else, and it was as if my mother's memories were annihilated, too. My mother took flight and became part of the hordes of refugees pictured in documentary accounts of the war, but she does not talk about this. The constant streaming of refugees left millions separated from their families, the vast majority of whom would never be reunited because

Waiting for assistance: 12,500 refugees.

they found themselves on opposite sides of the thirty-eighth parallel in 1953. But millions more died during their search for safety. They drowned crossing rivers, perished from disease and starvation, or were targets of military strikes. Some of the lost simply vanished or joined the millions of unclaimed bodies buried in mass graves. Among the dead and disappeared is my mother's brother, and perhaps other family members who have not been memorialized through a narrative about what was lost during the war. But rarely does my mother speak of the war or of any of the details about her life before America.

The Condition of Diaspora

Ramsay Liem's groundbreaking oral history project involving Korean War survivors and their children revealed that for the first generation—those who had experienced the war firsthand as children and young adults—memories of the war were still very much alive but had remained buried in silence for the duration of their lives in the United States. The second generation, however, having grown up in the United States with neither their parents' storytelling nor a public discourse about the Korean War, told a collective oral history in which they felt affected by some inarticulate presence that had left its imprint on what seemed to be their normal everyday lives. One man said that because of his parents' refusal to talk about their life experiences, *their past* acted on *his present.* "For me," he said, "it is not the past. It carries forward into my life. It carries forward into my sisters' lives . . . as a hole."[15] This experience of the children of Korean War survivors—having been haunted by silences that take the form of an "unhappy wind," "a hole," or some other intangible or invisible force—reflects the notion that an unresolved trauma is unconsciously passed from one generation to the next. Abraham and Torok's original theory of transgenerational haunting was based on work conducted in the 1960s with the adult children of Holocaust survivors, as well as others whose collective histories were traumatic. Their clients' preoccupation with silences in their families, or their acting out of traumas with which they had no direct experience, provided evidence of their being haunted by the unconscious of others. What is important to note here is that the haunting effect is produced not so much by the original trauma as by the fact of its being kept hidden. It is precisely within the gap in conscious knowledge about one's family history that secrets turn into phantoms.

While the traumas inherited by the second generation in Abraham and Torok's work were personal, they were also located within the legacy of the Holocaust as the paradigmatic collective trauma of the twentieth century. I want to offer the Korean diaspora in the United States as another site of transgenerational haunting, one that parallels the site in Abraham and Torok's original research in that the ghost is engendered in the private realm of family secrets, secrets that are inextricable from the abuses of political power. Every family has its ghosts, but this particular population serves as an interesting test case for Abraham and Torok's theory within the contexts of contemporary U.S. society and renewed expansion of the U.S. military. Especially significant is the fact that Koreans have been social scientifically constructed as one of the most successful immigrant groups to land on U.S. soil during the second half of the twentieth century, one whose measurable success has eclipsed the effects of trauma. While sociological literature on immigration often classifies Koreans as part of the post-1965 demographic trend that diversified the ethnic and national makeup of immigrants in the United States, the main impetus for Koreans' arrival came before the 1965 Immigration Act. The often omitted aspect of the story is that the Korean War, and particularly the United States' role in it, is what set Korean migration into motion. But this is something that we do not talk about—not in sociological stories of immigration and assimilation, not in public discourse about U.S.–Korea relations or military practices, and not in families like mine where someone survived the horrors of war to bring us here. The naming of the Korean War as "the Forgotten War" in the United States marks this event as a black hole in collective memory. Neither the general population nor second-generation Koreans in the United States have much conscious awareness of it. When such forgetting is made official, one must question what the psychic implications are for the diaspora that arrived here as its result.

The Korean diaspora in the United States has been haunted by the traumatic effects of what we are not allowed to know—the terror and devastation inflicted by the Korean War, the failure to resolve it, and the multiple silences surrounding this violent history. But it is not enough to say that the diaspora is transgenerationally haunted by the unspoken traumas of war; it is constituted by that haunting. If the historical condition of possibility for Korean diaspora is the Forgotten War, the psychic condition is that of enforced forgetting. The acknowledgment of a traumatic past is systematically disavowed by a matrix of silence, the major components of which include the institutions of U.S. global hegemony and social scientific knowledge production, along with the more intimate forces of familial desire and shame. The result for the Korean diaspora in the United States is that one is often an unwitting participant in one's own erasure. But by the same token, the act of disavowal often proliferates the very trauma that is being denied. The tensions produced by this vexed relationship are nowhere more palpable than in the diaspora's uncertain kinship to the yanggongju and the unacknowledged traumas that she has come to embody.

Diasporic Articulations

There are endless ways to begin telling this story, but the three historical entry points that lay out a story about how the yanggongju came into being also begin to articulate how the Korean diaspora came to be conditioned by transgenerational haunting.[16] September 1945, the Korean War from 1950 to 1953, and sexual labor's acquiring a voice in the early 1990s form temporal links between the peninsula, the population that was displaced from it, and its kinship to the yanggongju. September 1945 marked the beginning of the U.S. military occupation of the peninsula, and more broadly of Koreans' psychic entanglement with the United States, one that intensified and grew increasingly ambivalent during the war as the United States came to symbolize both destruction and possibility. The subordinate relationship to the United States that was generated on the Korean peninsula through war and imperialism laid the ground on which Koreans could participate in the American dream.

The war created the conditions for the forced migration of civilian populations, as well as for increasingly frequent sexual encounters between American soldiers and Korean women, some of which led to marriage and migration to the United States, enabled by the War Brides Act of 1945.[17] But these encounters were not motivated simply by personal desire and romance. They were thoroughly implicated in the power dynamics of U.S. military dominance, the material destruction of war, and the whitewashing of violence through the narrativization of the United States' role in Korea as benevolent. During the early 1950s, for example, the United States constructed a media image of itself as a kind protector to Korea while erasing evidence that the American military routinely killed civilians. Further bolstering the notion of American generosity and friendly U.S.–Korea relations was the picture of the happy interracial couple—the Korean war bride and her American GI husband—newly inserted into the narrative of the normative (white) American family.

This story of the Korean war bride who shows gratitude toward her hospitable new family and country, who later brings the rest of her Korean family to the United States so that they, too, can enjoy America's gifts, makes sense only if we draw clear boundaries between forced and voluntary migrants, if we do not question the extent to which the war bride is a displaced subject, and if we forget the brutality of war altogether. The story I want to tell is also one that shows that such a story can make sense only through exclusions. It is this narrative of the grateful immigrant, who achieves success by working hard and valorizing the institution of family, through which Koreans are incorporated into the national discourse of the American dream. The flip side, of course, is that the Korean immigrant now tenuously incorporated as a national subject must not betray her new nation by exposing its secrets. But this obligation is easy to fulfill when her own private secrets are implicated too. The yanggongju is the bearer of secrets about the traumas of the Korean War and of U.S.–Korea relations—and, in many cases, about her own past. The power of the family cannot be underestimated in this particular aspect of silencing. Both the Korean and U.S. dominant cultures severely stigmatize the overt exchange of sex for money and, to a lesser extent, the more subtle exchange of sex or companionship for material goods. That is true, of course, unless such exchange takes place within the context of marriage. Immigration to the United States through marriage represents an opportunity for the Korean woman who is associated with military sex work to shed the stigmas of the past by legitimizing her sexual labor, to the extent that it is no longer legible as sexual labor. Once in the United States, this woman becomes sanctified by giving her family in Korea an opportunity to participate in the American dream. The war bride, as the pioneer of Korean migration to the United States, then operates as a figure for the disappearance of geopolitical violence into the realm of the domestic. And what better place to bury a social trauma than in the closely guarded space of the family?

The unintended consequence of such an elaborate system of erasure is that the burial ground becomes all the more fertile for generating ghosts. During the 1990s, when the movements against militarized prostitution were sparked in Korea, many second-generation Korean Americans were coming of age and visibly populating institutions of higher learning. By this time, Asian Americans had been constructed by the mills of sociological knowledge production as hypereducated and successful model minorities. The yanggongju's children in the United States were, on one hand, personifications of the immigrant success story into which their historical and familial traumas had been made to disappear. On the other hand, they, too, had become knowledge producers who contested their own erasure. As Lisa Lowe argues, "The material legacy of the repressed history of U.S. imperialism in Asia is borne out in the 'return' of Asian immigrants to the imperial center. . . . Once here, the demand that Asian immigrants identify as U.S. national subjects simultaneously produces alienations and disidentifications out of which critical subjectivities emerge."[18] While the work of diasporic Korean scholars broadly questioned Korean Americans' complicated relationship to the United States, some of their work specifically looked at the figure of the yanggongju, especially as issues of militarized sex work in Korea became the focal point of transnational activists. In some instances, these authors explicitly questioned their possible relation to a yanggongju, perhaps as a means of vindicating the mother for having lived her life in the shadows.[19]

The Concentration of Silence

My mother identifies herself as being from the countryside of Gyeongsang, a southeastern province in the southern half of the Korean peninsula, yet most of her life was spent being displaced from her hometown by the forces of colonization, war, rural poverty, and migration to the United States. The town of Changnyeong in Gyeongsang province is where my family clan originated. Although I was born in Gyeongsang, in the southeastern port city of Busan, where my mother relocated as a young adult, I had never been to rural Gyeongsang until recently. But memories of Gyeongsang province have thoroughly saturated my unconscious through the course of my research for this project. As I began reading reports about massacres of Korean civilians by the U.S. military during the Korean War, I came across a finding that the highest incidence of massacres in what is now called South Korea took place in Gyeongsang province. In this part of the country in particular, there is a reported phenomenon called *honbul*, or "ghost flames," in which flickering lights rise up from the ground, usually at the site of a massacre. The folkloric explanation, generated since the Korean War, lies somewhere between science and the supernatural. In places where buried bodies are heavily concentrated, the remains have changed the chemical makeup of the earth, causing the soil to ignite. Through ghost flames, the spirits of the dead release their grief and rage, their *han,* into the world.

I returned to Gyeongsang province in 2002 to listen to these ghosts. According to Shoshana Felman and Dori Laub, "It is thus that the place of the greatest density of silence—the place of concentration where death took place—paradoxically becomes, for those children of survivors, the only place which can provide an access to the *life* that existed before their birth."[20] Not only is Gyeongsang province the part of the country where the most unclaimed bodies are buried in the ground; there is another way in which the taking of lives is concentrated there. Gyeongsang province boasts "the dubious honor"[21] of possibly having experienced not only the highest incidence of civilian massacres by the U.S. military during the Korean War but also the highest concentration of girls conscripted into sexual slavery for the Japanese military during the colonial period.[22] This place is haunted by the two most significant historical traumas of twentieth-century Korea, both of which would become buried and later embodied and transmitted by the figure of the yanggongju. This is the place my mother locates as her origin.

Assembling the Unconscious

And so I begin writing this uncertain history, this assemblage of my unconscious and the unconsciouses to which I am bound. I want to tell you a story about the role of the yanggongju in international migration and geopolitics, about the history of militarized prostitution in Korea, and about how these stories haunt my family history. But this telling is also a failure to tell these stories in their entirety, because there are too many uncertainties, and the very act of telling them in a way that makes sense would involve smoothing over the gaps. Rather than filling in these gaps, I am compelled to enter these empty spaces to find out what emerges, what one can learn from listening to silence.

While the threads of U.S. imperialism and militarism, scientific progress narratives, and familial shame are woven together into a fabric of erasure that covers up the traumas of the Korean War embodied in the yanggongju, they are not so tightly woven that the threads cannot come undone. The act of laying bare the components of silence can allow for something new to come forth in its place, but that is not to say that it exposes a singular truth. Because this book is a study of what cannot be known with certainty, I want to be explicit about what this text does not attempt to do. While this work treats questions of repressed histories of militarized violence in the U.S.–Korea relationship, particularly the sexual aspects of the relationship, it does not attempt to rewrite those histories, nor does it claim to offer new social scientific findings about populations of sex workers, intermarried Korean women, or their families. It does not ask people to speak about their experiences in order to reveal the contents of their secrets, because there is as much power in uncertainty as in knowing the truth, because secrets have a way of revealing themselves even when the subject who carries the secrets never speaks of them. In these respects, this is not a social scientific text in any of its familiar forms. Rather than writing a sociological narrative of military prostitution, I am making a shift away from traditional sources of data and forms of writing my interpretations. Instead, I would like to tell you about the ways in which the yanggongju has been a spectral agency acting on and interacting with various unconscious forces. [illegible]aveling of the effects of trauma [illegible] c figure of the yanggongju has bee[illegible] hrough her very erasure, has als[illegible] the Korean diaspora.

In c[illegible]t," I elaborate a discussion of the [illegible] he power of the ghost that taken-[illegible] to come undone. I lay the theoretical groundwork for understanding what produces haunting and what, in turn, is produced by it. While the theory of transgenerational haunting is the central theoretical concept I use for understanding how unspoken and shameful family secrets generate ghosts, the practices of knowledge production have played an equally important part. I engage critiques of the ways in which ghosts have been both ignored and created by the discipline of sociology, as well as by the more general practice of writing a narrative. A challenge then arises: how can one look at ambiguous personal and collective histories, and the traumas that reside in the spaces of not knowing, without reproducing the same kind of epistemic violence that induced those traumas?

I take up the task of piecing together a story about the yanggongju and showing that she became a figure who would be very much present yet obscured in the diasporic unconscious. Although I cannot deny that even a stitched-together story is a narrative, I am less interested in the explicit content of narrative than in the traces of trauma left on it. How, for example, is trauma transmitted across time and space through vehicles other than the speaking subject, such as the interviewee or the historical record? Do alternative methods of sociological inquiry and experimental writing such as autoethnography, psychoanalysis, fiction, and performance bring us any closer to an affective understanding of the yanggongju that cannot be conveyed through traditional narratives? In chapter 1 I also lay out the methodological groundwork for recognizing a haunting force and making it material through the practice of writing. One way in which to convey haunting is through the use of nonlinear temporalities, repetition, fantasy, and fiction; therefore, I use both narrative and nonnarrative methods of unfolding the layers of the multiple, often competing, stories about the yanggongju that have developed over more than sixty years. She is a ghost who is not just an apparition of the dead or a melancholic reminder of the past but also a productive and powerful force of the present. As much as this is a project *about* trauma, it is also an experiment in writing that attempts to traumatize the text itself, to animate the very ghostly traces and traumatic disturbances about which I am theorizing, and to encounter the ghost as a voice from the future.

Chapter 2, "A Genealogy of Trauma," is an example of a traumatized text. It is an enactment of *honbul,* of the ghost flames, through a writing experiment that begins to unearth concentrated traumatic memories that are sedimented in the land along with the blood and bones of the massacred. It weaves together narratives of survivors of the Korean War to look at the ways in which transgenerational haunting creates a scattering of memory that is material and affective, even if not fully articulated. This memory lives in the bodily matter of the survivors and in the earth from which ghost flames arise, and it stretches across time and place, linking disparate sites of militarized violence. The text moves disjointedly to mirror the massive displacement of refugees and to invoke a temporality in which the past is in the present, returning over and over to a traumatic moment—July 1950, which was when the most famous civilian massacre took place in Gyeongsang province near the village of Nogeun-ri.[23] The early part of the war was also the period of the most intensified killing and destruction of civilian life. Indeed, early on in the war, American soldiers had already been identified by Korean civilians as "*maengsu,*" or "monsters," so the chapter also unfolds the mounting anxieties at the time about U.S. soldiers' capacity to kill and rape. It was in the summer of 1950 that Korean villagers began the practice of hiding their daughters or, alternately, offering them up to American GIs to pacify their desires. These stories are interrupted by quotes from wartime propaganda disseminated by the United States, thereby demonstrating the tension between the official narrative of the United States in the Korean War and the unofficial narratives that survive in the diasporic unconscious. Memories of civilian massacres perpetrated by the U.S. military reveal a hidden history and thus instigate a radical rupturing of the fantasy of the American dream and of friendly U.S.–Korea relations. The U.S.–authored fiction that the United States is the Third World's savior disintegrates against war survivors' memories that conflate rescue and annihilation.

Even as "A Genealogy of Trauma" repeats the traumatic moment of July 1950, it also anxiously "dreads forward," in the words of Lyndsey Stonebridge.[24] One of the temporalities of trauma is an anxiety in which there is a sense that a trauma from the future is about to arrive. Just as a new trauma can trigger an older one, inducing a flashback, it can also flash forward, projecting itself into a future haunting. The traumatized memories of July 1950 resonate with the present geopolitical moment in which abuses by the U.S. military are not so hidden, nor is the U.S. military's agenda for permanent war and global domination.[25]

At the same time, the memories of July 1950 recall the fact that the Korean peninsula has been in a state of permanent war since 1950 despite the war's having been written into U.S. history as "the Forgotten War," which implies that it is long over.[26] As long as the division along the thirty-eighth parallel remains, Koreans on the peninsula cannot forget that they still live in a war zone. This failure to resolve is amplified by the silences surrounding it in the United States. The trauma of permanent war simultaneously calls up the past and the future in that the current status of North Korea, as a nuclear threat as well as part of the "axis of evil," has provoked anxiety about the destruction that is poised to unfold, but it is also a reminder of the unhealed wounds inflicted by the division.

Ultimately, chapter 2 establishes the war as the ground against which the yanggongju became enfigured, as a ghost composed of the material remains of 1953 and the residues of the daily practices of war. The war's obliteration of normal ways of life created the economic necessity that would lead Korean civilians to the military bases to look for employment, and thus the psychic and material conditions were set in place for the beginning of U.S. military prostitution as an institutional practice. Although it has been more than fifty years since the signing of the armistice agreement to bring a cease-fire to the Korean War, a peace treaty has yet to be signed. The deferral of the war's resolution serves as the geopolitical rationale for the continued U.S. troop presence in Korea, and therefore for the continuation of military prostitution. Having arisen from these conditions, the yanggongju is a painful reminder of Korea's division, destruction, and subordination to the United States over the past half-century, so she carries the weight of this history. Because this history is part and parcel of the institution of prostitution for the U.S. military, national struggles around reunification and the withdrawal of U.S. troops are often waged around and on the yanggongju body. I turn to these issues—the historical and political conditions of camptown prostitution and the way in which the body of the yanggongju became a site of contestation—in chapter 3.

A war without end. A division that permanently separated more than one-third of the population of the peninsula from homes and loved ones. Repeated and frustrated attempts to put the two halves back together. What Theresa Hak Kyung Cha calls an "exile fixed in the perpetual motion of search."[27] These are some of the traumatic forces that have constituted the changing terrain of the yanggongju's body since 1945. Chapter 3, "Tracing the Disappearance of the Yanggongju," outlines a history of camptown prostitution in which the figure of the yanggongju is constructed and reconstructed in the service of competing forms of Korean nationalism. On one side is a nationalism that has bought into the story line about the United States as benevolent protector a nationalism that Valerie Walkerdine says "wants to live that fiction, basking in the gaze of the Other who constitutes it."[28] On the opposing side is an anti-U.S. nationalism that positions the yanggongju as the symbol of a nation raped by the United States. Both camps have used this figure for the purposes of their political agendas—as a body in service of national security or as a body in need of saving. In both cases, she is a figure that is overinvested with fantasmatic longings for a unified and liberated homeland, and underneath this longing are the gaping wounds of the division as well as internal divisions about the road to reconciliation and reunification. But this is a story told through a diasporic lens by those displaced from the homeland, who have also become invested in making the yanggongju seen, thus adding another layer of fantasy to the telling of the story. These desires are projected onto her, and she makes apparent the ways in which Korean national identity has been built on a repeated fracturing of the nation. To borrow the words of Cha, "She would become, herself, demarcations."[29] No longer relegated to the dark alleys of American towns or the back booths of GI clubs, the yanggongju is not only the screen that allows other ghosts of Korea's traumatized history to be seen; she is also the figure that takes center stage in national and transnational scenes as she moves in and out of visibility.

As the anti–U.S. base movement in Korea disseminated images of sex workers killed by the U.S. military as a method of gaining support from different communities, the dead yanggongju became a trope of diasporic memory through which both the fantasies of the future and the horrors of the past are played out. Images of dead yanggongjus are inscribed on the bodies of the living in a diaspora haunted by "necropolitical" practices of routinely killing civilians during the Korean War and continuing to let camptown women die.[30] But in this particular distribution of haunting, there comes a radical break. As Korean sex workers marry American servicemen and exit Korea via migration to the United States, the yanggongju slides from hypervisibility back into the shadows again.

Between chapter 3 and chapter 4, "The Fantasy of Honorary Whiteness," there is an absence, a sense that some link has been broken. How do we get from the yanggongju as a body of nationalism to the narrative of assimilation in the United States? There is no smooth transition between these two stories, because the yanggongju's migration to the United States constitutes a severing from her history as a "Yankee whore." Chapter 4 demonstrates this attempt at erasure and its ultimate failure. The yanggongju's seeming absence in the United States is only a shift in the frame of visibility from a mass mediated gaze toward the unconscious knowledge of transgenerational haunting. By the end of the chapter it becomes clear that the Yankee whore who was the body of a fractured nation is entombed in the body of the GI bride. "The Fantasy of Honorary Whiteness" explores the ways in which the yanggongju has been constructed as a "statistical person" in the sociological discourse of assimilation—the intermarried Asian, the approximately white.[31] The abstractions that render her history invisible leave traces of trauma that are passed down to her children, and in the work of diasporic Koreans, particularly biracial Korean Americans who are presumed to be one step closer to whiteness, the yanggongju appears as a mark of ambiguous personal history and traumatized collective memory.

The history of Korean migration to the United States troubles the sociological fantasy of honorary whiteness in a way that sets Koreans apart from other Asian groups. By sociological standards,

Koreans are coded as the most assimilated of all Asians, thereby reinforcing the label of "honorary white" for Asian Americans more generally. The yanggongju as GI bride and her kin make up about half of ethnic Koreans in the United States, meaning that Koreans as an immigrant group arrived in the United States primarily through means of American military domination.[32] Of course there are other groups, such as the Vietnamese, Cambodians, Laotians, and Hmong, whose paths to the United States have been determined by similar military interventions, but the violent histories of these ethnic groups have not been covered over for more than fifty years by an illusion of interracial romance and international cooperation. Those of us who have literally been born from the U.S.–Korea relationship are not the living proof of harmony across lines of difference as much as we are bodies bearing the marks of militarization. If born on the peninsula and recognized by our fathers, we are simultaneously immigrants and U.S. citizens by birth whose identification papers signal our affiliations with the U.S. military. For those who are children of the violent and intimate relationship between the United States and Korea, assimilation is a homogenizing project that is impossible, because we have inherited the traumas that are sent into the diaspora by the yanggongju, and trauma is precisely that which is unassimilable.

In chapter 5, "Diasporic Vision: Methods of Seeing Trauma," I begin by raising a question about the psychic costs of assimilation and show that the wish for America is an impossible wish whose fulfillment yields tragic consequences. Social work narratives about Korean military brides suggest that there is an unusually high rate of mental illness among these women who are assimilated by sociological standards, and indeed, my autoethnographic observations are consistent with this claim. While acknowledging the problems associated with mental illness, I also turn to the notion of the irrational perception, whether it takes the form of a ghost or that of a schizophrenic hallucination, as a model of thinking that offers productive possibilities.[33] My intention is not to reify images of the yanggongju as always and only a tragic figure (indeed, this text seeks to show that the figure has varied meanings) but rather to use these familiar stories of madness as a point of departure. Can we reconceive of hallucination not just as psychotic abnormality but also as a method for reading erasure? Throughout this project, I struggle with the question of how one can see and hear a trauma that the subject of trauma herself cannot. How does one work through this paradox of telling a story about loss that is unnamable and trauma that is dislocated and materializes in forms far removed from the traumatic event itself, often through sensations, emotions, and unconscious thought? In chapter 1 I begin laying out methodologies that call forth the ghosts, and I conclude the book with a performance of trauma that is not just subjected to methods but also produces new methods for summoning the ghosts.

Applying Gilles Deleuze and Félix Guattari's notion of distributed perception and John Johnston's idea of machinic vision, I theorize that through the haunting of the Korean diaspora a method of seeing and speaking of trauma is composed of scattered images, affects, and voices. The yanggongju, as both the shameful secret that is passed down unconsciously to her children and the agent that ruptures the very story lines from which her history has been erased, distributes her haunting across bodies in the diaspora. Contemporary trauma studies has shifted its focus from trauma as a wound that is only a loss or lack to one that is also an excess, and therefore potentially productive.[34] From this theoretical understanding of trauma, the yanggongju's haunting generates a new kind of visibility. The inability to see and speak of her own trauma distributes this seeing across bodies that are affectively connected to her, thus creating a diasporic vision that engages the productive possibilities of trauma.

The purpose of what Johnston refers to as a "schizophrenic multiplicity of voices" and of what I call diasporic vision is not to tell a story but rather to register the nonnarrativizable.[35] Both the traumatic images and the traumatic affects of the yanggongju that circulate in the diaspora and the hallucinatory voices that speak through her body demonstrate the ways in which her trauma is a creative force that assembles new forms of perception. This assemblage implies a shift in writing form as well, from narrative to another kind of writing that registers the unassimilable of trauma. Throughout the chapters that follow, I attempt to make moves from a narrative about loss to an affective expression that registers the "loss of loss."[36] At the same time, I engage in a conversation about official narratives and counternarratives in which the yanggongju is present or absent.

The intent of this book, therefore, is twofold. On one hand, this study of a diaspora haunted by the figure of the yanggongju aims to challenge taken-for-granted narratives of the family, assimilation, and U.S.–Korea relations, all of which make up part of the larger fantasy of the American dream. The second goal of the book is to make a departure from the narrative told by the writing or speaking subject to an exploration of the affective potential of haunting. The accumulated grief and rage (*han* in Korean) transmitted by the yanggongju creates spaces of possibility within the ruptures she has made but also in a realm beyond narrative. Patricia Clough describes this movement toward affect as follows:

> The affective turn throws thought back to the disavowals constitutive of Western industrial capitalist societies, bringing forth ghosted bodies, and the traumatized remains of erased histories. It also sends thought to the future—to the bodily matter and biotechnologies of technoscientific experimentation . . . to grasp the changes that constitute the social and to explore them as changes in ourselves, circulating through our bodies, our subjectivities, yet irreducible to the individual, the personal or the psychological.[37]

Rather than abandon one model for the other, I want to hold in tension questions of telling a story about trauma and speaking from a subject position, on the one hand, and a mode of memory that comes out of a diaspora of trauma that is deindividualized, on the other. While these two ways of thinking about trauma are different, they are not oppositional. In fact, the self that speaks is also always an assemblage. As Deleuze puts it, "The collective assemblage is always like a murmur from which I take my proper name, the constellation of voices, concordant or not, from which I draw my voice. . . . To write is perhaps to bring this assemblage of the unconscious to the light of day, to select the whispering voices, to gather the tribes and secret idioms from which I extract something I call my self."[38]

1.
Fleshing Out the Ghost

Something like her shadow breathed through the empty spaces . . . in the secrets and suspicions left unsaid.

—Nora Okja Keller, *Fox Girl*

Something like her shadow breathed through the empty spaces, but it was not the shadow itself. The physical form of her body was somewhere, dislocated. As the years wore on, the wind that blew through the house became increasingly like her shadow breathing. Meanwhile, her body grew more fixed, sitting still on the couch for hours on end while she watched the time pass. She looked upward at certain moments, reading the time on the clock, repeating the time on the clock at those moments once the hands had come full circle. The shadowlike thing whose breath blew through the house acquired voice and soon began to whisper clues about things that had been left unsaid. She repeated dates in tandem with the clock's display, moments in history evoked by watching time tick toward the future. The historical marks left on the present were the very words that gave more breath to that thing that was like her shadow.

I want to tell you how this female form came to be so ghostly and at the same time so alive. The figure of the yanggongju, as an embodiment of trauma and the secrecy surrounding it, is paradoxically central and shadowy in multiple narratives about Korea's history and the Korean diaspora's present. This chapter lays out the theoretical and methodological frameworks for studying the ways in which the traces of trauma embodied in the yanggongju can become legible or, at the very least, their presence can be felt if not fully interpreted. Before I tell the story of how the ghostly figure of this woman haunts the Korean diaspora in the United States, I want to address a more fundamental question: Why study a ghost at all?

Blind and wounded Korean girl in the arms of an American GI.

The Meaning of the Ghost

To ask this question presumes an underlying faith in the existence of phenomena that are typically beyond the scope of social scientific analysis and often contrary to its aims. In Jacques Derrida's words, "There has never been a scholar who really, and as a scholar, deals with ghosts. A traditional scholar does not believe in ghosts—nor in all that could be called the virtual space of spectrality."[1] One notable exception to the social sciences' dismissal of the irrational is Avery Gordon's groundbreaking book *Ghostly Matters: Haunting and the Sociological Imagination,* in which she creates a detailed account of haunted sociality and challenges other sociologists to study that which is unacknowledged or otherwise absent at first glance.

According to Gordon's definition, hauntings are not rare supernatural occurrences but, more often, the unexamined irregularities of everyday life. If the craft of sociology is to animate the social world, a study of ghosts is a revision of what we normally see as the social world, and a softening of its edges. Like the shadowy thing that lives in empty spaces, haunting is a phenomenon that reveals how the past is in the present, "how that which appears to be not there is often a seething presence, acting on and often meddling with taken-for-granted realities, [and] the ghost is just the sign, or the empirical evidence . . . that tells you a haunting is taking place. The ghost is not simply a dead or missing person, but a social figure, and investigating it can lead to that dense site where history and subjectivity make social life."[2] From this point of view, it makes sociological sense to study a ghost, but making sense alone does not quite get at the question of why one should study a ghost.

If, in the most basic terms, studying ghosts allows us to rethink a society's relationship to its dead, particularly to those who were subject to some kind of injustice, the ghost and its haunting effects act as a mode of memory and an avenue for ethical engagement with the present. Drawing on Max Horkheimer and Theodor Adorno's "On the Theory of Ghosts," a postscript to *The Dialectic of the Enlightenment,* Gordon expresses the political and ethical urgency of "mourning modernity's 'wound in civilization' and eliminating the destructive forces that open it up over and over again."[3] For Gordon, the aim of telling ghost stories is to "represent the structure of feeling that is something akin to what it feels like to be the object of a social totality vexed by the phantoms of modernity's violence."[4]

This study of the Korean diaspora is, in part, a response to Gordon's call that sociologists take seriously our haunted social legacies, as well as an elaboration of Abraham and Torok's theory of transgenerational haunting. In the intersection between these two frameworks of thinking about ghosts is an imperative to come to terms with an unacknowledged history of violence, whether that violence took place at the level of the social or the familial. As Nicholas Rand remarks, the study of transgenerational haunting "enables us to understand how the falsification, ignorance, or disregard of the past—whether institutionalized by a totalitarian state . . . or practiced by parents or grandparents—is the breeding ground of the phantomatic return of shameful secrets."[5]

With the psychoanalytic framework of transgenerational haunting contextualized within broad ethical issues of state-sanctioned mass violence, the notion has been extended to other locales of political trauma such as South Africa under Apartheid and the Japanese American internment camps of World War II.[6] Jacqueline Rose's work, for example, demonstrates how trauma can travel from the Holocaust to present-day Israel-Palestine via the Jewish diaspora, thus affectively connecting Israeli Jews and Palestinians through an unconscious entanglement. Identifying transgenerational haunting in the writings of Palestinians who dream about Nazi concentration camps, Rose observes, "In this case the haunting works not just down through the generations, but *across* them; and not inside one family, but creating a monstrous family of reluctant belonging."[7] Seemingly incomprehensible acts of violence are thick with a history of collective trauma that refuses to remain fixed in the past or in its original place. Rose's work on the transgenerational haunting of collective groups implies the dissolution of the boundaries of individual bodies and takes us into the realm of the social, moving trauma beyond the family unit and moving the notion of a familial unconscious beyond bloodlines.

While the Korean diaspora provides another test of Abraham and Torok's theory in that the second generation is haunted by what their parents will not talk about, the secrecy around the first generation's trauma travels well beyond the boundaries of the family to pervade an entire society. Unlike the effects of the Holocaust on the Jewish diaspora, however, the ongoing conflict of the Korean War is not apparent to most Americans, nor are its state-sanctioned practices of mass killing. The failure to recognize the brutality of the Korean War is elaborated to such an extent that what we remember about it first and foremost is that it is "forgotten." But as much as this project attempts a reconciliation with the past, it also asks that we interrogate a present world order in which ghosts are being mass produced. Just as the Korean War has yet to end, so does the abuse of political power around which shameful family secrets become ghosts. Within the context of U.S. military expansion and renewed commitment to permanent war, the language of ghosts has made its way into common parlance. Iraqi and Afghani bodies that disappear from military prisons have been made into officially nonexistent entities, never there according to a rational bureaucratic logic but occasionally reported in the media as "ghost prisoners." On a geopolitical stage whose backdrop is U.S. imperialism, "the phantom represents the interpersonal and transgenerational consequences" of a disappearance that is produced by both the material obliteration of war and the epistemic violence of erasure.[8]

I am particularly interested in the effects of this multiplicity when the apparent absence of violence is the result of another act of violence, such as a subjugation or explicit erasure. The ghost that haunts this project lies at the crossroads of multiple forms of violence—the social and familial, the psychic and epistemic. Such a critical juncture invites us not only to explore the past that produced the yanggongju but also to consider what new things this alchemy of violence allows her to produce.

The Production of Haunting

The act of paying attention to the ghosts around us can be deeply unsettling on many levels, and might even be met with ridicule by those who are trained to see the world through a strictly positivistic lens. The mainstream of social science would dismiss the notion that something that is seemingly absent or nonexistent can be a powerful force in shaping empirical reality, let alone that this unseen presence can itself be the object of study. But, as Gordon says, "The ghost or the apparition is one form by which something lost, or barely visible, or seemingly not there to our supposedly well-trained eyes, makes itself known or apparent to us."[9]

What we can and cannot see is always partly a function of the limitations of our technologies of seeing in that the empirical reality that scientists observe is never disarticulated from their apparatuses of observation.[10] Despite these technical limitations, we should also recognize that not seeing is not done innocently. The dominant model of seeing creates both invisibility and blindness, and the disavowal of what cannot be perceived through our usual frameworks of observation generates ghosts as much as it dismisses them. As elaborated in the work of Gordon as well as the tradition of criticism that she draws on, narratives of Western progress play a large part in producing ghosts through this very process of epistemic violence.

While the traditional methods of social scientific research necessarily exclude what is not immediately observable, so does the practice of putting one's findings into narrative. As Butler remarks, "A certain problem of loss emerges when established narratives begin to falter, suggesting that narrative functioned once as a way of containing loss. . . . Other narratives of progress and development have proven to be contingent, have produced through their own excess, sites of exclusion as sites of resistance."[11] Narratives that consciously or unconsciously seek to discipline ghosts "give sustenance to the phantom," according to Abraham and Torok, because the gaps make room for that which has been excluded.[12] What gets subjugated, erased, and generated through these forms of knowledge production are the undocumented, illegible, and irrational. A project such as this writes against sociology's own tendency to create ghosts by looking to sites of exclusion. Therefore, an exploration of the yanggongju's haunting effects presents a test not only of the theory of transgenerational haunting but also of various postmodern and postcolonial critiques of science and reason.

Like traditional social scientists, some cultural critics might also question the value of a project that aims to unveil ghosts, charging that revealing the hidden is now politically passé, irrelevant, or even paranoid. Eve Sedgwick, for example, points out that many forms of violence are not hidden, but rather "offered as an exemplary spectacle," and that "visibility itself constitutes much of the violence."[13] As many Foucauldian critics would argue, seeing always implies "relations between vision and supervision" both in realist literary representations and in empirical social scientific practices in which the observer becomes the "Surveillant Other" whose watching regulates the bodies under observation.[14] It is precisely what escapes these technologies of seeing, however, that is the ghostly matter Gordon is interested in. Emphasizing that questions of invisibility are still crucial to understanding the workings of power, she writes: "In a culture seemingly ruled by technologies of hypervisibility, we are led to believe that neither repression nor the return of the repressed, in the form of either improperly buried bodies or countervailing systems of value or difference, occurs with any meaningful result."[15]

The yanggongju is neither completely hidden nor free from the forces of social repression. Instead, she vacillates wildly between overexposure and a reclusive existence in the shadows. Her presence or absence raises questions about the psychic and political forces behind the shifting frameworks of visibility, in which the yanggongju is put on display in some contexts but in others made invisible. Against conscious efforts of institutions such as the U.S. military or the media to expose or hide her, the yanggongju also moves in and out of visibility through a spectrality immanent to a diasporic unconscious that is constituted by trauma.

Because psychoanalysis is, as Gordon says, "the only human science that has taken haunting seriously as an object of analysis," I put a psychoanalytic study of trauma at the center of this work because it can infuse intelligibility into that which is normally unspoken or unspeakable and, in so doing, open up the creative possibilities of trauma.[16] More specifically, the theory of transgenerational haunting demonstrates how a silenced trauma can become a dynamic force—one that produces "countermemory," disruptions, articulations, visibilities, assemblages, and new configurations of kinship.[17] I now turn to what happens to that which is erased or obliterated, to what gets sparked by the remnants of the dead.

> All the departed return, but some are destined to haunt: the dead who were shamed during their lifetime or those who took unspeakable secrets to the grave. . . . It is a fact that the "phantom," whatever its form, is nothing but an invention of the living . . .

> meant to objectify, even if under the guise of individual or collective hallucinations, the gap produced in us by the concealment of some part of a love object's life.
>
> —Nicolas Abraham and Maria Torok, *The Shell and the Kernel*

> Finding and getting former prostitutes to talk with me was one of the most difficult aspects of the research because many had died and others had been forgotten by family members and camptown residents who had once known them. Many who are still living in camptowns experience ill health and loss of memory. . . . Moreover, the women often lie about their camptown experiences because they are ashamed of revealing the past and because they have grown accustomed to lying as a means to survive in the camptowns.
>
> —Katharine Moon, *Sex among Allies*

Behind the image of friendly and cooperative U.S.–Korea relations, 27,000 women sell their sexual labor to U.S. military personnel in the bars and brothels surrounding the ninety-five installments and bases in the southern half of the Korean peninsula. This system of militarized prostitution has been described by American scholars in terms of what is kept quiet and hidden—"silent but deadly," "so obvious and so soundless, making barely a cat's-paw imprint on the literature and lore of Asian–American relations," in the words of Bruce Cumings.[18] Although this form of prostitution is "silent" and "soundless," Cumings believes it is also "the most important aspect of the whole relationship and the primary memory of Korea for generations of young American men who have served there."[19] The female sex workers, who collectively have been one of the most important and unacknowledged forces in the geopolitical alliance between South Korea and the United States, are made objects of play, hostile aggression, and romantic desire by the American soldiers who purchase their services. They have been called "the women outside" and "the women in the shadows" by diasporic Koreans who study military prostitution, thus highlighting their marginalized social status.[20] The fact of being narrativized as invisible and soundless, yet consistently present, demonstrates the extent to which the yanggongju is a ghostly force that exceeds our normal capacity to see and hear. As David Eng and David Kazanjian remind us, "Abject and unlivable bodies do not simply lose intelligibility but also continue to be haunted by creative possibilities," so that, even if they seem to have disappeared, their "meanings emerge from interpretations of their persistent and volatile material remains."[21]

As one of the subjects produced by the traumas of twentieth-century Korean history, the yanggongju has been a central figure in the Korean diasporic unconscious yet virtually nonexistent in official discourses about U.S.–Korea relations and Korean Americans. She has inherited the unspeakable horrors of Japanese colonialism and the Korean War, but even in silence and shadows she distributes these traumas across the time-space of the diaspora. As the histories of camptown women are consciously or unconsciously forgotten, the traumatic origins of the U.S.–Korea relationship return to haunt other bodies to whom the yanggongju is affectively connected. For those who are the subjects of her haunting, it is the phenomenon of her secrecy that is the most vexing.

> What is your ethnic mix?
> *I am Korean/Caucasian. My mother is Korean.*
>
> How did your parents meet?
> *I'm not exactly sure how they met. All I really know is my father was stationed in Korea when he served in the Air Force.*
>
> —From an interview published on http://www.halfkorean.com

The Web site www.halfkorean.com, dedicated to exploring the "unique issues and struggles of biracial Koreans," offers an example of the same kinds of silences that haunted Abraham and Torok's clients. One of the standard questions asked of the "prominent half Koreans" interviewed is "How did your parents meet?" The answer is always some variation of "I don't know." But so often we do not even know that we are haunted by what we do not know. From the unconscious space sheltering the unspeakable trauma, the taboo "words giving sustenance to the phantom" return to haunt the bearer of the other's secret.[22] According to Abraham and Torok:

> Produced by the secret, the gaps and impediment in our communication with the love object create a twofold and contrary effect: the prohibition of knowledge coupled with an unconscious

> investigation. As a result "haunted" individuals are caught between two inclinations. They must at all costs maintain the ignorance of a loved one's secret; hence the semblance of unawareness (nescience) concerning it. At the same time they must eliminate the state of secrecy; hence the reconstruction of the secret in the form of unconscious knowledge.[23]

Abraham and Torok's method for revealing a phantom is to focus on gaps, on that which was suggested but still silenced in their clients' speech, and their treatment of haunted individuals involved wresting the phantomized secret from its hold over the individual's psyche by "staging" it and, thus, releasing it into the world. The psychoanalytic work of making ghosts public "implies uncovering... shameful secrets [of the dead or loved ones]," yet the paradox of transgenerational haunting is that the haunted person is unconsciously driven to know and speak the unspeakable even at the risk of betraying the person who has transmitted the secret.[24] This effort to speak the contents of one's psychic tomb is an example of what Abraham and Torok would describe as "reducing the 'phantom' [which] entails reducing the sin attached to someone else's secret and stating it in acceptable terms so as to defy, circumvent, or domesticate the phantom's (and our) resistances, its (and our) refusals, gaining acceptance for a higher degree of 'truth.'"[25] The tension produced in the unconscious of the haunted can prove to be a positive force, because ghosts become articulated not only through the avenues of everyday speech but also through creative work.

The appearance of the yanggongju in the scholarly and artistic works of diasporic Koreans, especially because she is the subject of a hidden or shameful history, suggests that diasporic Koreans have inherited the entombed secrets of other generations. The theme of confronting the silences of one's collective past is now a common one in Korean American scholarship, particularly around traumas of the Korean War and Japanese colonization, and the yanggongju is the ghost that symbolizes both the larger historical traumas and the trauma of keeping quiet about the past. The materialization of the yanggongju in the work of diasporic Koreans shows the ways in which this writing and speaking constitutes an attempt to speak the contents of the other's psychic tomb, to act out someone else's trauma, and thereby to "reduce the phantom."

While the yanggongju has been a powerful figure in shaping certain discourses, such as Korean discourses of nationalism (as I elaborate in chapter 3), particularly around issues of U.S. military involvement, she has been absent from many official U.S. accounts about Korea, such as that of the history of diplomatic relations between the two countries and that of Korea's economic miracle, as well as from U.S.-centered feminist debates about sex work. Since the early 1990s, however, there has been a proliferation of writing and filmmaking about prostitution and the U.S. military by diasporic Koreans as well as some non-Korean U.S. scholars.[26] This recent knowledge production about militarized prostitution in Korea, in which the yanggongju is the central figure, demonstrates Gordon's claim that writing about ghosts can "not only repair representational mistakes, but also strive . . . toward a countermemory."[27]

The yanggongju, repressed in many dominant U.S. discourses, returns via counterhegemonic discourses. This phenomenon could easily be explained away according to the dominant beliefs of academic culture—that the glaring absences in public knowledge about military prostitution in Korea provoked writing about the topic in order to fill in the gaps. The 1990s was an era characterized by new voices speaking about that which had previously been unacknowledged, but the new discourses also created new lacunae to be filled. While discourses of global sex work and women's rights as human rights flourished in the 1990s, for example, questions of military prostitution were largely ignored in those discussions.[28] Perhaps new work about the subject of the yanggongju was simply a matter of academic colonization.

But I would like to propose another reading—that this relatively new body of work is evidence of the transgenerational haunting of diasporic Koreans. During the same period in which this scholarly work was being produced, the arts community of diasporic Koreans took up the subject of the yanggongju and militarized prostitution, particularly in film and fiction. Many of these works were partly autobiographical and questioned the writer's or filmmaker's own family history and uncertain relationship to the yanggongju. Virtually all of these scholars and artists belonged to the generation of children who migrated to the United States via intermarriage between U.S. servicemen and Korean women or through adoption, and both of these trajectories of diaspora depend on the yanggongju as an unacknowledged force of movement. One might say that the materialization of the figure of the yanggongju in the work of diasporic Koreans signals the ways in which we have inherited the unconscious and traumatic memories that belong to someone else, and the writing of the imagined secrets is a way of "reducing the phantom."

The first time I envisioned my mother's past was before I had ever heard the word *yanggongju*. I did not know all that this word would come to mean, that a whole literature would be written about her, that ten years later I would begin writing about this figure in the Korean diasporic unconscious, or that the page would become a place for the figure to take shape from my own unconscious. The first time I envisioned my mother this way, the fears and fantasies about all that I had not known about my family history came to matter. It was, in fact, at the same time that the yanggongju began making her presence felt in the fiction and film of the Korean diaspora and in anti–U.S. base movements in Korea, so my history of engagement with this figure was born out of a larger historical moment in which the ghost began to matter most. In the early 1990s, women in militarized sexual labor, both the comfort women who had "traveled from fifty years in the past" and camptown sex workers who were being abused or murdered by American GIs, became subjects of grievance in the landscape of South Korean politics.

For the first time, in the early 1990s I heard a vocalization of taboo words that spoke to the traumas of my diasporic history, and thus the yanggongju emerged from "the space between social and psychic history."[29] This was perhaps the only moment of clarity I ever felt about what had happened in my family. But as I started listening to these voices, the story of what had happened

became increasingly loaded with information and at the same time more obscure. This contradictory tendency has been productive, however, in allowing multiple stories to come forth.

While the yanggongju was the vehicle for the migration of trauma across both generational and geographic borders, the countermemory of her was unevenly distributed among diasporic Koreans. In most families, she is still hidden in the gaps. Certainly the scattering of memory is imprecise, whether it be traumatic memory transmitted by the yanggongju or countermemory created as a result of transgenerational haunting, but perhaps this unevenness in itself is a particular quality of diaspora. Brent Hayes Edwards's work on the translation practices of the African diaspora offers a useful counterpoint to the psychoanalytic gap. He argues that diaspora necessarily "involves a process of linking or connecting across gaps—a practice we might term articulation . . . non-naturalizable patterns of linkage between disparate societal elements."[30] These gaps represent "the trace or residue perhaps of what escapes translation," but they also act as joints that facilitate movement and connection.[31] Particularly relevant for this project is the way in which the gap connects geographic and psychic spaces of diaspora through haunting. It is the place from which the transgenerational phantom emerges as well as the space across which the yanggongju, once ghosted, articulates links across different sites and forms of violence.

Perhaps the most important articulation is that which connects the geopolitical and the familial. In this gap, the yanggongju's haunting produces new forms of kinship and new kinds of bodies. To use Jacqueline Rose's phrase again, transgenerational haunting on a geopolitical scale creates a "monstrous family of reluctant belonging."[32] While half of those comprising the Korean diaspora in the United States are related by blood or marriage to a woman who married an American serviceman, the ghostly quality of this relationship is that one cannot know her past with any certainty. Others who arrived in the United States through a different trajectory may also be affectively connected to her through the larger unspoken traumas of the hidden history of U.S.–Korea relations.

The patterns of connection across the Korean diaspora are the result of an uneasy configuration of traumatic effects; thus, the yanggongju articulates a monstrous family—a diaspora that is bound together precisely through what cannot be known.

The capacity of the trauma to move across boundaries of time and space, however, implies that the ghost has an agency of its own that can be more powerful than either the subject who first experienced the trauma or the inheritor of the secret. Abraham and Torok's work moves haunting beyond the realm of the individual, and in fact it is an explicit challenge to Freud's individualized notion of the return of the repressed, in that the ghost is alien to the subject's own psychic landscape. I want to deindividualize haunting in another direction to consider not only the collective unconscious but also what Patricia Clough calls "subindividual finite forces" such as matter and energy.[33] If "technicity, the machine, the text, writing" are "bearers of unconscious thought," where else might we look for evidence of transgenerational haunting, and who or what is the agent of that haunting?[34] What are the subindividual finite forces of haunting that do not take the shape of a woman, and how is haunting at the micro level of perception transfigured into the ghost of the yanggongju?

Turning to the work of Gilles Deleuze and John Johnston for a moment, I want to suggest that haunting can be understood in terms of Deleuze's notion of the machinic assemblage or the dynamic nonorganic body assembled from disparate elements in an environment in order to produce something. The bodies of diaspora, and particularly the Korean diaspora, are constituted by unremembered trauma and loss. When an unspeakable or uncertain history, both personal and collective, takes the form of a "ghost," it searches for bodies through which to speak. In this way, the ghost is distributed across the time-space of diaspora. I want to rethink the ghost not just as the psychic representation of the dead or repressed but as a body assembled to transmit traumatic memory or a force of "desiring production."[35] The ghost is an assemblage in that it is not an individuated body but rather a spectral agency made up of different material and immaterial forces. As I explore in chapter 2, for example, the trauma of the Korean War is an assemblage of the remains of the massacred, the ruins of bombed-out cities and towns, the memories of survivors, affects of fear and hope, and the ongoing daily practices of the war, all of which have become ghosted in the yanggongju. The ghost is an assemblage, and at the same time it calls into existence new listening and speaking bodies that the ghost requires as witnesses to its own exorcism. These assemblages are produced in and against the resounding silences of unacknowledged histories of trauma, such as the Nogeun-ri massacre of July 1950 and the sinking of the *Ukishima Maru,* the first naval vessel of Korean slaves to return to Korea after World War II. They are bodies whose purpose is to see and speak the traumas that could not be seen and spoken by those who directly lived them.

Above all, what is produced in this notion of haunting is a constellation of affective bodies transmitting and receiving trauma. As Jill Bennett says regarding the force of trauma, affect flows through bodies rather than simply being located in a traumatized subject.[36] These are ideas I elaborate especially in chapter 5, but in all the chapters that follow I map out some of the constellations that make up a haunted diaspora. Perhaps as a result of my own haunting gaps, I articulate a link between somewhat disparate theoretical pieces—psychoanalytic notions of trauma and a Deleuzian concept of the body. While I explore this link, I also must recognize that they are not always reconcilable, and therefore, the modes of thought sometimes alternate between these two concepts and at other times bring them closer together. In the end, there is movement toward a decomposition of the psychoanalytic subject rather than a completed arrival.

Method: Dream Work, Fiction, Autoethnography

How does one detect a haunting that has been so dislocated and finely dispersed? How does one study that which is unseen and unspoken, that which has been lost, forgotten, made to disappear? How does one tell a story about something that cannot fully be known? The key to studying a ghost lies in our apparatus for recognizing it, reading it, and communicating its effects. While each of the methodological approaches I use in this text aims to see and listen to what lies in the gaps, the gaps vary, as do the methods for studying them. That is not to say, however, that these methods are discrete. On the contrary, methods of the unconscious lend themselves to condensation, whereby different objects and places blur into one, as do the elements of a dream.

When confronted with a gap, one must employ what Eng refers to as "radical new methods of looking . . . in order to see something else," such as "focusing on personal memories and the dream work—on the unconscious aspects of looking."[37] What is broadly termed "dream work" seeks a remembrance of that which has been violently repressed or made to disappear. If one method of looking at a gap is remembrance, the discussion thus far has already enacted this methodology. According to Gordon, "Perhaps the key methodological question is not *what method have you adopted for your research?* But what paths have been disavowed, left behind, covered over and remain unseen?"[38] The most fundamental method by which to flesh out a ghost is to investigate what produced it and expose the fictional elements of what is taken for granted as factual sociological knowledge. When one operates under the assumption that fiction is "at the heart of documentation," in the words of Trinh T. Min-ha, there is room in which to acknowledge the spectrality of data.[39]

The ghosts of my family history are thoroughly enmeshed in this work even when there is nothing in particular that appears to be autobiographical. The questions, the sources of data, and the theories used to inform the research are all driven by my own position as a Korean diasporic subject writing about the Korean diaspora's being haunted by the figure of the yanggongju. But I have made these choices within the context of a body of postpositivist criticism in which claims of scientific objectivity and authorized knowledge are called into question.[40]

Gordon suggests that one of the legacies of this tradition of criticism for the social sciences is "an understanding that the practices of writing, analysis, and investigation, whether of social or cultural material, constitute less a scientifically positive project than a cultural practice that organizes particular rituals of storytelling told by situated investigators."[41] As an investigator who is situated between sociology and literary criticism, between national disidentifications and unconscious inheritances, I have made it

Girl and baby with a tank.

part of my practice to put fantasy and fiction at the center of this project. Despite the lessons of postmodernism, not all intellectual work is self-reflexive. Many researchers still do not question the extent to which their work is informed by academia's cultural practices, and even when cultural bias might be acknowledged, the unconscious continues to be largely disavowed.

Valerie Walkerdine, for example, looks at the ways in which social science is driven both by a fear of the other being observed and a perverse desire for power (a will to knowledge) on the part of the researcher, yet this psychic dynamic is disavowed in the name of science. The object of observation is always a "fantasied image of the other," which then is narrativized into a regime of representation that is part of a fantasy of truth and therefore always part fiction.[42] Or, put another way by Gordon, "These facts are always in imminent danger of being contaminated by what is seemingly on the other side of their boundaries. . . . When sociology insists on finding only the facts, it has no other choice than to pursue the fictive, the mistake it seeks to eliminate."[43] This is not to say, however, that these critiques set up binaries between the "happened" and the "imagined."[44] Rather, they initiate a destabilization of the realist narrative in which, as Clough writes, "the indefinite mix-up of fact and fiction, fantasy and experience, is restored in what might be described as a ghosted or haunted realism."[45] Such a confusion about what is in fact true demonstrates the extent to which the unconscious is a powerful medium.

Walkerdine and other social scientists such as Jennifer Hunt have made explicit the "problem" of transference and countertransference in qualitative social science research.[46] A more recent turn in critical social science methodologies, however, moves a step beyond this paradigm of the unconscious as problem, thus acknowledging that, as Jackie Orr says, "fieldwork never occurs outside the fields of desire, dream, phantasmatic perceptions, compulsed repetitions, the imaginary."[47] Rather than treating the unconscious as something that needs to be reconciled when doing research, I go directly to the unconscious as my object of study while at the same time recognizing that all research and writing is informed by fantasy, even that which critiques the disavowal of the unconscious.

Within the chapters of this text I use short semifictional vignettes to give body to the uncertainty of a diasporic memory that bears the traces of erased histories. These vignettes are based on oral histories of Korean War survivors and Korean women who have married U.S. servicemen, interviews with Korean military sex workers and surviving comfort women, popular media accounts in which the yanggongju is a prominent character, and fiction and film by diasporic Koreans about the yanggongju. Some of these vignettes are my readings of a social scientific narrative or of a story spoken by an interviewee, while others are pieces of my creative or performance-based work that animates what I imagine to be my unspoken family history and the multiple variations of it. This method of mixing up factual accounts with fictionalized narratives is, to borrow Saidiya Hartman's words, "a combination of foraging and disfiguration—raiding for fragments upon which other narratives can be spun and misshaping and deforming the testimony through selective quotation and the amplification of issues germane to this study."[48] But besides offering examples of both the disaggregation of social scientific data that fixes the yanggongju as a statistical person and the way in which first-person testimony always implies some level of fictionalization, this method is also an enactment of traumatized memory itself. The distinctions between one source of information and another are not always clear in this text, just as the exact origin of a ghost cannot always be located. Marianne Hirsch's work suggests that it is "a powerful form of memory precisely because its connection to its object or source is mediated not through recollection but through projection, investment, and creation."[49] This is perhaps one of the only ways in which to document a history that has not been officially recorded.

Because haunting is dynamic and particularly because the gaps from which the ghosts emerge can be both negative and positive spaces, a study of haunting requires multiple methodologies. Therefore, I combine the process of disaggregating the social fact to reveal its hidden fictions with alternative methods of sociological inquiry that grew directly out of the critique of authorized knowledge production. The writing of the self, particularly in the tradition of feminist methods, has long been used to challenge the assumptions of dominant histories, thus using self-reflexivity as a form of critique. Autoethnography, as one of the primary methods used in this text, has proven to be a means not only of engaging the unconscious but also of disrupting the unspoken power dynamics of social scientific research by obscuring the subject/object distinction while opening up questions about what counts as evidence. In Clough's words, its "aim is to give a personal accounting of the location of the observer, which is typically disavowed in traditional social science writing. . . . It does this by making the ethnographer the subject-object of observation, exploring experience from the inside of the ethnographer's life."[50]

I am not interested in merely telling a story about my family history, nor do I claim to even know that history, but rather I experiment with forms of autoethnography that reconceptualize the self as necessarily entangled with other bodies and unconscious experiences. Particularly useful are Alisa Lebow's notion of "indirect memory" and "transitive autobiography," in which imprints of the past can be found everywhere, while the autobiographical subject herself is unlocatable, and Ann Cheng's idea of "anti-documentary autobiography," which presents the kind of "evidence that registers loss, even as it recognizes the unrecognizability of the content of loss."[51] This kind of displaced autoethnography is well suited to the study of haunting because it enacts "a relation to the world that is melancholic: a trace of something that cannot be named" and thus forces us to consider agencies in the environment that are usually presumed to not be there.[52]

While there are methods for fleshing out the ghost, I do not want to fetishize any of them as the correct alternative to standard practices of sociology. When not practiced self-critically, any method can run counter to the goals of my project—to study unconscious thought and dislocated memory, to see what emerges from the holes in history, and to explore the possibility of a witness to trauma that is an assemblage of disparate elements rather than an individual speaking subject. I therefore use multiple methods of dream work and experimental forms of autoethnography to explore the yanggongju's haunting of the Korean diaspora. But in order to bring alive these methods of remembering trauma, they must not only be written on the page but also expressed through other bearers of unconscious thought such as embodied performance. The field of performance studies, for example, has explored the relationship between trauma and performance, showing that performance, in many cultures, is a way of summoning ghosts.[53] It also suggests that the constellations of affect between performers and audience in a live performance embody and transmit trauma.[54] If trauma is an experience that is folded into the body but never quite reaches cognition, or thought that is stored but cannot yet emerge because it precedes the technological apparatus required to decode it, performance is one such apparatus that allows that unconscious experience to emerge.[55] As Jill Bennett says of the performance artist who treats the subject of trauma, "The artist does not merely *describe* an inner experience but allows such experience to fold back into the world in a manner that can inform understandings both about the nature of relationships to others and about the political nature of violence and pain."[56] This project combines elements of writing history and memory that are performative in their iterations to allow unconscious experience folded into the body to then *fold back into the world,* thus creating affective circuits between bodies.

As important as it is to use multiple methods, it is just as important to employ "multiple drafts." Johnston suggests that a contemporary psyche no longer inscribes itself in text through stream of consciousness but rather does so through the reworkings of multiple drafts.[57] The methodological byproducts of this process are unexpected juxtapositions, repetitions, discarded thought fragments, and the same story told differently each time. In order to engage the repetition of trauma, the same moments must be revisited, the same phantomized words reiterated. The result of these practices is a performance of traumatic effects—temporal or spatial dislocation, projection, hallucination—in order to unravel the haunting silence that generates ghosts. While such effects are evident throughout the book, they are most notable in the concluding chapter, in which disaggregated pieces of social facts are reassembled, repeated, and laid alongside remnants of an entirely different story. This method of juxtaposition creates unlikely connections and makes gaps more apparent. It exposes the fractures in what was previously a sensible story about the Korean diaspora, and it does so in order to make way for a violently submerged memory to come to the surface.

This is a project that must speak in more than one voice. It calls the reader, in Orr's words, "to turn an other ear toward what might (im)possibly be heard of *spiraling effects, of inarticulate experiences of more than one story at a time,* . . . the chattering stammering conversation with the dead and about death."[58] The presence of a ghost compels us to listen to these voices and to hear more than one story at a time. Therefore, some of the chapters are somewhat experimental in terms of the voices used, while others are presented in a more "academic" voice. Sometimes the voice is my own, but often my voice is interrupted by the multiplicity of unconscious thoughts that threaten the integrity of a single authoritative voice. Many of the voices in this text are inauthentic. As in Theresa Hak Kyung Cha's *Dictée,* there are borrowed voices that are a nagging presence in these pages—those of other authors such as Abraham and Torok, Gordon, and Rose, as well as Cha herself.[59] Alongside and in conjunction with these speak other borrowed voices that have not enjoyed the same privileges of authorship, those whose words were never legitimated through print. Some of the voices in this text are seemingly irrational to the point of madness, but if a ghost can take on the guise of a hallucination, what might we venture to gain by listening to what those voices have to say?[60]

As that thing that was like her shadow breathed life into the empty spaces of my house, the vocalization of taboo words grew a little bit louder. The sound of that voice was eerily familiar, like my mother's, or perhaps like the ones that spoke to her. For the first time, I was privy to the content of their speech. They compulsively repeated dates in synchronicity with time displayed on the clock, mostly marking birthdays and special events in my family's private history. But then there were dates that were not immediately recognizable, which I might have let go under other circumstances. For the first time, in the early 1990s, something like her voice emerged from the empty spaces to speak to the traumas of my diasporic history. I did not yet know that my history was also my future. But I began to sense something that I could not yet recognize—pieces of some incoherent story about incoherent stories, of which I could not make sense but that I want to tell you anyway.

I want to tell you a story about the yanggongju, but I also want to resist the tendency toward creating a piece of work whose politics remain at the level of representation about a lost or suppressed history. To tell a story of trauma is not to tell of what was lost but to meditate on the ways in which, as Cheng says, "cultural trauma . . . recurs as a profoundly unlocatable event."[61] Rather than claiming to uncover the truth about what really happened to Korean women during the history of U.S. military involvement or to recover these women's lost memories, I hope that this work will look for the traces of haunting around us. To give form to the haunted spaces marked by trauma creates openings for trauma's productive possibilities. Rather than privileging research methods that are organized around the argument, this project shifts the focus of research from content to affect. I am just as concerned about what the presentation of evidence *does* as what it *says.* What affects are produced in listeners, and what affects get stored away to be released in the future? As Gordon writes, "Being haunted draws us affectively, sometimes against our will and always a bit magically, into the structure of a reality we come to experience, not as cold knowledge, but as a transformative recognition."[62] What is produced in this process, I hope, will be new bodies that can offer insight about the present and that "make the irrecoverable the condition of a new political agency," in the words of Butler.[63] This project is a staging of words, of traumas Clough calls "too deeply embodied for an I to speak them."[64] Where flesh and paper meet and unconscious is rendered into text, I share the stage with these ghosts.

2.
A Genealogy of Trauma

So I've gone around in circles—China, to North Korea, down to O-san and to Seoul, then to the United States, back to North Korea. . . . It's all a painful story; there's no pleasure in it. Sometimes I want to forget it but I just can never forget.

—Helen Kyungsook Daniels, as quoted in "So I've Gone Around in Circles . . . Living the Korean War"

After the war I returned to Paekdu . . . but there was no one. No village. No home. Our house and fields were burned to the ground. . . . We decided to make our way south; somehow it was easier for us to keep moving, to keep busy, to keep not remembering.

—Nora Okja Keller, *Fox Girl*

The two quotes above suggest a repetition of trauma that resists all attempts to erase it from personal and public memory. The two speakers, in fact, have much in common despite their divergent outcomes. One is a Korean War survivor who married a U.S. serviceman and was a participant in Ramsay Liem's oral history project; the other is a Korean American writer's fictional representation of a postwar military sex worker.[1] One of these women moved to the United States to realize the "American dream," while the other never made it out of the camptown. Although one speaker is a real woman vocalizing her life experiences and the other is a character in a novel written by a Korean American writer, the similarity between the two quotes suggests a continuity between those who lived through the war and those of the second generation who give creative expression to the traumatized memories they have inherited. Perhaps more important, the language of being caught in circles evokes two important aspects of trauma that have set the stage for this chapter. The disintegration of progressive time and the inability to locate (and thereby erase) the content of memory play out in such a way that the distinctions between the actual interview and the imagined story become less important than the traumatic effects communicated by the words themselves. Both speakers are constantly on the move, in a state of physical and psychic exile that unsettles one's sense of being grounded in place and time, in which neither forgetting nor fully remembering the traumatic events of the war and its aftermath is possible. Under such conditions, what are the mechanisms of remembering? Where is memory stored? What story can one tell about that which the subject does not want to remember?

This is a story about what we have been made to forget and what we have never even been allowed to remember, about what has been covered over by official narratives of the United States' role in the Korean War and the ways in which the enforcement of forgetting sometimes falters. Indeed, it is impossible to forget completely, because the Forgotten War is not yet over, either in geopolitical terms or in its psychic effects.

While the Korean War is arguably the least understood war in American military history, this chapter does not attempt to rewrite that history. Rather, through an act of memory it looks to sites of unacknowledged loss in order to piece together the remnants of the Forgotten War—the memories of its survivors, the bodies of its dead, and the charred remains of the American scorched-earth policy. Such an act of memory reveals not only hidden histories of grief but also continuities with contemporary geopolitics, and thus it raises questions about the ways in which the United States is a neocolonial power rather than a peacekeeper bestowing the gift of democracy. As the first conflict of the Cold War, the Korean War served as a testing ground for future wars, particularly for what Bruce Cumings refers to as the United States' "capacity to be a good anti-communist manager."[2] Vietnam was already in the works in 1950, and the technologies of warfare developed during the Korean War were later used in the Vietnam and Iraq Wars. The Korean War was both a launching point for an intensification of U.S. military dominance in Asia and a continuation of what had already been initiated by the Japanese colonizers. For example, in the war crimes tribunals led by the Western Allies after World War II, the Japanese were exonerated for testing the technologies of human torture and biological warfare on the bodies of forced Korean laborers, many of whom had been comfort women. According to Sheldon Harris, the condition for Japan's exoneration was to share these technologies with the U.S. military, which later redeployed them against Koreans during the Korean War.[3]

Although the Korean War resonates with other wars, most scholarship on the subject has neglected to deal with what is perhaps the most remarkable thing about it—the magnitude and intensity of the destruction, which were, in many ways, greater than those of any other war of the twentieth century. Although World War II was much deadlier, the proportion of collateral damage was greater in the Korean War. By one estimate, 70 percent of the Korean War's death toll was composed of civilian casualties, compared to 40 percent for World War II.[4] While the Vietnam War is well known for brutal tactics directed at unarmed civilians, the same tactics were used against civilians in the Korean War, and more intensely, resulting in a larger death count in a much shorter time span. According to Sahr Conway-Lanz,

> Unlike the writing about the Vietnam War, historians have largely ignored the cost of fighting in Korea. They have not drawn attention to the war's ferocity, the devastation it inflicted, and the ways in which the conflict was anything but a limited war for Koreans. . . . Most histories of the war have left the aerial devastations, the large number of civilian casualties and refugees, the toll of post traumatic stress for American veterans, the destruction of entire communities, and the problems posed for the UN forces by guerrilla warfare as a footnote in their accounts.[5]

More recently, however, some scholars have created works that evoke the experience of the war from the perspective of the Korean civilian who survived it.[6] Ramsay Liem's oral history project, in particular, involves a kind of remembering that acknowledges the destruction of the Korean peninsula and the loss of life at the same time that it makes room for what is in excess of loss.

In order to flesh out a memory of the Forgotten War, Liem assembled a group of second-generation Korean American artists, activists, and scholars (myself included) to create an art exhibit around his oral history research. The exhibit, titled *Still Present Pasts: Korean Americans and the "Forgotten War,"* brings the traumatic effects of the war into public discourse through a collection of visual and performance art pieces. While these works are based on historical research, including the oral histories, they also press against the boundaries of what counts as history. Many of the artworks in *Still Present Pasts* use Saidiya Hartman's method of "foraging and disfiguration."[7] They take pieces of the oral histories recorded by Liem and invest them with the artist's creative vision to animate that which has been lost or forgotten and to recognize the ways in which, in the words of Jill Bennett, "the past seeps back into the present, as sensation rather than representation."[8] Likewise, I am interested in addressing the history of the Korean War not by offering an authoritative account of what happened during the war but by making palpable its traumatic traces.

This chapter is a writing experiment that encourages the past to "seep back," to use Bennett's phrase. While there is a certain chronology to keep in mind, I unfold this story through a temporality of trauma that is nonlinear, one that operates at the level of what can be neither forgotten nor fully remembered. I do so with the recognition that what hovers in the liminal space between forgetting and remembering can open up to inform histories and current practices of domination. I use historical accounts about less-known aspects of the Korean War, such as those revealed by Liem's work on the psychic impact it has had on survivors, as well as the artworks inspired by his oral histories, popular journalistic writing about civilian massacres, and testimony offered in war crimes tribunals to evoke the traumatic sensations carried by those who survived the war and those who would later be constituted by it.

In particular, I focus on the early days of the war, for it was the first five months of conflict that was most devastating to civilian life. I insert layers of vignettes that return again and again to the summer of 1950 with others that come from moments in the future that are haunted by this past. These vignettes are based on historical sources, as well as my own uncertain family history and my mother's memories of the war, especially her memories of the kind of minutiae that seem uncanny in the absence of a larger narrative about her experience as a displaced refugee child. I also draw out the stories of Korean civilians who witnessed the Nogeun-ri massacre as well as other less notorious incidents involving the killing of civilians. Through "foraging and disfiguration" I spin a story about a diaspora of trauma in which it becomes unclear whose memory is being recounted.[9] These mixed-up experiences are an expression of a "generalized unconscious" in which trauma is carried forward along with the movement of bodies, thereby evacuating the sense of progress that is associated with the passing of time.[10] Although this chapter deals primarily with events that took place on the Korean peninsula between 1950 and 1953 from the perspective of civilian war survivors, I also approach this history by connecting disparate points in time and space. What these moments have in common is that they are articulated by a similar haunting, tenuously held together by some ghost that emerged from the space of evacuation.

This is a story about the figure of the yanggongju and how she was constructed largely out of the ruins of war, at the same time becoming the ghost that carries the history of the war forward into the future and across trajectories of movement. In so doing, she disrupts the narratives that go unquestioned about the Korean War and U.S.–Korea relations. What is articulated through these disruptions is a story about the yanggongju and the multiple discourses that have brought her into existence while also disavowing her. I begin this atemporal chronology, of trauma and Korean diaspora and of the making of the yanggongju, with the Korean War because of its relationship to broader forms of collective trauma for Koreans and because this unresolved conflict is the underlying geopolitical rationale behind the current system of prostitution around U.S. military bases in South Korea. I also want to point out that naming the Korean War as a starting point is somewhat paradoxical, because the war itself is a traumatic event that obscures notions of linear time. It is the first and last conflict of the Cold War, whose beginning is uncertain and whose end has not yet arrived.

The Forgotten War's Monstrous Family

silence children—
never utter another word
your fathers and mothers are no longer with us
and they will not come back
such is the lot of many of us here

> it's a secret
> lock it deep in your hearts. . . .
>
> remember that these things didn't happen. . . .
>
> dry your tears and learn to forget
> we are alone and frightened
> from the terrors we witnessed. . . .
> who will believe
> who will speak for us
>
> silence children—silence.
>
> —YONG YUK, "Cheju Do," unpublished poem

June 25, 1950, is written in history as the day the Korean War began. In Korean, the date "yugi-o" (six twenty-five) is a metonym for the entire war, thereby fixing this date as an originary moment in Korean public memory as well. Organized guerrilla war began much earlier, however, as did American involvement in anticommunist hostilities. The peasant uprising on Jeju Island on April 3, 1948, and the subsequent counterinsurgency authorized by the Rhee Syngman regime and backed by the U.S. military, formed one of "the darkest yet least-known chapters of post[–World War II] Asian history."[11] The mass killing of Jeju villagers in the name of anticommunism was a precursor to the events of June 25, 1950, one whose visibility casts doubt on the accepted narrative about when and how the Korean War started.[12]

According to typical accounts, the war began on June 25, 1950, after the North Korean Army crossed the thirty-eighth parallel and perpetrated a surprise attack on South Korea in an attempt to forcibly reunify the peninsula under a communist regime and the south resisted the north's invasion.[13] The extent to which the North Korean attack was a surprise has now been called into question; some historians have shown that U.S. and South Korean forces had advance knowledge of the attack and that U.S. officials had been speculating about a Korean war as early as 1946.[14] Even reporters who investigated the war as it was unfolding hypothesized that the United States did in fact know what the north had been planning.[15] Conspiracy theories aside, the United States was, at the very least, complicit with the division and massive destruction of the Korean peninsula, even if not entirely responsible. As Cumings writes:

> The Korean War did not begin on June 25, 1950, much special pleading and argument to the contrary. If it did not begin then, Kim Il Sung could not have "started" it then, either. . . . As we search backward for that point, we slowly grope toward the truth that civil wars do not start: they come. They originate in multiple causes, with blame enough to go around for everyone—and blame enough to include Americans who thoughtlessly divided Korea and then reestabilished the colonial government machinery and the Koreans who served it.[16]

What Cumings alludes to here is the fact that the "civil war" that escalated into the Korean War was aggravated by a U.S. intervention that simultaneously disabled the indigenous independence movements that had begun prior to September 8, 1945, rewarded Korean officials who had collaborated with the Japanese, and turned the peninsula into a playing field for its power struggle with the Soviets, thus sowing the seeds of armed resistance. Although the historiography of the war has been contested on various counts, what is indisputable is that it was a cultural trauma that directly affected nearly the entire population of the peninsula. Decades after the end of fighting, incidents from 1950–53 continue to surface, resonating with current events, as if the traumas of the Korean War were already entangled with horrors that were yet to come.

America's First Vietnam

I. F. Stone's book-length investigative report titled *The Hidden History of the Korean War* was first published in 1952, thus revealing the unpublicized events of the war as it was still being waged, but the appearance of the book was "met with an almost complete press blackout and boycott."[17] It vanished as soon as it could materialize. It is rumored that even copies of the Spanish translation were bought up en masse and destroyed by the U.S. Embassy in Mexico. In 1970, a second edition was published with a publisher's note that the rerelease of

the book was "urgently relevant to the Vietnam peace negotiations." Prefacing the title on the cover of the 1970 edition are the words "America's First Vietnam."

Korea's My Lai

In September 1999, the Associated Press (AP) broke the Pulitzer Prize–winning story of the 1950 Nogeun-ri massacre, in which U.S. troops had opened fire from the air and ground onto civilian refugees near the village of Nogeun-ri. An estimated four hundred villagers were shot dead. The media reports draw striking similarities between the mass killings in Nogeun-ri and the 1968 My Lai massacre of the Vietnam War.[18] Other investigations followed this disclosure, and there is speculation that Nogeun-ri is merely "the tip of the iceberg" of the war crimes committed on the Korean peninsula.[19] Thirty-seven other civilian massacres have come to light in the southern part of Korea, along with "countless massacres" in the north.[20]

The Korean Vieques Called Maehyang-ri

Maehyang-ri is a small fishing village located near the Kun-ni range, the largest U.S. Air Force (U.S.A.F.) bombing training site in Asia. There it is not uncommon to encounter people whose body parts have been torn off by misfired bombs or whose hearing is impaired by the sound of low-flying planes. In this sense, it is a village of bodies created by the daily practices of war. During a bombing exercise on May 8, 2000, a U.S.A.F. fighter pilot began losing control of his plane and, in an attempt to rid the plane's cargo of excess weight, dropped six five-hundred-pound bombs over Maehyang-ri. In this most recent episode in the fifty-year-long history of miscalculated bombings, 170 homes were damaged and seven people injured.[21] Ismael Guadalupe, an antimilitary activist from Vieques, Puerto Rico, site of a U.S. Navy bombing range, visited Maehyang-ri shortly after this incident

and commented, "It is a situation that you have to see in order to believe. . . . Before the struggle increased in Vieques [in 1978], we had a situation similar to the one in Maehyang-ri."[22]

These comparisons of Korea to Vietnam and Vieques speak to the ways in which the trauma of militarized violence can traverse boundaries of time and space so that the effects of military bombing practice can at once be embodied in two seemingly distinct geographical and historical locations: Maehyang-ri in 2000 and Vieques in 1978. They also illustrate how one occurrence can evoke another moment that has not yet happened. While Maehyang-ri is reminiscent of an earlier Vieques, Nogeun-ri evokes a future My Lai. According to Jacqueline Rose, this temporal or spatial shift suggests a transgenerational haunting in which trauma can be unconsciously passed "not just down through the generations, but *across* them; and not inside one family, but creating a monstrous family of reluctant belonging," so that the past is future and Vieques is Maehyang-ri.[23] A temporality in which past and future collide is the temporality both of an unconscious haunted by trauma and of the affective experience of a traumatic event, in which the past opens directly onto the future because the present moment happens too quickly to be perceived. Events and their contexts are folded into the body as potentialities, and the present moment is accessible to conscious experience only through its traces.[24]

Korean history articulated through the more familiar stories of Vietnam and Vieques also raises a series of questions about perception. Why is Korean history so little known in the United States and other parts of the world? Why is the official history of U.S.–Korea relations so riddled with holes, so full of silences that take fifty years to be heard? Are these stories told through Vietnam and Vieques because a history of conflict between South Korea and the United States is unintelligible on its own?

The official script of U.S.–Korea relations reads that the United States has always been a friend to South Korea, a friend that has come to its rescue many times: to liberate a country left demoralized by Japanese colonialism, to fight the communist north in the name of freedom and democracy, to rebuild a country left devastated by war, to grow its economy to miraculous proportions, to save its orphans, to marry its women, to take them to the land of opportunity where they are welcomed with open arms and assimilate quickly. This story line of cooperation between the two countries relies on metaphors of familial relations in which the United States is always cast as the dominant male figure—older brother to the Korean military, husband in the interracial romance, and father figure to orphaned children.[25] While many parallels can be drawn between the Korean War and the Vietnam War, Vietnam was an example of the U.S. military's failed masculinity, whereas the narrative of Korea as a successful rescue mission restores the United States' dominance in the patriarchal family of nations. In the words of Philadelphia-based reunification activist Sung Yong Park, "The American people are used to hearing stories of the bravery of the American military in war. They believe the myth that the Korean War was one of the most successful actions in American military history and that any atrocities were performed by the communists but not by their own army. This myth has been created by the U.S. Army's concealing and/or disguising the truth."[26]

While in the United States unofficial histories about the violence that is part and parcel of the U.S.–Korea relationship remain largely unseen and unspoken, in Korea stories and images of a traumatic history are all too visible and can also create a state of not seeing. As Hosu Kim's work in *Still Present Pasts* suggests, the continuing effects of the Korean War have become so ingrained in the fabric of everyday life in Korea that they have become almost imperceptible to those who live under the regime of stalemated war. In either the U.S. or the Korean case, what we are looking at does not always register through standard measures of observation, thus requiring different methods of seeing. David Eng's approach of "focusing on . . . the unconscious aspects of looking," for example, implies a shift away from looking at a clearly identifiable object of analysis to looking at effects that reverberate beyond the field of vision.[27] Bennett describes this register as "seeing feeling," which "yield[s] information to the body" about that which cannot be precisely located.[28]

The team of AP investigative reporters on the Nogeun-ri story, for example, employed these methods of perception because the incident had been covered up in the United States. They found evidence that both the military and the media had heavily censored reports documenting the deliberate destruction of civilian ways of life or the targeted killing of civilians themselves. The AP reporters spent a year analyzing both the gaps in military reporting and the traces of evidence that remained after the erasures. They looked at the unpublished accounts of dead journalists who had recorded the brutality of the Korean War only in personal diaries and letters to their families due to the level of media censorship during the 1950s. Beyond that, the AP reporters retrieved the psychic records of witnesses, both Korean and American—evidence in the form of nightmares, visions, auditory hallucinations, and nagging memories of things they wished they had not seen.[29] *The Bridge at No Gun Ri,* the book based on their research, allows these irrational forces to speak and thereby push against the rational bureaucratic authorities who have continued to deny that the massacre took place.[30]

The American veterans involved in the incident reported that their memories had been plagued by visions of the people they had killed, the faces of people they had known were not the enemy but looked like them. Several of the veterans talked about a little girl. She had been one of the refugees who had counterintuitively run toward the soldiers during the massacre instead of hiding from them. "You should have seen those guys trying to kill that little girl with their machine guns," one of the veterans recalled.[31] The man who ultimately claimed responsibility for killing her explained, "We understood that we were fighting for these people, but we had orders to fire on them, and we did."[32] Edward Daily, another veteran who had been involved in the massacre, returned to Korea in 1999, shortly after the AP story broke, so that he could make peace with the victims.[33] For almost fifty years, he said, he had not been able to let go of his guilt for the lives he had taken, nor had he known that there were any survivors to whom he could apologize. The fifty-year silence around the civilian massacre and the psychic ties among the victims and perpetrators of the crime is another example of how transgenerational haunting has created "monstrous families of reluctant belonging."[34]

Warning: We Are Here

> My first contact with Americans came in the form of fliers dropped from planes. The fliers read "You are safe. We are here."
>
> —Chong Suk Dickman, "Thank You," in *I Remember Korea*

Park Sun-yong was a young mother of two in July 1950 when she fled south from her home village toward Nogeun-ri. She remembers that at the start of the war she had felt comforted knowing that the U.S. soldiers were there to protect them. On the first day of the massacre, when she saw U.S. airplanes above, she believed the Americans had come to transport them to safety, but moments later the bombs fell. After that, the ground troops ordered the surviving refugees onto a train trestle where they waited for several hours before the troops fired on them again, this time with their guns. Those who tried to run were shot down, and so were those who waited under the bridge. A few survived by escaping at the right moment or hiding beneath the bodies of the massacred. Sun-yong had watched her mother-in-law and her two-year-old daughter die and had made a decision to try to save her remaining child. With her four-year-old son strapped to her back, she ran away from the trestle and was fired at repeatedly. Both mother and child were hit and fell to the ground. "Blood was spreading from the small body of my child," she said. "That day I saw the two faces of America."[35] Another survivor, Chun Choon-ja, also experienced the stunning contrast of these two faces of the United States. Ten years old at the time, she witnessed the killings of her mother, grandfather, and baby brother. Between rounds of shooting, the soldiers offered her something to eat. "Maybe chocolate," she said. "But I didn't eat it."[36]

> Warning: Yellow food parcels and cluster bomblets may look alike. . . . Please exercise caution when approaching unidentified yellow objects. . . .

BooDaeChiGae. Copyright Ji Young Yoo/Still Present Pasts, 2005. Video, Korean rice paper, Korean table, C-rations can, video monitor. The outlines of three Korean War orphans eating from relief goods are burned into rice paper. On the dining table, a video monitor sits inside a C-ration can. The video captures a pair of hands making "BooDaeChiGae" (military-base stew). The voice-over features a Korean War survivor talking about living off the garbage on U.S. military bases. The artist describes this piece as "a distorted relic of the drastic social change derived from the U.S. intervention."

> Aid is being dropped by plane at a very high altitude using large parachutes. . . . Do not stand directly below them. . . . If you follow these instructions you will not be injured. . . . The United States cannot warn you enough about the danger that you will put yourself in if you do not stay away from the bundles until they land. . . . These supplies are being sent to help you.
>
> —Radio broadcasts during the "War on Terror" in Afghanistan

The two faces of America—murderous and benevolent—loom large in the memories of Korean War survivors, although some recall one face more readily than the other. Perhaps the narratives of U.S. benevolence have proved more powerful than psychic evidence that suggests the contrary. Perhaps they are evidence of a defense mechanism, what Freud called a protective fiction, yet this discrepancy is about more than just an internalization of one story over and against another. Rather, the inability to see is one of the workings of trauma. According to Cathy Caruth, "Traumatic experience . . . suggests a certain paradox: that the most direct seeing of a violent event may occur as an absolute inability to know it," so many of those who witnessed the unjust killing of civilians are unable to make sense of it, or even to remember it.[37]

When I ask her about the war, she says practically nothing. Sometimes she cannot remember, does not want to remember, or remembers things that are conspicuously out of place. I do not know for sure what horrors even belonged to her, if she had been witness to her brother's death or to the deaths of neighbors or strangers traveling with her.

After fifty years, some of these memories have begun to be documented in an effort often led by those of the postwar generations who have been haunted by the uncertainty of their pasts. One of the difficulties in documenting the scale of the civilian massacres, however, was that entire families were killed, leaving no one to officially register the deaths. How does one piece together a history that is always rendered incoherent by what is missing and unknowable? How is a traumatic event such as mass killing remembered when there is no one recording it, no speaker to speak of it? According to Marc Nichanian and David Kazanjian, the documentation of history through the archive always privileges "the executioner's logic" in that "the victim is obliged to appeal to the archive to prove that what was conceived as not having taken place did indeed take place."[38] The method of dream work, however, moves beyond this paradigm by looking for evidence of the "Forgotten War" that is recorded not on paper but in body memory, in what is "expressed fugitively in all its obscure fullness, in people's eyes and the horror they reflect."[39]

You Are Safe; We Are Here

June 25, 1950. That was not the beginning of the war for those who lived near the border. The conflict was at least as old as the division of the peninsula after World War II, and the first Korean's life was taken in September 1945, the same day that the American occupation began. The border fighting was especially intense right before the war. June 25 was not a beginning as much as it was an escalation toward the unresolvable. "Brother against brother" gave way to superpower against superpower. And those who lived near the border had already learned to bear witness to how the splitting of land demanded blood.[40]

Choon-ja lived in a southern province more than three hundred kilometers south of the thirty-eighth parallel. She was far away on the official first day of fighting, so she did not witness the first American bombs fall, and she took for granted that the Americans were there only to help. She was nowhere near womanhood and so had not yet contemplated death—the departure of the spirit into the next life and the decomposition of the corpse. She certainly had never imagined the particular form the flesh takes when it is drained of blood and submerged in stagnant water. Over the days and months that followed June 25, 1950, she would come to know death—and loss. She would become intimate with the disarticulated limbs that she could only guess belonged to her mother, and the wholeness of her own body by contrast, the capacity of her own two hands to cradle the flesh already falling off her father's bones.

The official rhetoric in the north was that the U.S. troops were hostile invaders who had divided and occupied the land. In the south the story was that they were allies who had come to liberate the Koreans. Some Koreans embraced one of these ideologies, but many did not care for either regime; however, they all had something in common by the time the fighting had erupted into full-scale war: they were targets of American military strikes.

By mid-July of 1950, news came that the war front was heading toward the southern provinces and that fleeing provided the best chance for survival. Conway-Lanz writes: "In the early weeks of the war, tens of thousands of civilians moved southward along with the retreating American units. Some civilians had been told to evacuate their villages by the South Korean government; others were fleeing the violence of battle; and still others had been directed south by North Korean soldiers hoping to hinder the UN forces."[41] Families who lived in the path of war packed whatever belongings they could carry and left the rest behind or buried them beneath their homes. Choon-ja was ten years old when everyone in her village started walking farther south. At first, this move appealed to her sense of adventure, but as her legs grew heavier and her feet blistered, the excitement withered away. At least they were getting out of harm's way. They did not know that by this time the U.S. military had already issued warnings that bands of refugees might be harboring enemies and should be treated accordingly. They did not know that orders from the highest U.S. command in Korea stated that regiments could exercise "complete authority. . . to stop all civilian traffic in any direction" and that "responsibility to place fire on them to include bombing" was in the hands of individual commanders. Nor did they know that "strafing fire from low-flying aircraft" was regarded by many officials as an effective means of "clearing a roadway" of civilians.[42]

Soon-hee was one year older than Choon-ja during the summer of 1950. They did not know each other, although they lived in the same southern province, only a few kilometers apart. But Soon-hee's hometown was large enough to be a town, while Choon-ja's was only a village. Perhaps this was the variable that determined the path of war, that Changnyeong was a town and Imke-ri a village. Perhaps this was the same variable that sent Choon-ja south toward her family's massacre and kept Soon-hee safe at home for the time being.

Warning: Yellow Food Parcels and Cluster Bomblets May Look Alike

"One midsummer morning in this year of the tiger, the Americans arrived in the valley."[43] So wrote the AP reporters of that time in 1950. This arrival was a premonition, a promise of something more to come. The Americans arrived with exotic goods in hand, giving Marlboros only to the men because women were not allowed to smoke. There was chocolate for the children. These were the same Americans who weeks later would extinguish entire families of refugees, even against their own sense of ethics, simply because they had been ordered to kill. Maybe they were the same Americans into whose arms Soon-hee would later run, these men who soothed little girls' tears with candy and tempted their desires for America.

Soon-hee's older brother had already disappeared, and by the time her family fled, she had been put in charge of caring for her brother's young son. She traveled by foot across mountains and rivers from Changnyeong to Busan, an eleven-year-old carrying a three-year-old on her back. In the mountains she encountered the Red Army, and what startled her most was that many of the North Korean soldiers were women. In the mountains, the girls with guns let refugees pass unharmed. Or, as some survivors recalled years later, the North Korean army, although brutal in its own right, had spared the lives of civilians.[44] Maybe it was a recognition of kinship, that these people belonged to one another, that kept the North Korean soldiers from shooting. And this was a recognition that most Americans could not register. Some survivors would say that it was the Reds who gave them tips on how to survive strafing from aircraft. "*Don't move and the pilot won't see you.*"[45] As much as those who lived south of the thirty-eighth parallel had been told to fear the Reds, it was the communist soldiers who let refugees continue on their paths through the mountains. But it was the Americans who guarded the crossings at the river.

You Are Safe

> We all came to the Imjin River and my brother-in-law said, we have to cross. . . . There's American soldiers, [South] Korean soldiers, and Korean women police—they're all there. They all had guns on us, saying you can't come. So we said, why? And they said because of North Korean soldiers, you can't trust who's a soldier, who's not. . . . Either we die here or we die crossing.
>
> —DANIELS, as quoted in "So I've Gone around in Circles"

Jin-sok was fifteen in July 1950 when U.S. troops ordered his village to evacuate and flee, but when his family reached the crossing at the Naktong River, all the bridges had already been blown up. The only way to get to the other side was to wade across, but U.S. troops fired on his group. His father was shot and had died by the time they reached the riverbank. Koon-ja was eighteen in

July 1950 when bullets showered around her, so she withdrew from the water and left the slain members of her group floating upstream. She headed north and encountered Nogeun-ri after the massacre, including the bodies of Hee-sook's family, whom she did not know but who on another day had also turned back at the river. Hee-sook was sixteen in July 1950 when her mother hid her in a gimchi jar because American men were passing through their village. Weeks later, Hee-sook encountered these men at the Naktong.

Warning: We Are Here

In 1950, 875 women were reported raped by U.S. soldiers stationed in Seoul.[46] But the evidence of rape and killing at the crossing of the river also lives in the material of memory—in Jin-sok, who still sees his father's blood coloring the river red; in Koon-ja, who retreated from the bullets and backtracked to find the human remains of her neighboring village; in Hee-sook, who was invited to go to the other side because her young body was just what the soldiers were looking for. The memories of what happened at the river are stored in the flesh of the survivors, in the flesh of the dead, and in the bloodied banks of the Naktong.

It was not until almost fifty years after the cease-fire in 1953 that written evidence began to confirm these memories. Declassified U.S. military documents show that army units made calculations to destroy bridges in order to block the movement of refugees, and in cases in which groups of refugees attempted to swim across anyway, deliberate decisions were made to kill them. Advanced directives ordered troops to "shoot all refugees coming across the river."[47] Bridges were sometimes blown up at the very moment that refugees were crossing. "*August 2, 1950: It was a hard decision to make, for hundreds of refugees were lost when the bridge was demolished.*"[48] While the Department of the Navy officially stated that "warring against civilians" in such a manner was "wholly abhorrent," they also believed that it was "wholly defensible."[49]

Military efforts to deal with "the refugee problem" resulted in a self-perpetuating cycle of destruction and displacement. The massive dislocation of Korean civilians meant that battle lines often became obstructed with hordes of moving refugees whose origins

Ghostly piles of ashes: a child standing where his home used to be.

could not be identified. As the bodies of Koreans from different sides of the thirty-eighth parallel became more and more mixed up, U.S. and U.N. forces increasingly justified the destruction of homes, hospitals, orphanages, schools, farms, fields, and all things necessary to the sustenance of life as a means of harming potential communists. "*As Korean civilians return to the north now in the wake of advancing forces of the United Nations and see what has happened in their villages, they stare in numb disbelief at the ghostly piles of ashes that were once homes.*"[50]

The more that the bodies of panicked Korean refugees blocked roadways and prevented the movement of military vehicles, the more the United States and the United Nations rationalized the use of lethal force against civilians as a means of clearing traffic jams.[51] As Jackie Orr writes: "Jamming the exits and inflaming fatalities, panic also permits those who preside over industrial-size disasters to account differently for the loss of life—and to render more obscure its financial and legal accounting—by offering a deadly psychological subtext to the malfunctions of increasingly massive, complex technosocial machineries."[52] The chaotic movement of frightened Koreans required stricter enforcement of the military's civilian control policy. In short, the more the new technologies of destruction were directed at civilian life, the more the refugee problem grew to monstrous proportions. But this is something that the U.S. military covered up during the war and would later deny as its genocidal practices became exposed.

Burn 'Em Out, Cook 'Em, Fry 'Em

Declassified memoranda show not only that the destruction of civilian life was indiscriminate but also that it was whitewashed by military officials. In a July 1950 memo whose subject heading was "Policy on Strafing Civilian Refugees," Colonel Turner Rogers expressed his concern: "Our operations involving the strafing of civilians is sure to receive wide publicity and may cause embarrassment to the U.S. Air Force and the U.S. government."[53] Rather than proceeding with discretion in order to prevent civilian casualties, the Air Force continued the strafing of refugees, the massacre of civilians, and the destruction of homes. By the end of the summer of 1950, the military's public relations office in Washington, D.C., had heard rumors that U.S. bombers in Korea were "promiscuous."[54] Ultimately, the Pentagon recommended that U.S. forces in Korea stop documenting the bombing of villages and begin calling them "military targets" in order to avoid negative press. One of the biggest challenges of fighting the Korean War was precisely that there were so few industrial and military targets, and most of these were destroyed within the first few months of fighting. As one U.N. official reported in August 1951, "In Seoul, . . . one of the most modern cities of the Far East, 85 per cent of industrial facilities, 75 per cent of office space, and 50 to 60 per cent of living space had been destroyed."[55]

Despite these challenges, U.S.A.F. operational summaries often reported "excellent results" in the implementation of the "scorched-earth policy" by which entire villages were routinely burned to the ground and cities were given "saturation treatments" if they were believed to be enemy occupied.[56] Scorching the earth, as well as the people who inhabited it, was facilitated by the use of chemical weapons that had been tried and tested a few years earlier against the Japanese. Thanks to these new technologies of killing, the scorched-earth policy yielded excellent results:

> *The first* damaging effect of a napalm bomb is, of course, a burn. . . .
> *The second* . . . is carbon monoxide poisoning. . . .
> *The third* . . . is a burn in the upper part of the windpipe. . . .
> *The fourth* is shock. . . .
> *The fifth* is an effect on the blood and internal organs. . . .
> *The sixth* is a change in the bones.
>
> —Masahiro Hashimoto, Vietnam War Crimes Tribunal

Napalm was conceived in 1942 in a science laboratory at Harvard, and then the U.S. government contracted Dow Chemicals to develop it into a weapon that would be the basis for a new form of warfare. The United States used it extensively in three wars, dropping it over Japan, Korea, and Vietnam, then used it to a lesser extent over Iraq during the 1991 Gulf War as well as during the current Iraq war. The weapon itself is composed of a highly volatile, sticky substance held inside an aluminum casing. When the substance combusts, the aluminum explodes and the "incendiary jelly" contained inside disperses and sets fire to everything with which it comes into contact. Over the years it was refined into "super napalm," a chemical weapon that would burn at increasingly higher temperatures, destroying the land and population more quickly with each war in which it was used.

Between 1950 and 1953, U.S. bombers dumped as much as 600,000 tons of napalm over the Korean peninsula; in Churchill's words, it was "splashed" over the landscape. This was more napalm than had been used against Japan in World War II and more than would later be dropped over Vietnam.[57] However, the use of napalm would not become an issue of widespread public concern in the United States until years later, when Americans saw images of Vietnamese children being burned alive. When social protest against the Vietnam War solidified, U.S. military practices during the Forgotten War began to resonate. But between 1950 and 1953, neither did the U.S. government exhibit restraint in its deployment of "weapons of mass destruction," a term that came into common usage in military vocabulary during this period, nor did the practices of warfare become public knowledge in the United States, despite the fact that weapons of mass destruction were largely what Cumings has said "accounted for the remarkable civilian death toll" in Korea.[58]

On November 30, 1950, President Harry Truman held a press conference in which he admitted that since the beginning of the war he had been planning to drop atomic bombs over Korea, but even before making this confession he had sent secret orders to the Strategic Air Command "to be prepared to dispatch without delay medium bomb groups to the Far East. . . . This augmentation should include atomic capabilities."[59] The plans Truman disclosed during his press conference sent murmurs of discontent through the international community, but despite the generalized disapproval of atomic warfare, the American public remained unaware of the mundane practices of the war. They did not know about the indiscriminate bombing of villages, schools, and hospitals; the rape and massacre of civilians; the burning of fields; or the torture and execution of suspected communists, nor were they aware of the particular damage that the new technologies of war were inflicting on the bodies of Koreans and on the population. The scorched-earth policy and the widespread use of napalm were unquestioned, even celebrated. The American war propaganda of the time unabashedly and affectionately termed its new weapon "flaming death" when captioning aerial photographs of napalm bombings.[60] "*Burn 'em out, cook 'em, fry 'em.*"[61]

Unidentified napalm victim.

Poison-and-Burn Pathology

The people who were being fried and cooked were "gooks," and as some veterans and war correspondents recall, "Every man's dearest wish was to kill a Korean. 'Today. . . I'll get me a gook.'"[62] Americans "never spoke of the enemy as though they were people, but as one might speak of apes. . . . Otherwise, these essentially kind and generous Americans would not have been able to kill them indiscriminately or smash up their homes and poor belongings."[63] According to military psychologist Dave Grossman, it is racial difference and a belief in one's moral superiority, perhaps above all else, that hinders the kinds of guilt responses that are normally exhibited when one human being takes the life of another. The perception of "the gook," constructed by both military rhetoric and 1950s American popular culture, was that of a racially and morally inferior class of beings who needed to be saved in the south and extinguished in the north, yet because of the constant movement of refugees across boundaries of conflict, north and south became virtually indistinguishable. The very Koreans who were purportedly being saved from communism were massacred by U.S. and U.N. forces and held as political prisoners by the South Korean and American armies. When British reporter James Cameron raised concerns with the U.N. Commission about the extreme human rights violations he had witnessed against political prisoners, the Commission's response was "Most disturbing, yes; but remember, these are Asian people, with different standards of behavior."[64] Similarly, Barrett wrote in response to Koreans' loss of faith in U.N. allies, "It is too much to expect the average primitive Korean to understand that most destruction is unavoidable with the tools of modern war."[65] These perceived differences enhanced the institution's capacity to let die, as well as the soldier's capacity to kill.

Although many veterans of both the Korean and the Vietnam Wars were haunted by the knowledge that they had killed innocent people, and though others refused to carry out what were euphemistically called "special missions" involving the murder of civilians, there were some whose willingness and desire to kill were almost pathological. One Vietnam veteran, for example, said that he had experienced a perverse pleasure in killing, in spewing bullets and penetrating the body of the other. By the end of his tour of duty, he had become addicted to killing. "It can consume you," he said, "just like sex can."[66] Other soldiers may have experienced indifference to rather than pleasure in killing civilians. After all, "What's a couple of gooks? A couple of goddamn gooks?"[67]

The poison-and-burn pathology of napalm is such that its combustion changes the chemistry of the air, so one need not be hit by the substance itself to be killed. Napalm produces lethal levels of carbon monoxide, deoxygenating the air so that everyone caught in a strike zone dies of asphyxiation almost immediately. If one does survive the poison, napalm can generate so much heat that breathing the air near a strike zone can burn the inside of the mouth, the throat, and the lungs. According to GlobalSecurity.org, "When incendiary weapons were dropped on bunkers in Germany, the intense heat literally baked and dehydrated the dead, giving rise to the German word 'Bombenbrandschrumpfeichen,' meaning 'firebomb shrunken flesh.'"[68] And direct contact on the skin results in a combustion of the flesh that penetrates the body quickly and deeply, so that even after the burn has been extinguished on the surface, the fire continues to spread through the tissues:

> *first degree:* the outer skin only
> *second degree:* the inner layer of the outer skin
> *third degree:* the inner layer of the inner skin
> *fourth degree:* the deepest hypodermic tissues
> *fifth degree:* the muscles
>
> —Hashimoto, Vietnam War Crimes Tribunal

Napalm ignites at such high temperatures, in excess of six thousand degrees Fahrenheit, that first-degree burns from napalm contact are impossible. In most cases, the substance burns its victims through the skin to the muscle and through the muscle to the bone. "*There is a phenomenon of bone-ashes dropping away and burnt bones fusing together or disappearing.*"[69] Expert testimonies from the Vietnam War Crimes Tribunal describe napalm as "a means of extensive undiscriminating destruction." Ironically, the remains of these bombs also served as a means of survival for Korean War refugees, who searched for aluminum casings that were only partially exploded so that they could use the residues of the napalm jelly as cooking fuel. Their will to survive outweighed the risk of getting burned.

On June 27, 1950, President Truman addressed the nation about the United States' role in Korea, framing all U.S. involvement in Korea as a defense against the threat of communism. For the Truman administration, the events of June 25, 1950, justified a permanent military draft and the quadrupling of military spending over the next three years. During this speech Truman also announced his decision to securitize all U.S. military posts in Asia, thereby accelerating the dispatch of troops not only to Korea but also to the Philippines and French Indo-China.[70] According to Don Oberdorfer, "Internationally, the bloody three-year Korean War... led the United States to shift decisively from post–World War II disarmament to rearmament to stop Soviet expansionism."[71] Korea was an impetus, and a testing ground, for Vietnam. Fifteen years later, the scorched-earth policy would be redeployed in Vietnam. "The American forces that poured into South Vietnam . . . soon viewed all 'gooks' as potential enemies."[72] An operational summary of the Eighth Cavalry Regiment, a prestigious unit of the U.S. Army assigned to Korea during the Korean War, might have read as follows:

Eighth Cavalry Regiment Log, Any Day, Late Summer 1950

> 0745: "U.S. bombers committed a saturation bombing of Seoul, killing 1,096 civilians, leaving 1,201 . . . wounded and rendering more than 7000 homeless."[73]
>
> 0900: "The inhabitants throughout the village and in the fields were caught and killed and kept the exact postures they had held when the napalm struck—a man about to get on his bicycle, fifty boys and girls playing in an orphanage, a housewife strangely unmarked, holding in her hand a page torn from a Sears-Roebuck catalogue. . . . There must be almost two hundred dead in the tiny hamlet."[74]
>
> 1015: A pan-Korean investigation into U.S. war crimes found that the United States deployed bioterrorist tactics, such as the airdropping of relief goods contaminated with smallpox.[75]
>
> 1120: An International Committee of the Red Cross investigation into the conditions of refugee camps and hospitals found them to be overcrowded with civilians suffering of disease and starvation whose faces and bodies were covered with "large festering wounds" and "pus-filled swellings." Most remarkable was "the silence of the hospital, a silence of the apathetic and the dying." The report concluded that the failure to provide food, medicine, and sanitary conditions meant that three to four million refugees were "slowly dying."[76]
>
> 1345: "More than 100 children were killed by bombs rained on a crowded orphanage in Seoul—apparently from United States bombers—early this year, Christian Children's Fund Inc., which operated the orphanage, reported today."[77]
>
> *Results: Excellent*[78]

Targeting a civilian population would be a strategy that the U.S. military "perfected" during the Korean War, leaving three million people, or 10 percent of the population, dead. The horrors that began to unravel on the Korean peninsula on June 25, 1950, were already reminiscent of a future of U.S. military domination in Asia, flashing forward to images of napalmed children running through the streets of Saigon, naked and burned to the bone.

"*Every deep burn is a wound that is vulnerable.*"[79] With a burn the magnitude of what napalm inflicts, the growth of new skin begins only at the outer edges. The wound attempts to heal itself from the periphery. New tissue grows around the outside, but it is not the type of tissue that can stretch itself over the wound, no matter how much time has passed. The wound heals slowly, sometimes not at all. Scar tissue that grows on the edge is extremely fragile, making the wound susceptible to being reopened again and again, with little provocation.

"*Every deep burn is a wound that is vulnerable.*" It heals sometimes not at all, but this state of never healing, of never making progress, is not even the worst-case scenario, because the wound has the capacity to spawn new pathologies. The trauma can spread into other parts of the tissue or into the blood, generating infectious agents that attack the immune system and resulting in what burn pathologists call secondary death. "*Such deaths can appear long after the trauma itself.*"[80]

Air Raid: By Order of the U.S. Military, You Are Instructed to Evacuate

Up to 90 percent of the population of the Korean peninsula survived the war, but more pessimistic estimates, particularly those from North Korean sources, say that it was closer to 80 percent. But what does it do to a person to live through such massive devastation? Perhaps the most enduring effect of the fact that civilians were targeted was the scale of their displacement. In March of 1951, U.N. officials estimated that three million Koreans had become homeless because their homes and villages had been destroyed, and by summer of 1951, five million Koreans had been displaced from their homes as refugees.[81] At the end of that summer, another U.N. official reported that of the nine million people who had lived in the northern part of the peninsula at the start of the war, one million were dead, while over half of those who had survived had sought refuge in the south.[82] Even eighteen months after the signing of the armistice, four million Koreans remained homeless.[83]

One of the most salient aspects of the Korean War in the accounts of both historians and survivors is the relentless bombing led by the United States. "*Americans were bombing every day and night. The Korean War was a bombing war. . . . North Korean army did not have much power to destroy, but American airplanes were indiscriminate, just flattened everything.*"[84] In this respect, the United States displayed more force than any nation involved in the war. Its forces had the technology not only to destroy the land and the people but, perhaps more significantly, to spread fear through the population. According to Jon Halliday and Bruce Cumings, "The USA had complete control of the air: everyone and everything that moved was subjected to constant bombing and strafing. People could move only at night."[85] The knowledge that one might be killed at any moment kept millions of refugees in a state of constant displacement, on the move without any particular destination other than beyond the reach of the bombs. The U.S. military also made careful calculations of the psychological impact of the bombing, especially in the north. Pyeongyang, for example, was the target of "operation insomnia," a bombing campaign designed to "exhaust the population."[86] The United States bombed continuously for forty days and nights, and by the end, only 10 percent of the population of the city of Pyeongyang remained. No doubt, many of them died, but many more fled to the south and would eventually renounce their identifications with the north for fear of being summarily executed. The displacement of civilians was not just about the movement of bodies but about psychic exile: survivors bear the lasting effects of trauma and are unable to be settled in the present moment. As Judith Butler has written, "All that happens has already happened, will come to appear as the always already happening . . . entangled and extended through time through the force of repetition.[87] The bearers of the traumatic effects of war are in a constant state of emergency.

So I've Gone Around in Circles

From Japan, where she was born, to Changnyeong, the town that her family called home. From Changnyeong to Busan after the evacuation, then back to Changnyeong, then to Busan again after the war. From the camptown at the naval base, where she eventually found work, to rural America, where her GI husband had been born and

Child caught in an air raid of enemy territory.

raised, back to Korea again—and again, until finally she could no longer return. But this small town would not be where her journey ended.

It was forty years after the end of the Korean War, the year she moved cross-country for the first time (the first of three such moves), after her second divorce from the American, her second divorce but one of five separations. She moved into a small one-bedroom apartment in a New England suburb, a quiet neighborhood except

for the routine sounding of an alarm that she could not identify. The noise did not increase in volume or frequency, but it grew increasingly disturbing. Any external noise bothered her, because it interfered with the sounds only she could hear, but this noise was particularly problematic. She began having flashbacks of air raids when she was nine years old. Although all reasoning told her that it was not 1950 and she was not in Korea, the siren told her that bombers were coming. During an air strike, civilians have to make quick decisions about whether it is better to seek shelter and possibly get caught in a strike zone or to run and be exposed. Of course, in order to really calculate one's chance of survival, one would need to know the exact moment of impact and the type of bombs used, and civilians are not privy to this information. The decision, then, is always a gut reaction, except in cases when verbal commands ordering civilians to evacuate are radioed from above. The siren, and the voice coming from the radio, told her to run.

Trauma evacuates memory in that it perpetually disturbs one's sense of being settled. Memory is poised to take flight whenever it is threatened, when there is a sense of a trauma returning or of a new trauma that is about to happen. This sense of impending catastrophe is an illusion, however, because the trauma never quite arrives. It never arrives because it has already happened; it is already in the present as an effect of some persistent past. The traumatized subject is continually uprooted. She might seem to be in a familiar place, in the sense that she has been there before, and she will most likely return there again and again through the force of repetition. Yet this place is neither an origin nor a final destination, keeping her suspended between a failed remembering and an incomplete forgetting. If trauma is understood as that which is in excess of frames of understanding, it is often impossible to positively speak one's memory of a traumatic event or to know what really happened. Yet memory is also not bound by the subject who forgets. It materializes in the most unlikely places or fixes itself to things with no logical connection to the traumatic event. It yields an overvaluation of objects, as Freud called it, the condition in which something becomes so full of desire and longing and fear that it is hardly recognizable.

"Let it die," she said. The potted wildflower had been a housewarming gift upon her arrival at her second residence in New England, to which she had returned after her third and final divorce from the American. Some might say that she was incapable of caring for the plant, or for any living thing. Or maybe it was not a question of her capacity or incapacity for sustaining the life of another as much as a willful refusal to allow this particular life to carry on. But killing it through neglect had proved difficult, and she could not bring herself to inflict direct violence on it. Even when left outside and untended, it hung onto life. In the wild, it continued to grow through winter and spring, producing new flowers month after month. "The name" she said. "I hate the name. It sounds like cycle." The plant survived most of the winter, then rotted into the soil by spring.

The summer of 1950 was unusually hot. This is how survivors of the war remember it regardless of what temperatures actually registered on the thermometer. It was the first "hot" war of the Cold War, and entire villages were evacuated. Families gathered children and grandparents at a moment's notice and carried sacks of rice and pieces of their homes on their backs. They walked south along paths that would soon be well worn by the millions of displaced persons. They packed up and traveled down the length of the peninsula toward Busan and then northward again, waded across rivers, and watched their children drown, finally to return to earth that had been scorched and to ghostly piles of ashes that had once been homes. The heat that summer was particularly memorable for what it did to the flesh that littered the landscape.

During the days and weeks after Nogeun-ri, the few survivors returned to the site of the massacre to gather the remains of their family members. Hee-sook was sixteen in the summer of 1950. She escaped after witnessing the deaths of her mother, father, sister, and niece. Perhaps it had been the few words in English she called out to the Americans that had prevented them from shooting her. She continued walking southward, dazed, hungry, and encrusted with blood, her white dress turned stiff and brown. She came to the Naktong River, where the American military were selectively allowing refugees to cross the river, but only if they were young and female. "People were saying everywhere that GIs did bad things to young women."[88] Hee-sook turned around and walked back to Nogeun-ri.

It had rained a lot that summer, so where the massacre had taken place there were pools of stagnant, bloodied water that contained the dead. There she waded through the stench of decomposing corpses and found the body of her father. "It seemed that the bones and flesh moved separately. . . . I virtually scooped up the remains of my father—like mucus—with the cup of my bare hands."[89] "The heat and humidity, the rain and the insects were all rapidly breaking down the bodies. . . . One nine-year-old girl returned to the scene and saw her dead mother's pregnant belly burst open, the fetus liquefying on the ground."[90]

After the War I Returned; Our House and Fields Were Burned to the Ground

To what did she return after this journey deeper into the south? After having avoided the lines of most intense combat in the area that the U.S. Army called "the Busan perimeter," she made her way back to Changnyeong. On rare occasions when she can remember anything of the war, she tells a story about being lost. She is nine or ten, depending on whether her age is measured in American or Korean years. Something happens that makes her disappear from her family's sight. Maybe they are crossing a river when the bullets order them to go back; maybe the air raid siren is screaming at them to run and she goes off in the wrong direction, and amid the dispersal of bodies and particles of dust, she is lost. The details of how it happens are left blank. In this story there is only an outline—fleeing, getting lost, and returning. The return was almost a year later, she says, because three

seasons had come and gone. She does not say what was left in Changnyeong when she made her way back in the spring. She says only that the photographs were destroyed, and that is why she has never shown them to me. Other families might have had enough warning to bury their belongings beneath their homes before leaving. After the war, there was nothing. No village. No home. Only remnants of burnt family photographs and bone ash seeping into the ground.

In the years following the massacre, residents in and around Nogeun-ri reported occurrences that might have been strange had they not been so frequent. Farmers dug up human bones. Villagers saw the flickering of "ghost flames." And the spirits were most restless in the summer. In Korean folklore, *honbul,* or ghost flames, often appear at the site of a massacre or unjust killing. There are theories about *honbul* that go beyond the supernatural. Some explain *honbul* as a visual hallucination caused by mental disorder or malnutrition. Others say that they are sparked when warm rain and wind agitate the bones buried in mass graves, causing phosphorus to ignite.[91] The survivors of the massacre were haunted by *honbul* that were stirred up each summer near Nogeun-ri. The ghost flames are perhaps a material expression of *han* (often translated as "unresolved grief and rage")—*han* of the dead for having been murdered and of survivors for having been witnesses to their families' slaughter.

Sun-yong dreaded the cycling of seasons. Cold weather offered her some relief, but summers were heavy with the promise of pain. When it was warm, she could no longer block out the visions of her four-year-old's body, perfectly still except for his hair trembling in humid air and his blood draining into the earth. The forward march of time was disrupted every summer by snapshots of July 1950. She perceived things that, by other norms of perception, were not really there to be seen or heard. Her son's bloody foot. His voice crying, "Um-ma." The white cloth bag that the U.S. soldiers placed his body in as she lay immobilized on a stretcher, watching.

The repetition of this scene agitated the *han* that reverberated within and beyond Sun-yong's body. If trauma is that which exceeds frames of reference for understanding, then it cannot be assimilated into a coherent narrative about oneself. For Sun-yong, images of her dead child were absorbed not just by her eyes but by the "resonating vessel" of her brain and skin.[92] So July 1950 permeates the cellular memory of survivors like Sun-yong and those to whom their trauma has been transmitted. While the traumas of war and militarism are often unremembered events rooted in lack and loss—the massive loss of lives and homes and the lack of public record of the atrocities committed—they also operate at the cellular level of affect. The failure to assimilate trauma is repeated through cycles of time, but trauma is unfaithful to these patterns in that it is also triggered by the senses. The sensation of heat, the sound of sirens, the smells and tastes of war incite a reliving of trauma that sends the present moment into flight.

The sound was familiar, yet nothing she had actually heard before. The siren signaled an emergency, and her body responded exactly as it had been trained to do when she was nine years old. She began having flashbacks of the air raid sirens screaming at her to make a decision: hide or keep on running. It was forty years after the end of the war when she stopped going outside because the prospect of being exposed induced severe panic attacks. But the thought of being trapped inside terrified her just as much, so she took drastic measures to fortify an escape route, breaking the glass out of the window to leave only a frame so that in the event of an emergency all she had to do was jump. There were times, however, when she grew uncertain as to whether she had executed the best plan of action, especially as mild September days gave way to nights of winter. But the empty window frame provided some relief. At least she knew that she was prepared, that at any given moment she would be ready for evacuation.

Relief: Our Bodies Were Purged

> I still remember the stamp on the top of the drums, the first English letters I ever saw: U.S.A. . . . We drooled at the thought of so much food.
>
> —DICKMAN, "Thank You"

During the 1950s, the popular press promoted images of Americans overseas as essentially generous and kind. Catherine Lutz and J. L. Collins have reported that "GIs in Korea were photographed giving chewing gum to children. American leaders traveled abroad with candy bars and soft drinks in their hands to distribute during photo opportunities."[93] At the U.S. National Archives, a repository for what officially is recorded as national memory, one can find hundreds of photographs depicting U.S. military personnel's charitable acts toward Korean civilians—feeding the hungry and clothing the destitute—but few photographs depicting the cause of their hunger and destitution.[94] Perhaps most impressing are the pictures of young American men, barely out of childhood themselves, presenting dolls, dresses, and lollipops to delighted little girls. They are delighted, the captions tell us, because a doll is what every little girl wants for Christmas, and Korean girls like suckers, too, because every Korean's favorite gift is food. Although the United States was producer and distributor of the discourse of the American dream and its accompanying images of American generosity, the distribution rests on a mutually lived-out rescue fantasy constructed not just through ideological impositions but also through sensory experiences that register at the level of affect. That relief goods emerged from the rubble as symbols of American luxury and freedom demonstrates that benevolence is also a tool of domination that is linked to ideals of a racialized moral superiority. But just as sensory perception can be a site of colonization, it can also be an important site of resistance precisely because it reveals the conflation of American rescue and annihilation in the body memory of the War. As a character in Kang Sŏk-kyŏng's "Days and Dreams" says:

> My mother told me that when I was a kid during the American military occupation I used to suck on hard candy from the relief

> goods until my tongue turned red. So she made me spit out the candy that colored the inside of my mouth." She'd get mad and say, "Do those little sugary things fill you up?" When I think about it now, it was our poverty that made her angry. . . . I got money from a GI for the first time, and suddenly I remembered the [candy from the relief goods] I ate when I was young. I realized vaguely that I'd gone back to where I started from.[95]

She was fourteen at the end of the war. Although she was not yet a woman, there were few places left for her to go. In 1953, U.S. military bases were centers of survival for the Koreans who were left alive at the end of the war, so she, like other Koreans, gravitated toward the Americans.

"In 1953, the Korean peninsula was a smoldering ruin," Cummings wrote, and the U.S. Army stayed there to protect Koreans south of the thirty-eighth parallel from the threat of the north, although many of those who had ended up in the south had been displaced from the north.[96] The American military provided relief in the form of food—staples like rice and exotic treats like powdered milk and chocolate. They rebuilt the schools and hospitals they had blown up or occupied, and they built orphanages and shelters for the people whose homes and families had been destroyed.[97] They helped reconstruct the economy to the extent that it was soon centered around U.S. military bases.[98] In 1953, the peninsula was a smoldering ruin, and the U.S. Army stayed there for years on end so they could continue to safeguard the South Koreans from the threat of communism, so they could maintain their dominance in Northeast Asia, so they could have a training ground for generations of young men and women in the U.S. armed forces.

The Americans were more likely to be generous to Koreans who spoke English, so she began studying English, painstakingly memorizing one word at a time from a dictionary in the hope that one day she might practice them with men who would buy her drinks at the camptown bar.

And then there were those English words that anyone could identify. Cho-co-late. Ci-ga-rette.[99] Words that came to be associated with the strange-looking men riding on military vehicles tossing candy and sugar-coated words into crowds of children who could have been their own flesh and blood. Sometimes they threw out words in Korean, too—like "saekssi" (young woman), which they pronounced "sexy."[100] She was not yet a woman and could not yet speak English, but maybe, like other girls who met Americans who became their husbands, she could learn how to entertain. Other girls as young as she did find work at the bases. They danced on stage and let the men admire their pigtails and call them by American nicknames or by Korean words that meant "virgin girl."[101] I do not know what happened in 1953, but at some point in the future, she would entertain the American men who stayed there.

> When the barrels were opened, we found that we had an endless supply of powdered milk. . . . This foreign aid, being foreign to our systems, caused all who drank it to suffer for days with diarrhea. Though our bodies were purged of all that we had, we were grateful.
>
> —Dickman, "Thank You"

> I hate powdered milk. The taste of it reminds me of war.
>
> —From a conversation with my mother

Within her own being she is fraught with contradictory impulses, to be grateful for the very thing that tastes like war. The yanggongju is the figure on which Koreans' desire and resentment is projected, who carries the violent and intimate history of U.S. military involvement in Korea folded in her body, who disseminates the contradictions of this history throughout the Korean diaspora. The primary contradiction is that the Korean War is forgotten in the United States but not over in Korea. But the trauma of war embodied by the yanggongju does not allow for this forgetting to be complete, even if rescue is that which is remembered over and against slaughter.

Out of the Ruins

> We are well aware of the American role in making the Korean peninsula peaceful, and we know that the presence of the American military forces is essential to our prosperity and peace. We will never forget you for what you did for us.
>
> —Dr. Suk San Kim, commemoration of the fiftieth anniversary of the signing of the armistice agreement, Seattle

> I have never seen such devastation. After I looked at that wreckage and those thousands of women and children and everything, I vomited. . . . If you go on indefinitely, you are perpetuating a slaughter such as I have never heard of in the history of mankind.
>
> —General Douglas MacArthur, speech to Congress, 1951

The Korean War was a war of nearly total destruction.[102] General Curtis LeMay, whom Halliday and Cumings describe as the "architect" of the "genocidal air war," reported: "Over a period of three years or so . . . we burned down every town in North Korea, and in South Korea, too."[103] More than half of the population of the peninsula were killed, wounded, missing, or permanently separated from their families. Millions of those who remained were left homeless. By the end of the war in 1953, the peninsula was in total chaos, forcing a complete reconstruction of Korean society. This new society was literally built by Americans. The confusion that Koreans had experienced during the war—terror, grief, shame, rage, gratitude, and longing—had created a deeply ambivalent relationship between them and the Americans who were largely responsible for both the annihilation and the re-creation of a divided Korean peninsula. This radical reorganization, both psychic and structural, had a particularly dramatic impact on the lives of women.

The magnitude of the destruction of the Korean War, as well as the failure to resolve it, solidified the grounds for the emergence of the yanggongju. A previous incarnation of this figure, namely the comfort woman, had already set the stage for a system of prostitution for the U.S. military, but the poverty of postwar Korea sent to the U.S. army bases millions of Koreans in search of livelihood, many of whom were women and girls who entertained soldiers, while others informally exchanged dates for American goods and dollars. A whole economy sprang up around these practices, and military prostitution continues to be a crucial part of camptown life in Korea. The yanggongju, as camptown prostitute, has been perhaps the most salient memory of Korea for generations of American men who have served there, while for Koreans the yanggongju has been perhaps the most salient figure of conflict in the U.S.–Korea relationship. She enacts a generalized overinvestment in the American dream and, even in her silence, threatens to expose the nightmare beneath the glossy image.

There is almost no memory that she can speak. Sometimes she cannot remember, does not want to remember, or remembers things that are conspicuously out of place. I do not know for sure what horrors even belonged to her, if she had been witness to her brother's death or to the deaths of neighbors or strangers traveling with her, if she was like the young people whose memories are documented here, who at every turn encountered bodies that were burned or ripped apart, who came to embody the ripped-apartness that was the Korean War, whether that war began on June 25, 1950, or in 1945 with the division of the peninsula. She has never recounted any visions of bone ashes falling from napalmed children, pregnant bellies burst open, or ghost flames flickering at the site of a massacre. The only detail about the war she has ever elaborated was her journey through the mountains. There were North Korean soldiers there, young women who looked like her older sisters. The vision of these girls with guns, she says, is the most horrifying image she can remember from the war. It was so terrible that she has been unable to forget it. It was terrible, she says, because women are not supposed to fight. A woman in combat was beyond her frame of reference for what counted as appropriate female behavior, but so was consorting with American men in bars. But this she does not talk about either. She does not talk about it, but out of her silence, something else emerges.

3.
Tracing the Disappearance of the Yanggongju

I am struggling to resurrect the pieces of some willfully forgotten story, to make sense of what happened in that space of absence. I have laid out all the little bits of what you said was your experience, arranged and rearranged them into so many uneven configurations. Still, no clear picture emerges. So I begin searching for words to fill in the blanks of this perforated history. In the absence of your telling, I dream you. "Mother, I dream you just to be able to see you. Heaven falls nearer in sleep. Mother, my first sound. The first utter. The first concept."[1]

The first time I dream this dream, it is inchoate. All I can remember is standing in the shadow of something that is burning, and an unseen presence leads me down a path to a strange and familiar place. I don't know which comes first, the burning or the movement, but I am terribly anxious. Each time this dream repeats, a different detail flashes up. Things fall from the sky—ashes or leaflets or slivers of flesh, shiny silver-wrapped chocolate bars or Christmas presents, and a thousand grains of rice raining down like tiny bullets. And burning photographs, or photographs of things that are burning, photographs of people and places I vaguely recognize. There are photographs falling to the ground, a multitude of female figures—napalmed women tightly wrapped in white gauze bandages, women living in squalor pressing oil out of sesame seeds, dead mothers with crying babies, delighted little girls sucking on lollipops, equally delighted big girls basking in the gaze of handsome American soldiers, hordes of frightened girls made homeless with no place left to hide. Sometimes they jump out of the photograph and into the landscape, but in the dream I can never

quite tell the difference between what is real and what is representation. At every stop along this path of search turned into research, I have found some unconscious evidence of an erasure, of a violently repressed history of violence. So many details, Mother, and I still can't find you pictured among all these women and girls.

This is a story about a collective struggle to resurrect the pieces of some willfully forgotten story and to render the forgotten visible. It is about searching for lost homes and histories, memories and mothers, and finding something else in their place. This chapter conducts a somewhat meandering search for the elusive female figure that haunts the Korean diaspora, drawn out along parallel paths that meet and merge somewhere across the Pacific.

The first path is located in the shadows of the U.S. military bases that are scattered throughout the southern half of the Korean peninsula. Along this path I look for the emergent new woman left in the wake of destruction, whose image was at first barely visible and, in this state of near-blankness, served to screen the collective fantasies of a post–Korean War nation still technically at war. But just as the nation was still divided, so were its collective fantasies. The search conducted on this path focuses on the various and changing figurations of the yanggongju since 1945, as a body materially and discursively constructed by competing ideologies of South Korean nationalism, a body that has itself become an object of violence and a site of contestation. It lays out the historical and political conditions of military prostitution to show that the yanggongju is both subjected to practices of hypermilitariziation and constituted by a history of collective trauma. In following her form through several critical periods of U.S.–Korea relations and the political contexts in which she is alternately made visible and kept hidden, we can see the ways in which the deployment of the yanggongju enacts South Korea's ambivalent relationship to the United States. She is simultaneously an erased figure of national development and an overexposed figure of national loss, both of which can be traced back through a history of war and imperialism. I want to point out, however, that the story I tell is necessarily an ambiguous one, for the yanggongju is a figure that has been largely invisible.

The second path is etched out through the movement of bodies, images, and ideas across the diaspora. On it I look for what happens to the fractured politics of the nation when its disjointed pieces travel across the Pacific and are translated into a politics of the "homeland." During the early 1990s, the yanggongju became a symbol of anti–U.S. nationalism, sparking not only action against the U.S. military in Korea but also knowledge production in the United States among diasporic Koreans. The yanggongju was made public for the first time, but the image of her was still unclear. The meanings around who she was and what she represented were contested through a process that Brent Hayes Edwards describes as "articulation," connecting across the gaps and differences that arise when discourses travel, when "they are translated, disseminated, reformulated, and debated in transnational contexts marked by difference."[2] What gets lost in translation when the yanggongju's new visibilities on the peninsula are distributed across the diaspora, and what new meanings and affects are generated by this "haunting gap"?[3]

> She allows herself caught in their threading, anonymously in their thick motion in the weight of their utterance. . . . She would become, herself, demarcations.
>
> —Theresa Hak Kyung Cha, *Dictée*

Using Cha's *Dictée* as one point of articulation between the national and the diasporic, on this path I explore the ways in which notions of home and homeland are endlessly fractured—how the dislocations that took place during the war and the permanent division of the peninsula have generated a state of serial displacements for both the Koreans who have "left home" and those who have stayed.[4] As Hyun-Yi Kang says, the work of Cha and other diasporic artists embodies the "recurring tensions between and expressed desire for this 'home' and an historically sobered acknowledgment of its manifold inaccessibility."[5]

> The population standing before North standing before South for every bird that migrates North for Spring and South for Winter becomes a metaphor for the longing of return. Destination. Homeland. . . . There is no destination other than towards yet another refuge from yet another war.
>
> —Cha, *Dictée*

The condition of being uprooted intensifies the longing to be settled, yet every effort to return home renders that space even more elusive. It is the sense of loss and impossibility that creates a psychic resonance between division and diaspora as post-traumatic effects. The quest for a reunification of—or, alternately, with—the homeland can be read as a working through of trauma, but it is a working through that is impossible in light of the unresolved nature of the war and its erasure from memory in the United States. It is perhaps more of a challenge for the diasporic Koreans who, in the words of Kang, "in addition to the lapses and distortions of personal memory over time . . . must often try to gain access to the homeland through the tinted lens of 'American' cultural and pedagogical accounts of Korea."[6] Similarly, because I am a diasporic scholar who can access information about Korea only in English, either through translated texts or those authored by Korean Americans, the first path I lay out is necessarily mediated by the second.

Where the two paths of searching that make up this chapter meet, the yanggongju becomes a figure of impossibility. Just as ideas of home and nation are revealed to be fantasmatic, the yanggongju has been made into a symbol of trauma even though the effects of trauma cannot be precisely captured in a symbolic representation. This is a story of how the yanggongju has been transnationally constructed and circulated as a body of division and of the ways in which a division can produce something greater than the sum of its parts.

Birth of the Yanggongju

> In 1953, the Korean peninsula was a smoldering ruin. . . . And still the war that ended in 1953 resolved nothing.
>
> —Bruce Cumings, *Origins of the Korean War*

> Thatched-roof houses gave way to all kinds of stores with English signs, aluminum cans replaced gourds, and a village full of shy maidens with their long braided hair instantly became a village full of *yang gongju.*
>
> —Oh Yun Ho, as translated and quoted in *Beyond the Shadow of Camptown,* trans. Ji Yeon Yuh

On July 27, 1953, the United States and North Korea signed an armistice agreement to bring a cease-fire to the Korean War, leaving the peninsula in a permanent state of war temporarily suspended.[7] After the mass slaughter of civilians and the burning of villages, it appeared that there was nothing left but ghostly piles of ashes and five million displaced Koreans. Bruce Cumings notes that the greatest tragedy of the Korean War was not the massive scale of the destruction but, after three years of fighting, the lack of resolution. In geopolitical terms, nothing was resolved, but the war has been productive in other ways.

Out of the ruins of catastrophic loss and evacuated memory emerged the remains that "animate history through the creation of bodies and subjects," in the words of David Eng and David Kazanjian.[8] And so a new female subject began to take shape, as did an institution populated by the bodies of working-class women who traveled from the country to the camptowns around U.S. military bases. Her traces can be found in the memories of those who witnessed the transformation of shy Korean maidens into brazen Western whores, but this was not the first appearance of this woman who had come to represent the body of a divided and dominated nation, a body assembled and reassembled by a fractured nationalism. She had already been there prior to the war, as a residue of earlier traumas. Since the war, she has gone through various transformations, from her early days as the struggling war survivor to later incarnations as sexual "ambassador" or victim of U.S. imperialism. These transformations have corresponded to certain episodes in South Korean national development, particularly during the early 1970s and the early 1990s, but they are also aftereffects of the period from 1945 to 1953.

I am uncertain about when or where she was first sighted or who first named her "yanggongju." There is some suggestion that she had been servicing American soldiers in the comfort station the Japanese Army had built in Itaewon from the moment U.S. troops arrived, but perhaps she went unnoticed because at this point she was still called "wianbu" (comfort woman), not yet "yanggongju." Maybe, like the refugees who tried to be inconspicuous

to American bomber planes, she went unseen because she did not move. She did not move from the country to the city in search of work because she had already been conscripted and confined. She was behind protected gates and therefore out of public view. But the comfort station was not yet called "gijichon," and this woman was not yet associated with the Americans who occupied the land.

This figure was born not only from the ruins of the war but also from the ghostly vestiges of Japanese colonialism imprinted on the bodies of the women who had been taken to serve as sexual laborers for the Japanese and on the psyches of those who had participated in and been shamed by this aspect of Korean history. The yanggongju, as the woman who sexually services American men, may have first been sighted during the Korean War, yet her figure had already been there in the form of the "comfort woman." The yanggongju's beginning is uncertain, and the story of her development is ambiguous. Both the recent literature on camptown prostitution and the narratives of comfort women and of early generations of camptown women suggest that there is no clear delineation between one system and another or one body and another. According to Cumings, when the U.S. military occupied Korea in September 1945, they also occupied the comfort stations that had been set up in Korea by the Japanese, taking over the women who were stationed there as well.[9] Likewise, Yoshimi Yoshiaki has written that, at the end of World War II, "rumors about the 'violence of American troops' were rampant, and [also] demands that 'complete comfort station facilities for the occupying army be actively expanded. . . . ' In short, by offering up the bodies of some women, people contrived to guarantee the safety of others."[10] On August 18, 1945, the Japanese government ordered the rounding up of women to serve in the comfort stations for the Allied forces.

And the women who were returning from Japan to Korea in 1945, to what did they return? Many of them never spoke of their experiences in the comfort stations, but among those who did, some said that they had nothing left to return to.[11] Having been banished by their homeland as national "traitors," and shunned by their families for having become "fallen women," many comfort women returning home to Korea returned to sexual labor. The return home was also a return to the past. The experience of returning comfort women was haunted by the ghosts of other women who had labored in the same way but in other times and for different nations. During the Manchu invasions of Korea during the seventeenth century, for example, Korean women had been forcibly taken to China, and those who returned were part of what Chunghee Sarah Soh calls a "centuries-old pattern of societal rejection of survivors of forced sexual labor. . . . The term *hwanhyangnyo* (literally, a home-coming woman . . .) degenerated into *hwanyangnyon* (a promiscuous woman, or a slut) to be despised and ill-treated."[12] The act of coming home marked her as a woman whose body had been invaded and contaminated by a foreign nation. For the Korean woman, the very meaning of *return* is tainted with the impropriety of having left home in the first place.

> You return and you are not one of them. . . . Every ten feet they demand to know . . . when did you leave this country why did you leave this country why are you returning to the country.
>
> —Cha, *Dictée*

The impossibility of return expressed in Cha's work is especially pronounced for the Korean female subject whose sexual labor is used in service of national development but is erased from narratives about national development. Elaine Kim notes that *Dictée* represents a similar paradox for the diasporic female subject: "Korean American women are continually called upon by the Korean nation-state to 'be Korean,' embraced and rejected in turn."[13] Perhaps it was a diasporic connection to the uprooted woman whose return implies her impurity that made her into a subject of inquiry in Korean American feminist scholarship. Despite such an impossible condition, I attempt to locate some origin or place called home. As Cha writes, "You leave you come back to the shell left empty all this time. To claim to reclaim, the space."[14] In their works Cha and Kim and a number of other diasporic Korean women who have followed search for a lineage of female transgressors who left home, forcibly or freely, and for the mother whose origins are unknown and whose passport is stamped "Displaced

Person."[15] As much as the yanggongju was born out of the Korean peninsula's traumas, she has also been brought to life through the search. The process of searching thus enables the search by bringing to matter the body of the yanggongju that is composed of trauma's historical sediments. It enables the search for the woman whose image is then refracted through the act of looking. As a result of such recursive longings, we now have a body of knowledge in the United States about the corps of women working at American military bases in Korea and about the yanggongju's possible origins.

So I begin a search for the female figure that haunts the Korean diaspora, tracing her back through the body of the comfort woman to the body of the home-coming woman, displaced and thereafter always homeless. Following these lines of backward movement connecting the wianbu to the *hwanhyangnyeo,* I arrive at the presence of twenty-seven thousand women who are currently selling their sexual labor exclusively to U.S. troops stationed at the ninety-five military bases and installments in South Korea.[16] The demographic profile of the women who make up the corps of military sex workers has become largely migrant over the last fifteen years, including growing numbers primarily from the Philippines and Russia but also from China and Thailand—women who have left homes in other countries to labor abroad.[17] For some of these women, ethnic Koreans formerly displaced to China, there is a bitter homecoming that haunts their movement, for much of South Korea's migrant work force now consists of North Koreans displaced to China, but who are officially counted as Chinese foreign workers rather than Koreans.[18] The vast majority of camptown sex workers, however, have historically been Korean women who have traveled from rural areas to urban ones in search of work, dislocated from their hometowns by the conditions of South Korea's economic development. By some estimates, over one million Korean women worked as prostitutes for the U.S. military between the early 1950s and the mid-1990s, but this number is likely to be conservative.[19] Not only were early generations of yanggongjus absorbed into the numbers of wianbu; many of these women turned to prostitution as a survival strategy during the war and were not yet the curious objects of data collection.

Although there is no clear distinction between the system of sexual slavery set up by the Japanese and the system of camptown prostitution for the U.S. military, in Korean cultural memory the birth of the yanggongju dates back to the early days of the war, when U.S. soldiers set up camp near small towns and villages. One camptown sex worker recalled that "U.S. soldiers would break into the homes of private Korean citizens and rape women—housewives and young virgin girls."[20] In recounting her memories, this woman traced the genealogy of her work to a popular belief rooted in wartime experiences—that camptown prostitution serves the social function of protecting "normal" Koreans from the unwanted sexual advances of American GI's. In other accounts of the war, sexually aggressive "beastlike" American soldiers are recurring characters, such as in Park Wan-so's short story "A Pasque Flower on That Bleak Day."[21] Park, who was herself a "saxi," or young woman, during the war, depicts the widespread fear of what American soldiers did to young Korean women, particularly in the absence of professional prostitutes:

> One day, there spread a rumor in the village that the occupying army at the elementary school was now neither the Republic's nor the communists', but that of the "big-nosed Americans."
>
> "Saxi have yes? Saxi have yes?"
>
> Whenever they spotted women they accosted them with such words, making lurid gestures. The horrified women hid deep in their houses. They trembled. The naked carnality that glowed on the faces of these big-nosed foreigners made them shudder. The big-nosed men seemed to be looking for professional prostitutes who catered to foreigners, but there could be no such prostitutes in this rustic village.
>
> Terror engulfed the village. . . .
>
> As night deepened, the big-nosed men's cry of "Saxi have yes? Saxi have yes?" took on an urgent and threatening tone, like the wailing of beasts in heat.[22]

The confrontation between a rustic village full of terrified virgins and a menacing invasion of monstrous Americans resolves peacefully, even joyfully, however, as the old village matriarch, disguised as a "saxi," sacrifices herself to save the young and innocent and becomes the unexpected object of American generosity. Upon discovering the truth about the old woman after "her shriveled body was revealed under the light stronger than daylight," the soldiers put the old woman's clothes back on and return her to the house with gifts of food. The matriarch further embellishes the story of what happened by saying, "It was thanks to their being Yankees that I returned alive and even received presents. If they had been Japanese . . . they'd have killed me a hundred times over. . . . If they had been Russians, they'd have raped me nonetheless."[23] The old woman makes this proclamation with confidence although this has resulted in her one and only encounter with foreigners. The village girls' memories of terror become submerged beneath the seduction of American treats, thus reinstating the narrative of U.S. soldiers as benevolent and elevating the status of the American military to that of the most merciful of all occupying armies. Reminiscent of Oh Yun Ho's observation of the chemistry between traditional Korean girls and American soldiers, a sudden transformation takes place in Park's text, too. The transformation is not that of "shy maidens with their long braided hair" into yanggongjus but rather its counterpoint—the transformation of "wailing . . . beasts in heat" into the best of all possible foreigners to whom a Korean woman could offer her body:

> The "Saxi have yes?" was by now a violent scream. . . .
>
> [The] women shook with mingled thrill and shame . . . and hid away in dark corners. . . .
>
> 'There was food in every box . . . canned fruits, canned meat, sweet preserves. . . . The old and young women looked at them ecstatically and hardly dared to breathe.[24]

Other memories of the war reveal a similar tension between feeling frightened of American GIs and attracted to the material things they had to offer. During the first few weeks of the war, Korean families began the practice of hiding their daughters when American soldiers passed through their villages or, alternately, sacrificing them to pacify the men's sexual appetites. Although most of the villagers did successfully "protect" their women, there were rumors about men who allegedly traded time with their daughters for American cigarettes and gum.[25] And from the perspective of some who remember witnessing such exchanges, this appeared to be a fair trade. Yun Jeong-mo's autobiographical novel, *Goppi* (A bridle), for example, portrays a little girl's adoration of Americans:

Every Korean's favorite gift is food.

> The child was fond of the war and the American GIs in the orchard to whom she used to go to request a chocolate bar. She could not understand Pilsu's father, who got angry at the American GIs when they asked him to borrow his wife. If he had lent his wife to them, he would have received a huge bag of chocolate bars and sweet cookies. . . . She was eager to put on high heels and run to yang-nom [Yankee].[26]

The seeds of desire for Yankees and their goods were planted in children from a very early age, and the threat of American men's sexual appetites served as a rationalization for many Koreans to condone prostitution as a necessary evil that would prevent the rape of "innocent" women and girls. As the war progressed, as the landscape and people became increasingly obliterated, Americans also began to represent survival, and U.S. bases became places where Koreans bought and begged for leftovers or sought employment and where women and girls would exchange companionship for American goods:

> I saw through the window. American soldiers with Korean lady. . . . They look just like a toy. . . . They don't know how to speak, only

> 'honey, kiss, honey, kiss' pretty cheap language. Then they kiss. . . . And after that, she has chewing gum and packs of Marlboros. Then they sell that on the street. . . . They can buy about 10 meals and some clothes you know. But I feel very bad for that. . . . I don't complain about that girl. She has to eat. She doesn't have good background, but she has to survive.[27]

The local population's fears and fantasies about U.S. soldiers as both benevolent protectors and "*maengsu*" (monstrous) rapists, coupled with the material realities of war, set up the conditions for yanggongjus to become what Katharine Moon has called "living symbols of the destruction, poverty, bloodshed, and separation from family of Korea's civil war" at the same time that they were associated with "never-before-seen material goods that American soldiers brought to an impoverished and literally starving Korea."[28] Public scrutiny of Korean women's sexual encounters with Americans was softened during wartime, for these women were sometimes excused as victims under duress of the war or as a price one had to pay for American "protection." The yanggongju was in full view then, but those who were watching looked the other way or, at the very least, did not call her a "Yankee whore." The survivor's testimony just given, for example, describes a series of events without directly spelling out any conclusions about the yanggongju's morality: first she kisses the GI, then she has American goods, then she sells them, then she buys food and clothing. Yet this description is ambivalent in that what goes unnamed here also implies that her actions are too shameful to speak, laying the grounds for the secreted words to phantomize, as Nicolas Abraham and Maria Torok would say. The exchange of sex for money or goods was increasingly commonplace during the war and postwar years, yet despite its public nature, the act of prostitution, particularly for the U.S. military, became the shameful family secret of Koreans who lived in the southern half of the peninsula. Like the comfort women before them, women who commercialized their sexual labor often faced rejection by their families and nation, even though that labor had become a primary source of income.[29] The composition of the "family" and the contours of the shameful secret would go through a series of transformations as camptown prostitution became systematized and highly regulated to meet the needs of the U.S. military servicemen on the peninsula during the 1970s, and as some sectors of the Korean public came to recognize the salience of military prostitution for anti-American politics during the 1990s.

The U.S. military, on the other hand, kept this aspect of their involvement in Korea under wraps, constructing it as an activity solely organized by the local population in Korea while making official statements such as "The U.S. military does not condone prostitution, but whatever Korean civilians make available is beyond our control."[30] By not acknowledging their role in creating and regulating the system of *gijichon* prostitution, the U.S. military effectively erased the yanggongju from all public records, thereby rendering her invisible to the general American public and disposable to U.S. servicemen in Korea. Despite the fact that prostitution has been absent from an official history, it is still very much present, even dominant, in unofficial histories. This flickering in and out of the public gaze made the shameful family secret difficult to keep secret, on the one hand, and increased the sense of shame, on the other. But such family secrets are never fully hidden or erased and often appear, in the words of Jacqueline Rose, as "forms of remembrance . . . which hover in the space between social and psychic history."[31]

There are few photographs of my family in Korea. They all burned up during the war, I am told. The handful of pictures that traveled across the Pacific with us are all from the postwar period, after 1960. There is an image of this young woman in a whole row of other women. She alone stands out. She is not wearing a *hanbok* or canoe-shaped rubber shoes. She does not have long hair pulled back in a knot. This woman is unmistakably Western. Short skirt. High heels. Heavy makeup and hair coiffed in a beehive. Between the hair and the heels, she stands a head taller than the rest of the women, and the child she is holding looks different than the other children, too. But she is smiling more widely than any of the other mothers, and it seems as if she is enjoying something that the other mothers are not, the other

South Korean entertainers.

mothers who look the way Korean mothers are supposed to look. Years later, she recalls a memory of that day, after she got her hair done at the salon, or maybe it was a different day, a different event for which she got her hair done. She is walking down the street, and a man shouts out to her, "Who do you think you are? Miss Korea?" After telling this story, she says, "I never liked Korean men, but I don't know why." She had already been marked (had marked herself) as a woman reserved for American men and the object of Korean people's envy and loathing.

Prostitute, Princess, Patriot: Transnational Figurations

> I went and got a job at the airmen's mess hall, the one for sergeants. At the time I had two pigtails. There was another girl there and they called us "chunyo" which means virgin girl. We were just young country girls, didn't know anything, but there were older city girls, too, looking for boyfriends. . . . One of the

> sergeants, he said, I'm gonna give you two girls names. . . . I still keep that name. . . . I carried it all this time, sort of a treasure to me.
>
> —Helen Kyungsook Daniels, as quoted in "So I've Gone around in Circles . . . Living the Korean War"

At some point during the Korean War, the yanggongju, as someone distinct from the comfort woman, was birthed. First she appeared as a war survivor looking to date American men or as a young girl who entertained them at the mess halls, but even as she rose out of disaster, she was already transforming into a woman who would be associated with the privileges and perceived moral ambiguities of American life. As "Yankee whore," "Western princess," "UN lady," and "GI bride," *yanggongju* has been given a variety of translations, expressing both the ambiguity of traumatized memory in the Korean diaspora and the materiality of the yanggongju's geopolitical conditions on the Korean peninsula. While the meanings of *yanggongju* have shifted over time, what these variations have in common is that each one has emerged from what Joan Nagle calls the United States and Korea's "militarized ethnosexual frontiers . . . collateral creations of the global defense and warfare system."[32] The yanggongju, in all of the word's connotations, is a figure that has been transnationally produced out of the unresolved traumas of war and division.

Tracing the development of sex work in Korea through the twentieth century, John Lie analyzes the shift from sexual labor performed by a caste of women for the elite landholding classes during the premodern/precolonial period to commercialized and militarized sex work during the colonial and postcolonial periods. While the Japanese colonization of Korea modernized the country, thus eliminating the caste system of sexual labor, it also gave rise to two new forms of prostitution—commercial sex work for businessmen and government officials and the sexual labor performed at "comfort stations" set up for Japanese soldiers. Lie reinforces the notion that *gijichon* are a continuation of the Japanese comfort stations, saying, "The U.S. dominance in Northeast Asian geopolitics ensured the privileged position of American soldiers (virtually all men in 1945) in the domestic sexual economy of South

Korea. . . . Under U.S. dominance, the primary organization of sexual work catered to American soldiers stationed in Korea. In the colonial period, Korean women served Japanese colonizers; in the postwar period, they entertained American GIs."[33] Although the U.S. occupation government officially outlawed prostitution in 1946, it is estimated that there were 350,000 prostitutes in Korea by 1953 and that 60 percent of them worked around U.S. military bases throughout the 1950s and 1960s.[34] According to Moon, the "sex slaves of the Japanese military serve as the historical prototype of U.S.-oriented prostitution in Korea."[35]

It was during the postwar period that women who consorted with Americans first became associated with the image of the "Western princess" because of their access to American products. But while American goods were the most valuable form of currency for postwar Koreans, these new objects also became ambivalent symbols of the way in which U.S. aggression and benevolence are conflated in cultural and personal memory. Chocolate was the peace offering that U.S. soldiers gave to little girls whose families they had just executed, and the taste of relief goods was tainted by sensations of loss, anger, and shame.[36] The yanggongju was transfigured into the privileged woman who enjoyed the resources of American bases and the Yankee whore who suffered from the maladies of greed and desire. The narrative of the yanggongju's fall from victim of circumstance to woman tempted by American excess is what Hyun Sook Kim calls an "allegory of the nation" and its vexed relationship with the United States.[37] In this instance, the yanggongju is the embodiment of a raped nation, and, like victims of rape more generally, she is always already morally suspect for being susceptible to her material and bodily desires. According to Nagle, her victimization is further called into question for crossing "national sexual boundaries" that dictate "what good citizens should and should not do sexually, and whom they should and should not have sex with."[38]

In the work of Korean filmmaker Shin Sang-ok, for example, one can see the yanggongju's transformation from war survivor to "Western princess" and "Yankee whore" through the shift in filmic representations of the yanggongju from his 1952 film *The Evil Night* to his 1958 film *A Flower in Hell.* The woman protagonist in the earlier film is portrayed as the prototypical victim of war—orphaned, homeless, impoverished, and forced to sell her own flesh to foreign soldiers. In the 1958 film, however, the protagonist expresses a conflicted agency in which she is not just a victim but thoroughly implicated in the budding system of camptown prostitution, succumbing to her longings for all things American: "Like a flower blooming in the swamp of hell . . . she has her material desire and American soldiers satisfy it. . . . Yanggongjus like Sonya . . . are all parasitic, living on American soldiers and even each other to fulfill their desires."[39]

Then they kiss. . . . And after that, she has "fruits, milk, sweet and sour, and fragrant powders, chocolates wrapped in silver foil, sweets, jelly, and crisp biscuits inside colorful boxes." . . . They kiss . . . and after that, she is so ecstatic that she hardly dares to breathe.[40]

Sonya, the fictional hell flower, demonstrates the way in which a Korean imaginary of the United States has historically been fraught with envy and loathing. Here the yanggongju is the figure of moral decay and erosion of traditional values, a morally bankrupt woman who violates Confucian gender norms, on the one hand, and enjoys the perverse privileges associated with her affiliation with the U.S. military, on the other. The yanggongju intensified collective feelings of shame and yearning that could not be fully acknowledged and, at the same time, became the screen on which Koreans projected these feelings of fear and resentment of the United States alongside their desire to become part of the American dream. Camptown prostitution, however, was not simply forced on Korea by the United States; it was tolerated by the public so that the yanggongju could be the buffer between respectable Korean citizens and the "beastlike" American GI's. Indeed, military prostitution became the only form of legal prostitution in Korea, highly regulated by both governments despite the absence of its official mention in U.S. military documents.[41] But this absence is perhaps the space of a larger fantasy about Korea's relationship to the United

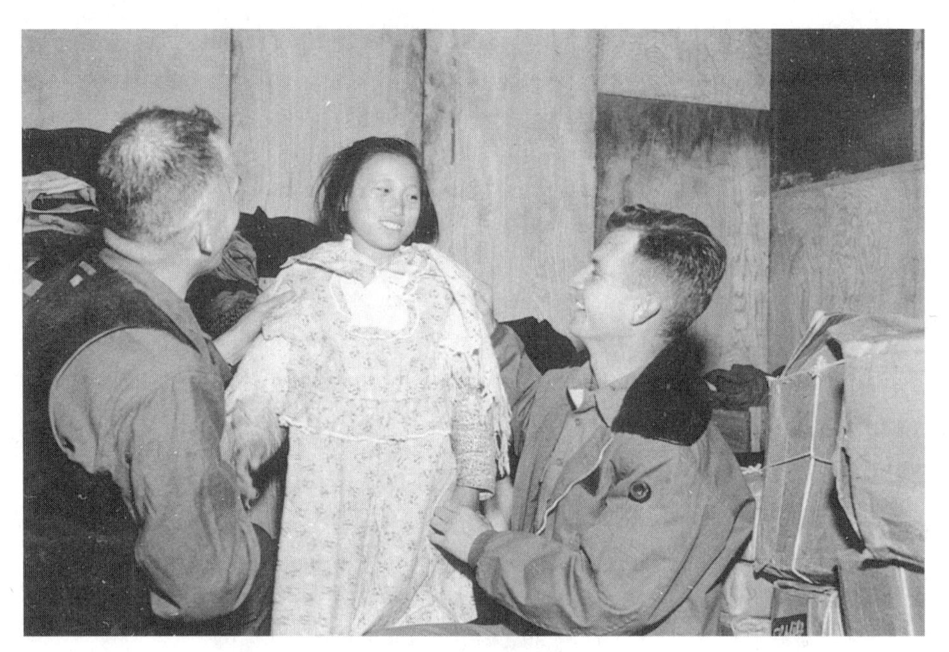

A new dress for Christmas.

States in which the United States believes itself to be the benevolent protector of South Korea while Koreans experience a simultaneous rejection of and desire for the United States. Despite this ambivalence, camptown prostitution flourished largely due to the South Korean government's desire for international recognition as well as its status of subordination to the U.S. military.

> From another epic another history. From the missing narrative. From the multitude of narratives. Missing. From the chronicles. For another telling for other recitations.
>
> —Cha, *Dictée*

While the use of women's sexual labor in service of the nation is not a new phenomenon in Korea, prostitution catering to foreigners gained legitimacy from the Korean government only as recently as the early 1970s, and now "generates more money than the state's annual budget," according to Chunghee Sarah Soh.[42] Young-Ju Hoang suggests that "current regimes of prostitution, designed to enhance Korea's economic prosperity, can be seen as part of such larger practices" rooted in "deeply seated linkages between prostitution, patriarchy, and militarism as an aspect of state violence."[43] She looks to traditional narratives about women and the state that suggest that "women's contribution has only been recognized when the state was in peril. . . . During ordinary times, women were often forgotten, excluded, or marginalized, but during national crisis or war, their positions tended to be 'elevated' by the state."[44] The dubbing of the camptown sex workers as "sexual ambassadors" during the early 1970s provides an example of the way in which women who were typically marginalized acquired an "elevated" status when the nation was under pressure.

As Moon shows in her seminal study of the camptowns during the 1960s and 1970s, the Korean government responded to claims by the U.S. military that the camptowns were breeding grounds of sexually transmitted diseases (STDs) as well as racial discrimination against black servicemen. Korean government officials used the "camptown cleanup campaign" or, alternately, "the camptown purification movement" (1971–76) as an opportunity to strategically manipulate sex workers as a tool of international cooperation and economic development, although the labor of camptown women has remained unacknowledged in official accounts of Korea's "economic miracle." During this period, the South Korean government began to recognize the role that camptown prostitutes played in building the nation and attempted to socialize camptown sex workers into a new identity—not as a struggling woman negotiating the poverty of postwar Korea but as a "diplomat" fulfilling her duties to the nation by keeping U.S. interests engaged. She served her country by "increasing Korea's foreign exchange earnings from the dollars spent by the men and contributing to security by 'providing comfort' to them."[45]

As part of the "camptown purification movement," it was mandated that sex workers attend government-sponsored "etiquette and good conduct" lectures designed to inspire the women to model their behavior after that of Japanese prostitutes who had served the U.S. occupation forces after World War II. Moon writes: "The Japanese prostitute, when she finished with the GI . . . knelt before him and pleaded with him to help rebuild Japan. The spirit of the Japanese prostitute spread to the rest of society to develop Japan."[46] In this context, *yanggongju* acquired another layer of signification, taking on the connotation of "UN Lady," and it was during this era that the official discourse of military prostitution framed the yanggongju as a symbol of Korea's national security whose body became a site of control as well as a playing field for negotiating international relations. While the Korean government used this figure as a behind-the-scenes actor in its struggle to gain international power and visibility, day-to-day practice in the camptowns remained quite contrary to the official suggestions that military prostitutes were "ambassadors." According to Hoang, "In the real world, the [sex workers] were degraded as 'dirty women,' exiled from the Confucian concept of virtue."[47] While Hoang's study primarily focuses on military sex workers for both the Japanese and the Americans, she situates them alongside the women who were the driving force behind Korea's rapid industrialization. During the early phase of economic development, factory workers tended to be women between the ages of sixteen and twenty-five who migrated to the city from rural areas to become "primary income earners, supporting their parents and, not infrequently, the education of their brothers."[48]

More generally, the government's manipulation of women workers was an absolutely crucial yet often invisible component of South Korea's national development, as well as the workings of masculinist geopolitics.[49] As Seungsook Moon explains, state-sponsored training programs for female factory workers, such as "The Factory New Village Movement, which started in the mid-1970s," emphasized compliance and domesticity as part of a discourse of patriotism and "industrial peace."[50] "Intended to depoliticize young single women working under extremely exploitative conditions, this movement involved the manipulation of reproductive and domestic femininity to make women docile and productive for the sake of building the industrial economy."[51] Regardless of these workers' contribution to the labor force, they were trained primarily as mothers and wives-to-be who would produce the next generation of citizens. The way in which exploited women workers were domesticated, whether they were the factory workers attending the Factory New Village Movement's workplace classes or the camptown workers who were attending lectures on etiquette and good conduct, reflects what Seungsook Moon calls "militarized modernity"—a state in which citizens are subjectivized as anticommunist patriots, on the one hand, and as docile bodies for capitalist interests, on the other. What distinguishes the two groups of women, however, is that the socialization of sex workers as patriots was not for the purpose of returning them to the domestic sphere as reproductive citizens who would fulfill societal roles as wives and mothers but rather for the purpose of separating them from society altogether. Their compliance as good national citizens would designate them as bodies for use by the U.S. military, too contaminated to be returned to Korean society.

Exile, Trauma, and the Biopolitics of the Camptown

> You return and you are not one of them. . . . They ask you identity. . . . Whether you are telling the truth or not about your nationality . . . they have the authority. Their authority sewn into the stitches of their costume.
>
> —Cha, *Dictée*

> Mother, you always tell me, don't stand in the front. . . . Don't lag behind. . . . Stay in the middle where it's safest.
>
> —Hyun Lee, "6.25 History beneath the Skin," in *Still Present Pasts*

You tell me be a good citizen and beware of the dangers of dissent. You tell me to be careful of the authorities upon my return to Korea. Be careful of the perilous conditions for wandering women. Better yet, just stay at home. Mother, you worry about my wandering but never reveal the source of your worry. You never tell me what led you to move away from Gyeongsang province, away from Korea altogether. Not of the unprecedented movement of the rural population to the cities, the growing gap between rich and poor, or the massive influx of women into the workforce that took place before you left.[52] In the absence of your telling, I read you in the stories about women whose participation in the national project resulted in their exile from the nation, stories

enabled by these women's exiled movements out of Korea. I read you in these circulating stories about the forces of displacement and the dangerous conditions for wandering women established when South Korea was a rising nation.

Bringing the notion of militarized modernity to bear on Katharine Moon's account of military prostitution, we can read the tightening of control over sex workers as a reflection of how the conditions of accelerated economic growth and authoritarian military control under the Park Chunghee regime (1961–79) brought South Korea into a state of militarized modernity and made the camptown into the biopolitical space that it continues to be today. During this period, the yanggongju became a body constructed by the state for the goals of anticommunist national security, economic growth, and cooperation with the United States, and also an embodiment of Koreans' conflicted feelings about a national project that was necessarily entangled with the United States. On the one hand, she was called a "diplomat," revealing Koreans' desire to be recognized in a global political economy, while on the other, she was a "Yankee whore" whose very being reminded Koreans of their status of subordination to the United States and of their legacy of war and colonial slavery.

If the yanggongju is "exiled from the Confucian concept of virtue" and this concept is a defining "national sexual boundary," it comes as no surprise that she is regarded, in the words of Katharine Moon, as "Korean in birth but no longer Korean in body or spirit."[53] She is banished from the nation to the camptown, a space sometimes described as an island that belongs to neither Korea nor the United States but whose borders are strictly policed. For the most part, Korean women cannot get out and Korean men cannot get in, and the only people who are granted unrestricted travel in and out of the camptown are American servicemen. As Ji-Yeon Yuh notes, the Korean nickname for the camptown is "bbaet-bul," meaning "a swamplike area that, once entered, is impossible to escape."[54] The material reality for military sex workers is that the camptowns are spaces of sanctioned violence against the women who labor in them.

Some of the disciplinary practices that were initially established during the "camptown cleanup campaign" of the 1970s include watching the women through peepholes as a means of ensuring that neither the client nor the sex worker gets away without paying the club owner and subjecting the sex worker to weekly mandatory STD testing at her own expense. She is tagged and quarantined if her tests come back positive, and she must carry a "passbook" at all times proving that she has been tested and is free of disease so that if a serviceman contracts an STD, he can trace the disease to the sex worker he believes infected him.[55] This testing regime, which clearly privileges U.S. servicemen, reinforces the image of prostitutes as "dirty women." Wendy Chapkis notes that "little attention has been paid to the fact that before sex workers can transmit disease, they must first themselves have been infected. The lack of interest in the 'contamination' *of* prostitutes—rather than *by* them—exposes the belief that prostitutes (like homosexuals) are always already 'sick.'"[56] Camptown prostitutes, on the other hand, are convinced that Americans introduced STDs to Koreans. One worker says, "We heard that the first AIDS patient was a sailor. . . . Koreans don't have it. We got it from Americans. In all cases, it's related to Americans. While we're here, we don't receive Korean customers. So AIDS and syphilis and things like that come from Americans."[57]

Both the official regulations and the comments of the sex workers highlight another discourse about disease—that it is something that comes from exposure to the foreign. According to Katharine Moon, besides the perceived function of preventing widespread rape, "In the eyes of so-called normal Koreans, the prostitutes . . . [contain] undesirable foreign influences on the greater Korean society."[58] The system of controls placed on the yanggongju body serve nationalist interests not only by catering to American soldiers who bolster the economy and securitize the border at the thirty-eighth parallel but also by minimizing the contamination spread by those very same Americans. Here Korea's response to foreignness is clearly marked by profound ambivalence—a simultaneous hatred of and desire for everything American. But because the body of the (willing) prostitute is always already diseased, it can be legitimately sacrificed as a receptacle for foreign illness.

Moon's portrayal of the camptowns around U.S. military bases in Korea as spaces of hyperregulation is supported by other ethnographic and historical accounts of U.S. military prostitution as well as by documentary films and fiction by diasporic Koreans, but even if we take for granted the tight controls placed on the bodies of women working in the camptowns, it is a system that disciplines imperfectly.[59] Ultimately, Korean officials failed to socialize sex workers into prostitute-patriots, and many of the women interviewed in Moon's study were in fact quite critical of this notion that selling sex is necessary to national security. They pointed out the hypocrisy inherent in this idea—that the women who are supposedly securing the country's interests with their bodies are put in the most danger. If camptown women were truly elevated to the ranks of "ambassadors," they would not be working under such harsh conditions, nor would they be faced with scant options for making a living. Moon reports: "All of the women . . . stated that their greatest need for [Republic of Korea] government protection (after the Korean War) was not from North Korean threats but the exploitation and abuse of club owners/pimps, local Korean police and VD clinic officials, and the power of U.S. bases."[60] As she notes, both camptown women and Korean feminists often describe the Korean state as a collective pimp but one that neglects to provides protection against abuse. The labor of camptown prostitutes during the time covered by Moon's study increased the foreign exchange earnings of the country while the women workers were incurring large debts that kept them bound to sex work under abusive conditions.[61]

The way in which camptown women are physically and psychically separated from the rest of society through the strict patrolling of camptown boundaries and stigmatization by "normal" Koreans reveals that camptown prostitution is a biopolitical practice—an investment in life that protects South Koreans against the threat both of North Korean communism and of sexual violation by U.S. soldiers, one that is contingent on marking sex workers as a disposable population. "In short," writes Yoshiaki, "by offering up the bodies of some women, people contrived to guarantee the safety of others."[62]

Ms. Pak worked in a camptown brothel outside of Seoul in the 1960s and 1970s. "Her sister, also a camptown prostitute, was mutilated and murdered allegedly by a U.S. serviceman, but U.S. authorities never turned the man over to the ROK authorities. . . . The U.S. military offered neither apology nor financial compensation to her family. . . . Camptown residents had to collect money from one another to pay for the funeral expenses."[63]

Another camptown worker of another generation tells a similar story. "When I first entered this world," she said, "I thought the Americans were well-educated and great people." But with time came disillusionment: "At first, I really treated them well. . . . I always used terms of respect when talking to them. Then I was tricked by them once or twice, and I saw many bad things happening. I saw people being killed. Like once, an Amore cosmetics saleswoman was walking to her job one day. On the way she saw an American GI burning trash; but it had a strange odor. She smelled hair burning so she got suspicious. She called the police. They found him burning the body of a woman. He had killed her during a fight."[64] By the time this incident took place, the killing of yanggongjus had already become a common occurrence. Often when camptown women turned up dead, there was no collection to pay for a funeral because there was no funeral. Families did not always come to claim the bodies of slain women, nor were the bodies always found to be claimed.

The highly regulated system of prostitution around U.S. military bases in Korea has produced the yanggongju as a subject disciplined by both the U.S. military and the South Korean state. Like Giorgio Agamben's figure of the *homo sacer,* the "bare life" that is included in the political order only through its exclusion, the yanggongju is the woman who is designated as the life that can be killed without being sacrificed and dies an unsanctified death in the biopolitics of U.S.–Korea relations. Agamben invokes the camp as the paradigm for biopolitics in that "the camp is the space that is opened when the state of exception which was essentially a temporary suspension of the rule of law on the basis of a factual state of danger, is now given a permanent spatial arrangement, which as such nevertheless remains outside the normal order."[65] In South Korea, the camptown is the paradigm for the state of the exception that has become the rule. It is a place designed by the temporary suspension of war that turned permanent, and the women working in them are deemed unworthy of life to the extent "that no act committed against them could appear any longer as a crime."[66] But it is also within this "zone of indistinction" that bare life becomes a force of resistance. The unclaimed bodies of yanggongjus have the capacity to haunt "normal" citizens beyond the camptown borders in order to expose the ways "in which the norm becomes indistinguishable from the exception."[67]

The Haunting Spectacle

For a long time I could not see her, but at some point her picture became very vivid, although still not entirely clear. An image of this woman began to circulate on the page and on the screen, igniting cyberspace with ghost flames. I have seen the scene replayed again and again, but each time with some slight difference. She was the tragic victim of U.S. imperialism, another woman drowned in the quicksand of *gijichon*. But not all accounts say she worked in a camptown. Sometimes she is called a sex worker or a bargirl, sometimes just "a Korean woman." She was twenty-six. The "cause of death was determined to be bleeding from her head, caused by repeated concussions inflicted with a Pepsi bottle." Or, alternately, with a Coke bottle. The bottle is a key actor in this story. The Pepsi bottle, or the Coke bottle, hits her in the head, causing her to bleed to death, but it is also used to inflict another kind of injury. Sometimes the scene depicts her rape with a Coke bottle, but more often it is a beer bottle, and in some versions of the story there are two beer bottles penetrating her, or occasion-

ally three: "As she lay dying, she was violated with the above mentioned objects."[68] There are many variations of this story, and a few details that are consistent: there are all kinds of foreign objects stuck in her body, and in fact I can see them in the picture. I see that she is naked on the floor with her legs spread open. And some substance is covering her—the reports say it is powdered laundry detergent, covering her dead body to somehow cover up the crime. And the strangest detail is that her mouth is full of matches. Fifteen years after she was found in such a state, on the Internet I still find pictures of this Korean woman with matches inside her mouth.

In October 1992, a camptown sex worker named Yun Geum-i was brutally murdered by one of her clients during a dispute. Yun was not the first camptown sex worker to be killed, but her death was made hypervisible, and the case set a precedent for U.S.–Korea relations in that it was the first time that an American GI was turned over to the Korean courts for a crime committed against a Korean sex worker.[69] The dead Yun became, in the words of Hyun Sook Kim, "material evidence of imperialist violence against the bodies of Korean women," thus opening "a new arena of discussing gender and sexual politics."[70] "Material evidence" certainly existed prior to this incident, but violence against yanggongjus remained unseen by a general audience because they were disposable women whose lives were restricted to camptown ghettoes and whose deaths were deemed unremarkable. The Yun case, however, was supported by a diverse range of organizations that formed the "Committee on the Murder of Yun Geum-i by American Military in Korea," a committee that later spawned the "National Campaign for Eradication of Crime by U.S. Troops in Korea." As hostilities toward the United States and the Korean government grew throughout the 1980s and into the 1990s, so did the conditions that would allow the figure of the yanggongju to be imbued with anti-imperialist desire. The Yun incident marked a turning point at which the yanggongju as a symbol of a colonized nation was transformed from the shameful sex worker in exile to the nation's daughter welcomed home. It was another moment that would mark a return to Korea's fractured past.

> Q. What kind of tenant gets free rent,
> doesn't pay their parking tickets,
> dumps formaldehyde in the backyard,
> plays with explosives without regard for their neighbor's safety,
> and can even get away with murdering their neighbor's daughter?
> A. The U.S. Army in Korea
>
> —People's Action for Reform of the Unjust ROK–US SOFA

According to Choi Jang Jip, the beginning of South Korea's "fractious history of state–society relations" can be located in the division of the peninsula and the Korean War. Choi writes: "The period from 1945–1953 was filled with political upheaval, ideological polarization, death, and suffering. The overall framework for all subsequent political conflicts in South Korea was established during this period of turmoil."[71] He outlines various "political cleavages" between a largely authoritarian and capitalist government regime in alliance with the United States and the *minjung*, usually broadly translated as "the people" or "the oppressed," which Choi defines specifically as the intersection among the working classes, those excluded from the political process, and those who are directly harmed by U.S. military intervention. The Yun Geum-i case brought the yanggongju out of hiding and into public view as a figure that embodied all forms of oppression, particularly because they were aftereffects of division and war. In Hyun Sook Kim's analysis of the nationalistic discourse generated in the wake of the incident, "the murder of Yun . . . indicates the urgent need for the divided Koreas to be unified, the peninsula to be de-militarized, and the American troops to be withdrawn as soon as possible."[72] With the rise of counterhegemonic *minjung* movements throughout the 1980s, the sensational murder of Yun Geum-i once again elevated the yanggongju's status, this time as a martyr of dissident nationalism.[73]

And so there was now a political imperative to see her, and in seeing her to expand a vision of the ways in which

the South Korean masses were being sold by state greed and crushed by U.S. military hegemony. The image of the dead yanggongju was widely circulated by activists who took on her case even as they claimed that "the condition in which her body was found was too heinous to look at with open eyes."[74] The language used to describe the body that was too brutalized to look at detailed every injury inflicted upon it: "In her uterus, two beer bottles. A coca cola bottle penetrating her vagina. An umbrella driven twenty-seven centimeters into her rectum."[75] "Her naked body sprawled on the floor. . . . Her body and face covered with blood."[76] "In an attempt to fake the evidence, [the perpetrator] filled her mouth with broken matchsticks, and spread white detergent powder over her body."[77] But in this effort to make her seen, she became, once again, an erasure.

In popular anti-American literature, Yun's murder is identified as both a moment of incipient action against U.S. military violence and a moment of awakening to the history of this violence.[78] As one activist writes: "The unmerciful and cruel crime, committed by a soldier whose commander insists that they came here to defend the freedom of Korea, shocked and angered the Korean people once again, as the worst of a long string of crimes perpetrated by U.S. military personnel in Korea during the last 40 years."[79] In another publication, a chronology of "U.S. GIs' criminal activities against civilians" begins with the murder of Yun and notes that for every high-profile case there are "numerous Korean civilians [who] have been stamped out noiselessly."[80] The viewing of violence committed against the yanggongju was central to a project of anti–U.S. nationalism in that Yun's murder became the primal scene that would recall all past violations of Koreans by the United States. Prior to this case, the yanggongju had been hidden in plain view, but this was an instance in which she was put on display and became, in the words of Rose, "symbolized beyond recognition . . . and then manipulated in fantasy to its purpose."[81] But such manipulation also runs the risk of undermining its own aims.

The overcirculated image of Yun's violated body turned into a "transnational macrospectacle," but in its travels it haunted the imagination of diasporic Korean feminists as well as anti–U.S. activists on the peninsula.[82] The yanggongju became the subject of contested meanings in diaporic scholarship, particularly around what it meant to turn her into a symbol of the nation. Elaine Kim, for example, observes that when women's sexual labor does appear in nationalist discourses, it is often depicted as rape rather than labor, and the women whose labor is unacknowledged are "unrepresentable except as the nation to be avenged by Korean patriarchal nationalism."[83] Hyun Sook Kim argues, perhaps most powerfully, that the deployment of Yun's image erases the subjectivity of the real women who work in the camptowns and refashions the yanggongju as a figure of populist struggle despite the absence of popular concern for living sex workers:

> When alive . . . Yun Kum-i was shoved to the margins of Korean society and viewed derogatorily as a "Yanggongju." The brutal way she was killed led Koreans to remember and reconstruct the image of her as a "good woman" passively victimized by "beastlike" *(maengsu)* American soldiers. This re-shaping of Yun's image is unusual: typically, Koreans and Korean Americans consider "Yanggongju" as "crazy women" *(mich'inyon),* "loose women" *(baramkkiga itnun yoja),* and "women plagued by the longing-for-America-sickness" *(migukbyong gollin yoja).* Children born of Korean "bar women" and American GIs are similarly viewed as "bastards of the Western Princess" *(yanggongju saekki),* "seeds sown by GIs" *(guninduri ppurigogan ssi),* and "darkies" or "niggers" *(kkamdungi).*[84]

After Yun's murder, however, *gijichon* prostitutes were exposed in anti-American discourse as victims of military domination whose suffering "embodies the collective suffering of Koreans and the Korean female."[85] This symbolization of the yanggongju, Kim argues, denies the camptown women's agency in negotiating the meanings of their own lives. As the yanggongju became a figure of populist struggle on the peninsula on whose body ideological battles were waged, the circulation of her image also meant that the yanggongju, as a symbol of fractious politics, would become further refracted through the diaspora. Diasporic scholarship about the figure of the yanggongju expressed a tense desire to engage in homeland politics while also being critical of dissident nationalism for appropriating the bodies of the oppressed for use as ventriloquists' dummies.[86] For feminists especially, the yanggongju became a site of negotiating meanings about female subjectivity in the Korean diaspora, about investing the female subject with the capacity to negotiate her own meanings.

I have read so many different interpretations, seen so many different visions, yet somehow I cannot find the real woman behind the image of these women who do not speak for themselves but who are spoken for, spoken through, as representations of someone else's longing. There is some suggestion that the real subject, the desiring sexual agent, is somewhere to be found. But I have not yet seen her distinct from the regimes of social stigma, battling nationalist discourses, and social scientific truth telling. So far I have found only a serial displacement of meanings—narratives edited, translated, framed, and distributed across travel routes and lines of demarcation.

The circulation and multiplication of meaning also destabilized categories of meaning. While nationalistic fantasies of "women as nation, as land, as property" are problematic, as Inderpal Grewal acknowledges, in that "the discourse of rape is acceptable in nationalist discourse only when the perpetrator is an outsider," the yanggongju complicates the boundary between insider and outsider, thus making her a volatile symbol of nationalism.[87] What happens to this narrative of the nation when the "raped woman" is mutually constituted by both the outsider-perpetrator and the violated nation she has come to represent? When the nation has also participated in the woman's having been violated?

As Sara Ahmed argues, "Emotions play a crucial role in the 'surfacing' of individual and collective bodies through the way in which emotions circulate between bodies and signs. . . . Emotions are not simply 'within' or 'without.' . . . They create the very effect of the surfaces or boundaries of bodies and worlds."[88] As a figure becomes invested with feeling, that figure increases in affective value the more it circulates in an economy of feeling to the point that the affect becomes autonomous and need not be bound by the subject. As affect travels, it "sticks" to bodies and creates over-invested figures that differentiate some bodies from others. These affectively produced bodies "threaten to violate the pure bodies; such bodies can only be imagined as pure by the perpetual restaging of this fantasy of violation."[89] The dispersal of images of the dead Yun acted both as a repeated drawing of boundaries between the yanggongju and the rest of the population and as a replay of the history of militarized violence. But the yanggongju also became invested with feelings of grief, rage, and shame that worked to dissolve those boundaries. She did not rest obediently where "normal" Koreans or government officials ordered her to stay. She would serve as a haunting reminder to those who tried to distinguish themselves from her by making her presence felt as the excluded outsider that threatens the boundary. In Cha's words, "She would become, herself, demarcations."[90]

From Labor Camp to Camptown: The Yanggongju's Ghost

Despite the rebranding of the yanggongju as a victim of imperialism during the early 1990s, her history as a "Yankee whore" could not be erased completely, and therefore she could not be restored to a state of innocence. She was a woman descended from fallen women, women imagined to have been innocent and unknowing before they were warehoused across Asia—in Japan, in the Philippines, and in their own country, where the U.S. Army now resides.

She was a peasant girl once, two long braids down the length of her back with brightly colored ribbons tied at the ends. Father was a rice farmer. Auntie had a peach orchard in North Gyeongsang. Under the rule of hostile invaders, they lost most of their land, but there was room for negotiation, as some men quickly learned. So Father made a bargain: he could keep the farm in exchange for the girl. He stayed in Changnyeong and sent her with the soldiers.

This is a history that she cannot speak. There are others who can, and their stories are made public generations after these events took place. They are given the utmost respect, because they are now elderly women, *halmonis,* who must be honored, even if they carried these shameful secrets hidden in the folds of their skirts for fifty years. "My story, as hidden as it is from those around me, will follow me to my grave."[91] But the story says that these *halmonis* were taken by surprise and detained against their will. And unwillingness excuses some of their sin. Unwillingness lets their shame be the engine of anti-imperialism. And the unwilling is made visible against one who is not. This is a history she cannot speak, and the unspoken is passed down from flesh to flesh, the unspoken already lining the inside of the womb.

This is a story about the fall, but it is not a fall from innocence, because the woman protagonist of this story was born bad. She was not forced by human hands or imperial guns, but walked with her own two feet to meet her destiny. She walked willingly from the labor camp to the camptown, where she would serve occupying soldiers from a different country. There she would work to endear her nation to them, to encourage them to fight for her freedom, to make them feel like this foreign nation was their home.

> Fraternization [in the form of prostitution] is near the core of troop–community relations here.... If a fellow is that far away [from home], his sexual appetites are met, and he'll serve better.
>
> —Katharine Moon, *Sex among Allies,* citing a "Human Factors research report"

In the early 1990s, two movements against militarized prostitution emerged in Korea—the *cheongsindae* (comfort women) movement (CM) and the *gijichon* (camptown) movement. While many scholars have noted the parallels between the Japanese occupation of Korea and the U.S. military presence, as well as between the experiences of the women for whom the two movements are fighting to gain recognition, the CM has refused to acknowledge any similarities.[92] Although both movements began as part of a larger struggle against the sexual exploitation of Asian women, the two have diverged because of the assumption that one group of women were "forced," while the others were and are "voluntary." Moon observes:

> The CM retained a traditional understanding of acceptable female sexual behavior. Many of the leaders and survivors emphasized that former "comfort women" were innocent victims whereas [gijichon] women were not. Chongsindae survivors were insistent that their cause not be linked to that of [gijichon] women, emphasizing that their identities as sex slaves were not to be equated with those of "willing whores." In the CM's view, the chongsindae survivors represent in body and mind the most humiliating, degrading, and painful colonial oppressions that were imposed on Korean people, not voluntary adventures into the world of sex.[93]

This dichotomy of forced versus voluntary sexual labor is an issue that has long troubled feminist debates concerning the "nature" of sex work. In Moon's study of the two movements, however, she argues that the demographic backgrounds, conditions leading women to work in gijichon, and long-term effects of the work are quite similar to the conditions experienced by the comfort women. Perhaps the most compelling piece of evidence Moon presents in favor of the notion of continuity between Japanese comfort stations and U.S. military brothels is that some of the women among the earliest generation of gijichon workers may have been former comfort women.[94]

The distinction between the raped woman and the fallen woman has come up again and again in the politics of the nation, but it is impossible to separate the good victim of imperialism from the bad Yankee whore.[95] The repeated drawing of boundaries, the repeated attempts to make oneself innocent, are futile, because there is no innocent past to which to return. The innocence of comfort women is soiled by the fact that they were not all forced into sexual labor. Some were traded by their fathers, some agreed as a means of supporting their children, and some, according to Soh, "chose to leave home, not out of economic necessity but in search of independence and freedom from domestic violence against and gendered mistreatment of daughters."[96] Nor were all camptown sex workers "willing." Some were deceived and others abducted, and, as Elaine Kim says, "they were blamed both for circumstances beyond their control and for the choices they made, for . . . leaving home."[97]

> Dear Mother,
>
> 4.19. Four Nineteen, April 19th, eighteen years later. . . . All this time we have been away. But nothing has changed. A standstill.
>
> It is not 6.25. Six twenty five. June 25th 1950. Not today. . . .
>
> Our destination is fixed on the perpetual motion of search. Fixed in its perpetual exile. Here at my return in eighteen years, the war is not ended. . . . We are inside the same struggle seeking the same destination. We are severed in Two by an abstract enemy an invisible enemy under the title of liberators who have conveniently named the severance, Civil War. Cold War. Stalemate.
>
> I am in the same crowd, the same coup, the same revolt, nothing has changed.
>
> —Cha, *Dictée*

A Spectral Agency

Ten years after Yun Geum-i's spectacular murder, another incident incited massive anti-American protests, this time involving victims who were not sullied by the shame of commercial sex. On June 13, 2002, Shim Miseon and Shin Hyosun, two junior high school students, were run over by a U.S. military tank along a road in Uijeongbu.[98] Although the U.S. military did issue an official apology, Korean protesters demanded that the two drivers of the vehicle be turned over to Korean courts, one of the concerns being that the spirits of the dead girls would haunt the perpetrators, the victims' families, and the nation until the deaths were brought to justice. As in the Yun case, graphic photos of the girls' dead bodies were circulated on the Internet.[99] The girls, whose deaths did not take place within the context of sexual exchange, became the new poster children of anti-Americanism. But as one New York–based Korean activist pointed out, if they had survived the incident they easily could have turned to military prostitution because of the pressures placed on females growing up around U.S. military bases.[100] Hyosun and Miseon were also haunted by the yanggongju in that they, too, had the potential to become "fallen women." The sudden slide between "shy maidens" and "yanggongju," in Oh Yun-ho's observation, demonstrates the way in which the yanggongju is composed of ghosted matter that flashes up from the past and carries forward into the future, poised to unfold at any moment within the militarized sexual economy of U.S.–Korea relations. The yanggongju may fade into the background as more innocent victims are exposed, but innocence becomes irrelevant in the context of an unequal power relation in which the abuses committed against Koreans by U.S. military personnel are not regarded as crimes. The dangerous consequence of designating the camptown as a biopolitical space where some bodies are sacrificed for the protection of the innocent is that there is always a possibility that the normal citizen can become confused with the person who can be killed.

Yun's murder sparked much anti–U.S. action in the 1990s, but prior to Yun's death the ghost of the yanggongju had been dwelling beneath the surface of a troubled history, one that haunted Koreans with an awareness of the fluidity of camptown borders. The day of Yun's murder in 1992 was not the first time a yanggongju was murdered, nor was it the first time Koreans felt hostility toward the United States. Layers of anti-American sentiment had been building, for the military dictatorship that had been propped up by the United States, for the 1980 Gwangju massacre in which as many as two thousand protesters had been gunned down, for the nearly fifty years of U.S. military occupation. The murder of Yun unleashed a well of affect from a growing generalized anger toward the United States, as well as from the piling up of dead bodies that had been unclaimed. The material disappearance of women and the resurrection of these bodies through the circulation of their images highlight the way in which the yanggongju became a spectral agent more powerful in death than in life. Her spectrality gains its force from the injuries inflicted on the bodies of a population left to die and from the accumulation of affect that adheres to her image. Ann Anlin Cheng has written: "What we are given . . . is the afterimage of the event . . . that has been placed in constant and uncanny circulation" as an effect of trauma and an excess that cannot be symbolized.[101]

Out of the ruins of catastrophic loss and evacuated memory emerged a sexual laborer, a symbol of a divided nation, and a ghost that haunts the diaspora. She became all of these things through a series of erasures that, paradoxically, also created an excess. In a state of near blankness, she became an absence upon which to project national fantasies, but with each erasure something was still left behind on the screen. The ghost that took flight from the camptown was composed of the relentless irreducibility of real violence to any kind of representation, and she scattered her traumatic residues across the diaspora. Visions of this elusive woman have come to permeate the memories of those displaced from the "homeland" to the United States, where the fantasy of the nation depends on a disavowal of the entire history that created her. And thus it is perhaps the Korean diaspora that has been most psychically invested in reading her mutually inconsistent fragments through a project of memory that projects a new image into the space of what has been forgotten. But as Edwards points out, a diasporic "frame of cultural identity [is] determined not through 'return' but through difference," and therefore her haunting effects have been uneven.[102] Some would seek to find this woman by creating a vision of her, and others would reject her, for not seeing her is a condition of the American dream.

I no longer remember the details, but sometime, somewhere, something was lost, and I started to look for it. An unseen presence led me to wander, and in the space of your absence I found half-formed images, fleeting outlines, and memories of events not quite the way they really happened. But these uncertain things became invested with so much feeling. I did not know exactly what I was looking for, but somewhere along the way I found a multitude of female figures hidden inside pages of books and boxes of photographs, hidden in plain sight, and painfully overexposed on the screen: A woman exiled

Operation Cookie Jar.

to live on a luxurious island, drowning in quicksand and laundry detergent. A little girl wading through a swamp to retrieve the remains of her father's rotting body. Then the Americans come to rescue her and offer her a pretty new dress to replace the mud-caked, blood-soaked one she is wearing. And soon she is a flower blooming in the swamp of hell. A blind and wounded girl lying breathless in the arms of a big-nosed soldier who is kind enough to feed her into ecstasy. And rows and rows of women ordered to get on their knees to threaten communists and fatten corporate wallets and beg forgiveness for their transgressions.

I found evidence of women whose sexual labor was written out of the narratives of national development and others whose sexual labor was also missing from the story of the Korean diaspora, women who had been exiled from the domestic sphere in Korea and therefore left to make homes elsewhere. And somewhere there are the dreams of no fewer than a million Korean women who have labored in the camptowns—dreams for America or for sexual freedom or simply wishes for something more than their circumstances allowed. I have found remnants of their dreams in the pages of texts written by their descendants and in the photographic documents of U.S. involvement in Korea.

I found a little Korean girl in Washington, D.C., hidden inside a box of photographs. She is poised on top of a pile of boxes full of food, a blonde baby doll at her side and a sucker in her mouth. In this picture she poses for the cameraman who is documenting the good will of American soldiers. But another time, in another box, I found the misplaced documentation of a mutual desire. The same little girl is returning the gaze of the American soldiers who ply her with their treats. I do not know who she is or who she belongs to, but I know she is far too young for such temptation.

But then again, I must also question the extent to which the author's dream is projected onto the girl's dream and then refracted through the dream of the audience.[103] Any of these narratives can be a representation only to the extent that an unconscious event such as a dream can ever tell a true story, and the contents are so mixed up anyway that I'm not sure I know where one dream ends and the next begins.

There is one that is clearly distinct, however. I am walking through a large empty space toward no known destination when a Korean man drives up in a black car, rolls down the window, and orders me not to go back to the place where I was born. I run away, and although he does not follow, I run as if my life is at stake. And, unexpectedly, I arrive at the house where I grew up. Everything looks exactly the same as it did when I left: the shag carpet and the grandfather clock and the fluorescent light in the kitchen illuminating the darkness in the hall. Something compels me to follow the projection of light to its conclusion, and where the hallway dead ends

it is dark once more—"in layers of forgetting . . . the opaque light fading it to absence, the object of memory." In every direction there is a closed door. I am terrified of finding what is on the other side, but by now I am also quite curious. The doors open one by one, and inside each room are members of my family, including those who are long dead or disappeared. My mother is the only one who is absent: "Her portrait is not represented in a photograph, nor in a painting." I ask where she is, but no one speaks. "Then slowly moving from room to room, through the same lean and open spaces" I keep walking, wandering in circles inside the house to look for her, and finally I find her in a room that never really existed. I come close to make sure she is still breathing, and then I lie down next to her and sleep.[104] "All along you see her without actually seeing, having seen her. You do not see her yet. For the moment, you see only her traces."

4.
The Fantasy of Honorary Whiteness

The area around an American army base is like an island between Korea and the U.S. . . . and those of us on the island are only whores for Westerners . . . we're temporary sweethearts, nameless "honeys" for the GIs.

—Kang Sŏk-kyŏng, "Days and Dreams"

After she saw her friends Tae-ja and Sun-hui die, both from unknown reasons, the deaths of four others followed. Some died from intoxication, some in a fire that a soldier allegedly set, and some committed suicide. "But God, I want to live," she found herself helplessly praying.

—Lee Min-a, from an interview with former camptown sex worker Kim Yeon-Ja

The camptowns around U.S. military bases in Korea are often described as "quicksand" and "islands"—"not part of the sea, not part of the mainland."[1] For some Korean women, they are exotic locales in which dreams of America are played out through a repeatedly performed romance between Korean women and American soldiers. For others, the camptowns are places haunted by death, from which there is no exit and in which marriage to American GIs is not a lived fantasy as much as a desperate attempt to find "a way out."[2] Although the camptowns are understood to be enclosures with tightly sealed borders, the effects of military domination are dispersed well beyond the confines of the camptown, especially because some camptown women do find their way out. It is through transgenerational haunting that the traumas that are inflicted, repeated, and repressed in the spaces of the camptown, as well as the historical sediments of war, take flight to circulate within the Korean diaspora. The yanggongju, as the primary vehicle of migration from Korea to the United States since the Korean War, has been one of the most important agents of this haunting.

I now shift my focus from the yanggongju as "Yankee whore" to the yanggongju as "GI bride"—and the gap between the two. The image of the injured body of the yanggongju that was salient among anti–U.S. activists in Korea disappears when the yanggongju as GI bride comes to America. Korean women who have married U.S. servicemen, many of whom met their husbands in camptowns, led the way for Korean migration to the United States, but the story of their arrival and rapid assimilation makes sense only through a willful forgetting of the everyday life of the camptown and of the violent and intimate history shared by Korea and the United States. This forgetting is quite apparent in American media accounts of the first Korean war bride to land on U.S. shores. A November 5, 1951, *Life Magazine* article titled "A War Bride Named 'Blue' Comes Home: Johnie Morgan Returns to the U.S. with a Korean Wife Who Once Walked 200 Miles to Be with Him" told an American public that Lee Yong Soon's sole motivation for walking two hundred miles during the war had been to be reunited with her beloved American soldier, who had renamed her "Blue" when they met.[3] He had been relocated to Busan from Seoul as the battle lines moved southward. "Three weeks later," the article continues, "her feet bare and bleeding, Blue reached Busan and Johnie Morgan. She had walked across country to Johnie. 'I knew then,' says Johnie, 'how much I loved the kid,' and he asked her to marry him."[4] This is the founding fairy tale of the intermarried Korean woman as the "Asian Cinderella."[5]

In this chapter I look at the ways in which the violence of U.S. militarism has been covered up through the reiterative practices of social scientific discourse and how these practices are disrupted by the unconscious memory of trauma. I show that sociological narratives about migration and assimilation in which Korean Americans are posited as honorary whites are fantasies that depend on a series of erasures of the yanggongju from both the geopolitical narrative of friendly U.S.–Korea relations and the micropolitical fictions of family life. What these erasures produce, in turn, is the Asian woman married to the white man as a social fact of assimilation. The story of honorary whiteness is a facet of the American dream, the larger fantasy of how the United States imagines itself as a site of liberation and a nation of saviors, a fantasy that is mutually supported by both the producers of this knowledge and the subjects that inform it. As much as the women who have led the way for their families to come to America have contributed to the discourse of honorary whiteness, they also occupy an unstable position in it. It is the figure of the yanggongju that most complicates this fantasy for Korean Americans in that she is heavily invested in the American dream, carrying the weight of a familial longing for America, yet at the same time her "assimilation" in the United States is contingent on her severing from the past, a past that is always present and threatens to turn the dream into a nightmare.

What I offer in this chapter is a reading of how different discourses in which the yanggongju is a spectral character create friction against one another and thus reveal the effects of unresolved trauma in the U.S.–Korea relationship. I pay particular attention to the gap between the two kinds of literature about the yanggongju—one that deals with sex workers as geopolitical actors and symbols in Korea, which I reviewed in the last chapter, and one that documents the life experiences of military brides in the United States. For example, Ji-Yeon Yuh opens her book with a discussion of the legacy of the Korean War and the system of camptown prostitution, and Katharine Moon includes in her book a chapter on marriages between U.S. servicemen and Korean sex workers. Both studies acknowledge the overlap between the two figures, as well as the difficulty in studying this overlap due to the women's reluctance to speak honestly about their life experiences. But neither book studies the gap between the two or the psychic consequences for the Korean diaspora of not knowing one's family history. It is precisely the gap between the "GI bride" and the "Yankee whore"—the silences among Americans surrounding issues of U.S. military prostitution, as well as the yanggongju's refusal to remember her traumatic histories when she comes to the United States—that create the conditions necessary for these traumas to be unconsciously passed across the diaspora.

I draw on the creative work of diasporic Koreans as evidence of transgenerational haunting and as a counterpoint both to standard sociological explanations of assimilation and to Korean military brides' own accounts of their experience. By linking analyses of existing literature on the yanggongju with examples of memory work by diasporic Koreans, as well as with short vignettes based on the life histories of Korean military brides, I explore the ways in which social science, testimony, autobiography, and fiction narrativize the fantasy of honorary whiteness. Some of the vignettes are based on one particular woman, while others are amalgamations of the experiences of several women. I fictionalize these vignettes to the extent that the life histories of Korean military brides are fictionalized by the women themselves as they are asked to reveal their lives to an audience of social scientists, historians, social workers, documentary filmmakers, and the general public in the United States. I intentionally blur the boundaries between one source of information and another to show how diasporic memory relies on porous boundaries to fill in gaps of what is not spoken, to disaggregate and reconfigure data collection about intermarriage, and to avoid "outing" any particular woman.

I also want to note that there is another haunting that takes place in this chapter. As a discourse that implicitly engages white supremacist ideology, the discourse of "honorary whiteness" automatically erases black–Korean intermarriages and the children of those marriages. Although sociologists have studied "segmented assimilation," in which an immigrant group assimilates to the norms of black culture or some other nondominant culture, it is often framed in terms of downward mobility. Sociologists commonly use *assimilated* interchangeably with *honorary white*, but there is no corollary of "honorary black" status, thus reifying whiteness as the benchmark of assimilation into the United States. Similarly, the American soldier in the escape-from-the-camptown fantasy is typically imagined as white. But as the three creative works I discuss in this chapter suggest, blackness is always present as the shadow of honorary whiteness, as another ghost that acts against and in conjunction with the yanggongju. Ultimately, my aim is to question whether marriage to a white American, as both a marker of prestige among camptown women and a marker of assimilation within the discourse of American sociology, allows the yanggongju and her kin to participate in the sociological fantasies of assimilation, upward mobility, and honorary whiteness. Does this trajectory of marriage and migration indeed represent a way out of the camptown, and if so, to what does the escape lead?

The Diaspora of Camptown

> The dead remain in the memory of the living and the threshold for flight is everywhere.
>
> —John Johnston, *Information Multiplicity*

The body of social science and social work research on U.S. military prostitution asserts that military sex workers view marriage to an American as the primary means out of the camptown, "an escape from prostitution and its stigma."[6] The fictional and autobiographical work about camptown life tells of another way out—death. This alternative to marriage suggests that these avenues are not disarticulated from one another and highlights some of the violence obfuscated by the romantic façade of international or interracial marriage. Together these narratives make linkages across time and space that show the ways in which the fantasy of America and the violence of U.S. military domination are bound together and how this entanglement is projected through the disavowed figure of Korean nationalism who is also the very foundation of the Korean diaspora in the United States.

> Since these islands have no roots, the girls living on them have no roots either. They know full well they can't rely on the islands, and that's why they have a pimp—or long for a one-way ticket to the U.S. Mi-ra and Sun-ja were just extreme cases of this.
>
> —Kang Sŏk-kyŏng, "Days and Dreams"

In the imaginary camptown of Kang Sŏk-kyŏng's fiction, there are three yanggongjus whose tales of escape are woven together—Mi-ra, the dead yanggongju who was murdered by her pimp before the story starts; Sun-ja, who desperately wants to be taken to America and hopes for romance with one of her American clients; and the narrator, who exhibits shamelessness at being a prostitute and is complacent enough to make no move toward leaving. For Sun-ja, the fairy tale of going to America nearly comes true, but

Kang adds an important twist. Sun-ja invests all of her hopes in one of her American clients, as the story often goes, but this client is not the white man that is the symbol of America for Koreans but a black woman named Barbara. Sun-ja transgresses the prescriptive fantasy of marrying a white male GI and enters into a relationship that defies norms even among the deviant women of the camptown. She pursues the relationship initially out of a desire to leave Korea but also because she encounters love for the first time. As the end of the story approaches, readers are led to believe that Sun-ja's dream will come true, but moments before meeting Barbara for their flight out of Korea, Sun-ja falls down a flight of stairs to her death, and "in this meaningless way, she left the world of the living for the eternal America of her dreams."[7] The day of Sun-ja's cremation, a letter to Sun-ja arrives from Barbara in which she makes Sun-ja's rescue fantasy explicit: "I love you and your agony. I hope I can be your savior. Think of our meeting as a blessing and please plan for our future."[8] But Sun-ja's alternative exit subverts their mutual dream and leaves Barbara to wonder why Sun-ja never appeared.

Unlike Sun-ja, the narrator indulges no escape fantasy. Her first sex-for-money exchange brings the realization that her movement is only circular, returning her to the same status of subordination to the United States from which she had started in postwar Korea, and she quickly becomes disillusioned about being saved. Although she takes pleasure in American men, she does not dream of romance or a married life in the United States. She even ridicules this dream in the final scene, when her married American boyfriend is about to return to his wife in the United States and promises to write: "I started giggling and told him I didn't need his letters. If he could just give me ten dollars, I'd call his name even in my dreams."[9] She defines romance as a commodity, placing sex and affection on the same plane in the business of militarized prostitution: "He stuffed two hundred dollars in my hand saying, 'Pay off what you owe your madam.' I gave him a violent kiss. I'd paid off my debt to the madam a long time ago, but I still had plenty of places to spend the money."[10] The final lines of "Days and Dreams" subvert the discourse of the American dream because we are confronted with a narrator who remains in militarized prostitution not because she is searching for a ticket out of Korea, not because she is debt-bonded, but because she already knows that she is going nowhere.[11] In Kang's narrative, marriage is not a viable option, and for those who dream of escape, the only way out is death.

Although Kang's work has been criticized for portraying the yanggongju as the tragic woman whose body represents a nation dominated by the United States, I propose a different reading in which the yanggongju is not simply a passive body or receptacle of national sorrow.[12] Kang's characters, in both their cynicism and their tragic outcomes, unsettle common-sense ideas of migration and marriage, particularly sociological assumptions about assimilation. The narrator, for example, harbors no notions of either romance or progress when it comes to marrying an American, thereby challenging the fantasy in which the white American soldier rescues the abject Korean woman from prostitution and the Third World and takes her to revel in the abundance of the United States. In both American and Korean imaginaries, according to Yoo, "marriage to [white] American soldiers symbolized eternal security and happiness, an insurance against suffering and want."[13] The discourse of assimilation in the United States also supports this story line that marriage to white Americans is a sign of assimilation and upward mobility; however, neither the narrator nor Sun-ja conforms to these desires. "Days and Dreams" challenges ideas about movement that equate marriage to an American with progress and raises questions about how death can be a line of flight out of the camptown.

Perhaps the deaths of Mi-ra and Sun-ja speak less to Kang's nihilism about camptown life and more to the ways in which the migration route of marriage to Americans is haunted by a history of militarized violence. In the sociological accounts of interracial marriage between Korean women and American men, as well as the oral histories of Korean military brides, there is an erasure of this violent past by both the women who are telling their stories and the researchers who are narrativizing the phenomena of migration and interracial marriage. Perhaps the "fictional" yanggongju who has been memorialized in the work of Kang and others, as well as the "real" yanggongjus who were murdered and made symbols of the nation, are spectral forces of memory against forgetting. Because there is movement in and out of the camptown, whether through marriage or through death, the traumatic effects of the system are carried forward through a diaspora descended from camptown women.

Imminent Arrival

> The Korean War sets up a first in matrimonial relations . . . for on the ship is Sergeant John Morgan and his bride Yong Soon, who becomes the first Korean War bride and the first to reach the United States. She was a telephone operator. She met Sergeant Johnie at a dance. Johnie's parents say, "If she suits him, she suits us." . . . So it's Mrs. Yong Soon Morgan . . . facing the cameras and given one of America's traditional family welcomes.
>
> —Archival news footage announcing the U.S. arrival of Yong Soon Morgan

One hundred thousand Korean women have migrated to the United States through marriage to U.S. servicemen, and upon their arrival in the United States they are absorbed into a story line about immigrant success and honorary whiteness, a story line that attempts to erase traumatic history and make the yanggongju as "Yankee whore" disappear altogether. But when she is made to disappear, what comes to occupy the space of her departure? In Eng and Kazanjian's conceptualization of loss, absence is not just a negative space but also a potential presence. The site of departure is also a signal of imminent arrival.[14] The departure raises the question of what rises up in the space of the yanggongju's absence, of what new forms of haunting are generated and passed along transgenerationally. But I also want to question the notion of "imminent arrival." If the yanggongju is a figure in perpetual exile, her arrival in the United States is always imminent without ever being complete, and the women who migrate to the United States through marriage to American servicemen never fully arrive at assimilation yet are made to appear assimilated within the discourse of American sociology. However, that which is left out in order to construct Koreans in the United States as statistical

American family welcome.

persons of honorary whiteness leaves residues of trauma that resist assimilation.

Yanggongju One **was a young girl during the Korean War.[15] She used to go to the U.S. military bases to buy leftovers from the mess hall. "In there you have toothpicks, napkins, there's all kinds of things—prunes, meat, everything. . . . That's how we lived month after month."[16] The bases were an outlet for survival, but also a promise of more. She got a job dancing for the sergeants. They pulled her pigtails and called her "virgin girl," and they gave her an American nickname. From a**

very young age, she developed a love for American men. Eventually she married one twenty-five years her senior and moved to America.

Yanggongju Two met her husband in a bar in Itaewon. He was a U.S. serviceman. She was an "entertainment hostess." She attended "etiquette and good conduct lectures" to learn the art of comfort, and although the lectures were mandatory, she looked forward to them with hope. Her studies paid off, because she found a man who wanted to marry her and take her to America. When she arrived in the United States, she wiped the slate clean and told no one about her past.

Yanggonggju Three moved with her two children to her husband's hometown in Kansas in 1979. A few months later, she gave birth to a baby boy, the first child by her husband. Her other children were legally adopted by her husband, and with that act of benevolence he won the right to raise them according to his rules. No Korean was to be spoken under his roof, so the older children learned English quickly and forgot their native language, while Three continued to speak broken English with Korean syntax and a thick accent. But Three could not argue with her husband's decision because she, too, preferred that the children speak English in order to "blend in."[17] As they grew, she became unable to communicate with them, and they became embarrassed by her and identified with their father.

Yanggongju Four sponsored six of her relatives who came to the United States, and they sponsored six more, until almost all her extended family were living nearby. When her brothers were coming of age, one of her friends had advised her: "You'd better marry an American, and take your brothers to America." "In those days," she said, "it was easy to invite one's brothers and sisters to America."[18] And so she joined the other "bar girls on U.S. mili-

tary bases . . . who built power bases for themselves by marrying U.S. citizens and then sponsoring family members as immigrants."[19] But few of Four's family acknowledged her after their immigration because of the relentless shame associated with her marriage to the American. Many of them became successful in one way or another—they opened small businesses or moved into respectable neighborhoods or sent their children to college. They attributed their success mostly to the abundance of opportunity in America, partly to their own hard work, and little to their yanggongju sponsor.

My father's hometown was not exactly the America of my mother's dreams. No one there had ever met a Korean, and her strangeness made her more determined to blend in, so she carefully studied the habits of American women. She cooked spaghetti and meatballs and made green Jell-O mixed with cottage cheese and fruit cocktail, hosted parties for the neighbors, smiled hello in response to people's stares, kept quiet about the goings-on behind closed doors, hung lights at Christmas, carved jack-o'-lanterns on Halloween, spoke only English at home so that we would grow up American, went to PTA meetings, donated to bake sales, volunteered for the United Way, and attended church, doing everything she could in the hope of becoming the perfect American wife and mother.

The Perfect American Wife, Korean Style

> After I have baby in the hospital, my husband, he abuse me by curtain [rod]. He abuse me by tennis racket. He abuse me by mop stick. . . . All over my body got abused.
>
> —Yang Hyang Kim, in *The Women Outside*

Like Kang's fictional story, J. T. Takagi and Hye Jung Park's documentary film *The Women Outside: Korean Women and the U.S. Military* narrates the lives of three camptown women. Two of them have grown jaded to the prospect of ever leaving the camptown, but the third finds possibility in marriage. Her first husband takes her to the United States, but he also beats her, thus showing her a nightmarish side of the American dream. She returns to Korea and to prostitution and eventually finds a second man who pays off her debts and marries her. Prior to her second departure, we follow her through classes in the camptown's "U.S.O. Bride School."[20] An article in the *Christian Science Monitor* titled "The Perfect American Wife, Korean-Style" describes the kind of training this woman might have received at the Bride School: "Yvonne Park bangs a head of lettuce against a table and extracts its core. . . . Twenty Korean women take note of the neat trick. They've never made an American-style salad. Next they learn how to baste turkey, slice canned cranberry gelatin, and bake pumpkin pie."[21] The women in this scenario are exemplary spectacles of hope who eagerly participate in the fantasy of America. The Bride School describes itself as a service to ease Korean women's assimilation into American culture, reinforcing the notion that escape from the camptown and assimilation into the United States are two sides of the same coin.

In *Beyond the Shadow of Camptown,* Ji-Yeon Yuh argues that military brides are the invisible backbone of the Korean American community in that for four decades following the Korean War the most common migration route for Korean immigrants was through sponsorship by one of the one hundred thousand Korean women who married American GIs. While she contextualizes the women's oral histories in the broader history of U.S.–Korea relations and military prostitution, she also acknowledges that the prevalence of former military prostitutes in the United States cannot be empirically proven because of the desire to keep this part of one's personal history secret: "One Korean wife of an American GI told a researcher that nine out of ten Korean women met their GI husbands at clubs catering exclusively to American soldiers, thus implying that they were prostitutes, and then added that nine out of ten will deny it."[22] As the title of Yuh's book suggests, these women have both moved beyond the camptown through migration, but they also seek to distance themselves from the stigmas associated with camptown life. When the yanggongju comes to America, she retreats into the private spaces of white middle-class domesticity, an achievement that sociologists of immigration have long considered a benchmark of assimilation. Although nearly half of the Korean community in the United States today arrived here through familial ties to the U.S. military, a trajectory born of the intimate and violent relations between the United States and Korea, the discipline of sociology has paid little attention to the role of U.S. militarism in Korean immigration and treats assimilation as an a priori desirable outcome. Asians in the United States are coded as highly assimilated and assimilable, even "honorary whites," despite a long history of Asian American exclusion in the United States.

In classical models of assimilation theory, assimilation is understood as a normal social process that is linear—"progressive and irreversible" in Robert Park's estimation, or incremental with each new generation ("straight line") according to Herbert Gans.[23] But diasporic subjects such as the yanggongju and her kin are often constituted by trauma, and the temporality of trauma is nonlinear. If we pay attention to the unconscious traumas that migrate along with Koreans in the diaspora, we can, in the words of Ann Anlin Cheng, "be attentive to the disjunctive and retroactive hauntedness of history.[24] The underlying assumption that assimilation is an almost inevitable and linear process has been challenged several times since assimilation theory's early days, both within and beyond the field of sociology, but notions of the assimilated Asian are still being produced in academic and public discourses.[25]

One of popular culture's most recent articulations of model minority success is the Kim Sisters' controversial book, *Top of the Class: How Asian Parents Raise High Achievers,* which was even glamorized in the *New York Times* style section.[26] Similarly, sociologists have called for a revision of assimilation theory, offering up Asian Americans as the test case. An assumption made by hegemonic sociological accounts of immigration is that Asians' "relatively high intermarriage rates . . . suggest their acceptability to many whites . . . and the absence of a deep racial divide."[27] While sociologists such as Pyong Gap Min and Mia Tuan caution against assuming that intermarried couples and biracial children are automatically "accepted," some leading sociologists of immigration continue to take for granted the standard indicators of assimilation.[28]

In a lecture sponsored by the Sawyer Seminar on Immigrants and the Transformation of American Society held at the City University of New York, for example, Richard Alba defended the notion of assimilation against recent waves of criticism about the model's ethnocentric biases. He asked the audience to consider Asian Americans as an example of a non-European group that is successfully assimilated. His evidence included statements such as "Asian kids don't speak Asian languages." On another occasion, Nancy Foner delivered a lecture in this seminar, stating that Asian Americans are "honorary whites."[29] Alba and Foner, as two of the top social scientists in the field of immigration studies, continue to adhere to the story line of the honorary white Asian, while scholars in other fields argue against these notions by bringing questions of political and psychic violence to bear on the assimilation paradigm.

Asian American studies scholars, for example, have criticized the notion of assimilation for erasing the traumatic aspects of diasporic histories and idealizing whiteness.[30] They suggest that assimilation is part of a national agenda of privileging white citizenship through the demarcation of racialized bodies, but one that is necessarily haunted because "these immigrants retain precisely the memories of imperialism that the U.S. nation seeks to forget."[31] The theoretical frameworks for studying assimilation used by these Asian American studies scholars contrast sharply with traditional sociological models that view assimilation as a normal social *process* that immigrants go through, rather than a normalizing *project* carried out by networks of discipline and control, in which the field of sociology is thoroughly implicated. Even if we take for granted the framework of assimilation, the yanggongju's history troubles the idea that assimilation can be quantified by intermarriage and the use of English only, standards by which Koreans are the most assimilated of all Asian groups.[32]

Some Korean American social scientists have challenged these indicators of "success," however. Sociologist Pyong Gap Min questions romantic notions of intermarriage, noting that among Korean women who migrated to the United States through intermarriage "the vast majority are married to U.S. servicemen. . . . Korean women who marry U.S. servicemen generally had low socioeconomic status. . . . Many of them were born and raised in rural

Napalmed women.

villages and migrated to Seoul and other large cities in search of urban employment."[33] Although Min omits any mention of the likelihood that the urban employment many of these women obtained, through which they met their husbands, was sex work in the camptowns, he criticizes intermarriage as a taken-for-granted indicator of Koreans' successful assimilation into the U.S. mainstream without questioning the quality or context of those marriages. Min goes on to say of Korean military brides, "Their language barrier and lack of assimilation make marital adjustment very difficult. . . . Moreover, many interracially married U.S. servicemen neglect and even abuse their Korean wives, deciding that the women who provided them companionship in Korea are no longer valuable to them in this country."[34] Jong Yeon Brewer, a social scientist who is also a Korean woman married to an American serviceman, contests the claim that speaking only English at home is a desirable outcome of assimilation. Instead, she argues that using English as the home language of such families results in a traumatic loss of language for children and communication for mothers. In other words, the cost of this kind of assimilation is the loss of "the intimate registers enjoyed by parents and children."[35]

What are obvious in these social scientific critiques are the ways in which indicators of assimilation whitewash discord and pain in these families, but less obvious is the way in which the discourse of assimilation is also implicated in the camptown's disciplinary logic. Not only does the narrative of Koreans' easy assimilation into the United States cover over instances of domestic violence; the performance of the successful intermarriage that begins in the camptown through practices such as "Bride School" domesticates the traumatic history of U.S.–Korea relations by glamorizing America for those living under the most oppressive conditions of U.S. military control. When these women are given the chance to go to America, they often go to great lengths to hide their pasts both from their children and from the gaze of social scientists who have coded the intermarried Asian woman and her children as "assimilated." Their quiet efforts to be thankful and unobtrusive and secretive about their pasts have earned them a leading role in the production of the fantasy of honorary whiteness.

***Yanggongju One* does not tell her interviewer many details of how she met her husband other than that it was at the sergeants' club, and when she first started working there she was a young virgin girl who was hired to dance for the men. And then she got a job as a telephone operator, and later she met Sergeant Johnny at a dance.**

***Yanggongju Two* agrees to tell her story as long as it is under a different name. She agrees to speak as "Erin" because her heart is full of knots, and if she cannot escape the past, she wishes to release it from the swamp of her blood history. But her chest is so tight that she can unwind only a small piece of the story, and it is about her one return to Gohyang and her brother's betrayal when she brought her biracial child from America: "When I visited my family in Korea... my brother asked us**

to hide our faces for a while when his friends visited, because in his position he was ashamed of the mixed blood. . . . He asked me twice to hide myself. . . . I was very disappointed in him. I had taken care of my family. My brothers had once told me, 'We'll take care of you, if you are poor and sick when you're old.' I was so disappointed."[36] All she can speak of is her brother's shame, his repeated requests for her to hide, and her unresolved grief that they had been alienated like this. There is a gap in the transcript. And then the interviewer asks about her husband, and more generally about how military brides meet their husbands. "Ninety percent of them," she says, "met through prostitution." But she, of course, was among the ten percent of women who were not prostitutes.

Yanggongjus Three and Four **say the same: "Most of those women were Yankee whores. But not me. Not me."**

The Denial of Grief

> Like the stories of untold numbers of others before her, my mother's personal history no doubt remained in silence and shadow because she was a commoner and because she was a woman. But I think she complied with the erasure because she did not want to unveil herself and her mother as "bad women." . . . I like to think that she was motivated by a wish to protect me from the legacy by not letting me know that I come from a long line of "bad women."
>
> —Elaine Kim, "Bad Women"

What is denied in service of the project of assimilation? David Eng argues that the history of Asian America is a history of exclusion—an exclusion of Asian bodies from the official history of the United States and an exclusion of Asian bodies from migrating to U.S. shores. He refers to these omissions as "a lack that threatens to consign existence to oblivion."[37] There are other exclusions to add to Eng's list. Asian immigrants are denied grief about the traumatic histories that precipitated their migration but also about their traumatic beginnings in a country whose national ideals are "sustained by the exclusion-yet-retention of racialized others."[38] In order to participate in the project of assimilation, Asian immigrants must perform the role of the "almost white" who never quite arrives at assimilation, the "excluded-yet-retained" racialized other. They suffer from the "deep-seated, intangible, psychical complications for people living within a ruling episteme that privileges that which they can never be."[39] They must deny their own grief and risk being consigned to oblivion.

***Yanggongju Five* did not find a husband. Neither Korean nor American wanted to marry her, so she stayed in Korea working the back rooms of camptown bars until one day she was found dead and naked, her body skewered like a pig's. The murdered Yanggongju Five mobilized anti–U.S. politics and became a household name in Korea—and among Koreans in the United States, too.**

***Yanggongju One* considered herself lucky. Her fate might have been like Yanggongju Five's had she not met the sergeant. Some of the other girls questioned how she could marry an old man like that. Instead, she took the advice of women who assured her that older men know how to take care of a girl.**

***Yanggongju Two* wiped the slate clean, but traces of what had been still ached, especially at times like this. She hid the shock of Yanggongju Five's murder. She hid it along with everything else because there was no way to explain why she had so much bad feeling. She pretended to not know anything about Yanggongju Five or the world in which she had lived or the national drama incited by her death. Instead, she kept quiet and raised her children to "never mind" about politics and just be good citizens.**

***Yanggongju Three* made every effort to shelter her children from things that were unpleasant. Still, she ended**

up losing them to her husband. But she was also to blame for pushing them away. On rare occasions when they asked about her life during the war, she did not give them any of the information that they had not found elsewhere. Instead she said, "Why you wanna know about those kind of things? We're in America now."

Yanggongju Four **divorced and remarried and relocated to New York City, far from her extended family. More and more, she found herself bruised and bleeding like Yanggongju Five, except that she did not die and have a whole country demand her vindication. The conflict carried out on her flesh was unremarkable. Her aggressor went unpunished and her wounds unnoticed by everyone except the social worker who referred her to a shelter, and there she would meet Yanggongju Six.**

Against the denial of grief that is the condition for a sociological narrative about Koreans as honorary whites comes the social work counternarrative, which paints a radically different picture of yanggongjus as women who are broken by the process of assimilation. The body of work done by social service providers in Korean American communities demonstrates the ways in which the unequal power relations in marriages between Korean women and American GIs often make assimilation more difficult, not less so, for the Korean women who have migrated to the United States. Takagi and Park estimate that 80 percent of such marriages end in divorce, and many of the women come out of these marriages abused, homeless, and/or mentally ill.[40] Although the research in this area is fairly new and much of the evidence is anecdotal, the services provided by organizations such as the Rainbow Center, a shelter for abused or homeless Korean women married to U.S. servicemen in New York City, and Duraebang, which provides similar services to women at a camptown near Seoul, attest to the fact that there is a population of intermarried Korean women who are in need of housing assistance, social services, and psychiatric care. The social work counternarrative suggests that the yanggongju as GI bride lives in equally abject conditions as the yanggongju as Yankee whore. Indeed, the mission of Duraebang is to attend to the needs of women who are either prostitutes or wives of U.S. military personnel, thus locating both types of sexual labor within the abusive conditions of the camptown. This newer body of knowledge illustrates what Lisa Lowe refers to as "the practices of resignification that the 'outside-within' condition of Asians in America enables" in the way that it resituates intermarriage not as a sign of progress toward full citizenship but rather as both the cause and the effect of violence.[41] The GI bride's abjection is not easily apparent, however, because of the way in which she is cloaked in the glitter of the American dream.

Yanggongju Six **married a man who left her almost as soon as she landed in the United States, so she started her new life with no resources and two young children. She found work in a massage parlor, and one night when she had left her children at home unsupervised, her youngest was killed in an accident. An accident, yet she was convicted of murder. There were things that influenced the jury—Yanggongju Six was a sex worker and a foreigner with a heavy accent in a North Carolina courtroom. Word spread about her conviction, and even Koreans on the peninsula began to rally around her as if it had been their Koreanness that was put on trial by the United States. After seven years, the International Committee to Free Yanggongju Six liberated her from prison.**

Yanggongju One **heard about Yanggongju Six while watching her daughter perform on television. Yanggongju One had proudly sent her daughter to college and then to graduate school, where she had earned a Ph.D. in English, but instead of becoming a professor as her mother had hoped, she became a spoken word poet who spoke her rage about everything except the circumstances of her own birth. Once the daughter was asked in a media interview how her parents first met. To Yanggongju One's relief, she answered, "I don't know."**

***Yanggongjus Two and Three* no longer paid attention to news about Koreans, either in the United States or on the peninsula. They had arrived in America, so there was really nothing left to complain about.**

***Yanggongju Four* had never heard of Yanggongju Six until they met at the shelter. Yanggongju Six had been out of prison only a couple years when she ended up on the streets, homeless and hallucinating. It seemed that the International Committee to Free Yanggongju Six hadn't considered all the implications of her liberation, but somehow she had managed to find a shelter full of other women like her. Yanggongju Four thought it strange that all the women there had married Americans, and she started to wonder if maybe she had been wrong all this time, thinking that American men were better.**

Korean diasporic discourses about the GI bride have begun to reveal what has been excluded so that the sociological story of assimilation can make sense, and they have also begun to unfold some of the ways in which there is a price to pay for honorary whiteness. The psychic violence experienced by diasporic subjects when they attempt to assimilate is perhaps what is most troubling about the project of assimilation. As Michael Fischer says about the experience of immigration for Asian Americans, the first generation participates in the project by always covering over their tracks in order to make their lives unintelligible to their children.

> Even though she didn't talk about it, I could feel the fear she had so many years ago. . . . She told us to do all the right things, just work and study hard, stay away from politics and social things. . . . So I learned, you're supposed to get an education so you get an education; then you're supposed to get a job so you get a job; then a house. . . . Then you ask yourself, "Now what, now what are you supposed to do with yourself?"
>
> —Chung Suh, as quoted in "History, Trauma, and Identity"

But what happens when the yanggongju as GI bride represses within her own body the yanggongju as Yankee whore and is haunted by the ghost of her own past? This type of psychic violence is not only what is most troubling *about* the project of assimilation; it is also what is most troubling *to* it, because the yanggongju comes to haunt the fantasy of honorary whiteness. She is ghosted by her own past covered up, as well as by all those yanggongjus left behind and those who have escaped the camptowns through death. The secret she harbors about herself and about the historical traumas she embodies is transmitted unconsciously across the diaspora. Even those deemed to have "made it" in America are still haunted by some lingering fear from another's past.

***Yanggongju Seven,* like so many others, does not tell her children how she met her husband. When one of them asks what she did for a living in Korea, she is silent and stares at a little spot on the wall as if to tune out the questions. But her daughter asks again. At first, Yanggongju Seven says that she was a waitress, but later she changes her answer to teacher, because teacher is a far more respectable profession. Whenever the question is asked, her fear is palpable. She is visibly disturbed, and her disturbance passes through the house like an unhappy wind.**

The Ghost and the Dream

> I dream of her still. . . . She drifts through my sleep almost nightly. . . . When I wake, I try to envision her face, but her features melt into one another . . . as if through several layers of photographic negatives. . . . At fourteen, peeking out from under the paper bag she had put on her head when we went to Dr. Pak's VD clinic; at seventeen when, with her mother's makeup smeared over her face, she taught me about "honeymooning" in the backbooths of the GI clubs; at twenty when she pushed a wet and wailing MyuMyu into my arms. . . . In every memory I have of her, I can hear her words, see her gestures, but her face remains a fragmented blur.
>
> —Nora Okja Keller, *Fox Girl*

When the yanggongju as GI bride represses within her own body the yanggongju as Yankee whore, she is haunted by the ghosts of her own past and these ghosts are passed down through the generations, haunting children with the gaps in knowledge about their family histories. According to Abraham and Torok, the tension of transgenerational haunting—that those who are haunted have been silenced by the "horror at violating a parent's or family's guarded secret, even though the secret's text and content are inscribed within"—is revealed in the dreamwork of diasporic Koreans, whose relationship to the yanggongju is likely but cannot be proven given the conditions of Korean migration to the United States.[42] As suggested by the protagonist of Nora Okja Keller's *Fox Girl,* this figure is not fully fleshed out but rather a fuzzy outline filled in by a suturing of memory flashes. The yanggongju seems to be less amorphous when one is in the dream state, but when the dreamer wakes she becomes ambiguous and phantasmatic. She hovers there, in the liminal space between sleeping and waking, between psychic and social history. She lives in the dreamer's unconscious as an assemblage of traumatic moments and a shameful family secret who threatens the waking fantasy of honorary whiteness.

Evidence of transgenerational haunting can be found in texts written by diasporic Koreans in which the yanggongju appears as a mark of a traumatized collective memory and an ambiguous personal history, suggesting that there is a shared theme of haunting around one's mother, or another relative, as a U.S. military prostitute. When the yanggongju appears, the author's relationship to her is often framed in terms of what remains secret or uncertain. For example, in one of her poems Ishle Park makes reference to the fact that her aunt's marriage to an American GI was a "family secret" even though it was that marriage that had allowed the rest of her family to migrate.[43] Questions of kinship to the yanggongju are particularly salient in the work of biracial Korean Americans who are the direct descendents of GI brides, such as Heinz Insu Fenkl and Nora Okja Keller, although this work is perhaps where she is also most ambiguous. Both Fenkl's memoir *Memories of My Ghost Brother* and Keller's novel *Fox Girl* address the ways in which loss and repression are the conditions under which the yanggongju and her kin participate in the American dream.

Memories of My Ghost Brother opens with a dream of a giant serpent that is about to tell Fenkl's mother a secret, but she awakens before it is revealed. It is the last dream she has before Fenkl is born—one that foreshadows the death of a cousin who commits suicide when a "yellow-haired soldier" gets her pregnant but refuses to marry her, as well as the novel's finale, in which Fenkl recovers a repressed memory of an older brother whose disappearance had become a family secret. In the end, the child narrator "sees" the lost brother by tracing a path in his unconscious, finding his brother not through a direct memory of him but through a memory flash of a family photograph taken when Fenkl was an infant, which then triggers a vague and momentary recollection that another child was present in the picture. The mother eventually confesses that she had given the older brother up for adoption in America as a condition of her marriage to Fenkl's father, a U.S. serviceman, who did not want to raise another man's child. This act of giving up a child in exchange for a ticket to the United States can be read by some as greedy and morally bankrupt, especially when the person in question is already stigmatized by her status as a prostitute, but it can also be read as an act of courage and love. When the grandeur of the United States is hyperbolized in the psyches of most Koreans, what better gift can a mother give than the chance to grow up there? But with this sacrifice, America comes to haunt her dreams even more, because "that's where all the wonderful things come from, and that's where he is. . . . Someday I'll find him. . . . That's why I'll go to America."[44] Thus, the sacrifice for a better future turns into a melancholic investment in the past.[45]

The lost brother is not the only ghost in Fenkl's memoir, however; it is teeming with them. But the other ghosts are not figures of deferred possibility like the lost brother. Instead, they operate as the violent and irrecoverable loss that lies beneath a fantasied image of America, particularly as that fantasy is colored by the "honor" of whiteness. Although the biological half brother may be the one that Fenkl dreams of at the end of his memoir, the ghost brother could just as easily refer to Fenkl's half-black childhood friend who mysteriously drowns at the bathhouse. This disappeared child is another nagging presence in the story, particularly after Fenkl's uncle insinuates that the child's death was not an accident:

> "Think about it. . . . You're a dungwhore and you catch yourself a GI by getting pregnant with his brat, but then he goes off to Vietnam and gets himself killed. That leaves you with the benefits from the great Emperor of America, but now you have a Black brat to feed, and it's not enough money. So now you want another GI husband to start things over—maybe a white guy with a higher rank, ungh?—but who would marry a whore a with a Black kid? . . .
>
> "Maybe she was trying to scrub the color off and she held his face down in the washbasin too long."[46]

In their desperate attempts to escape the camptown in order to participate in the American dream and its racial hierarchies, these mothers attempt to sever themselves from their pasts as prostitutes to become more marriageable, even if it means getting rid of the biracial children that are the material evidence of that past. While Fenkl ultimately makes it out of the camptown with his mother, he remains haunted by both the white Korean brother sent to live in America and the black Korean brother left to die in Korea.

The camptown of Fenkl's memoir as well as of Keller's fiction is the camptown of the 1960s, which in a few years would become the target of "clean-up campaigns" to smooth out racial tensions between black and white soldiers, as discussed in Katharine Moon's *Sex among Allies* (see my chapter 4). Bruce Cumings's diary from 1968 offers another portrait of the camptown during this era:

> The areas near the American military base are drastically deprived. . . . Here the local parasitic population lives . . . [in] filthy, backward, shameful "living establishments." The worst aspect, though, is the whoring district. . . . There are clusters of "clubs" catering only to Americans. Rock-and-roll blares from them, they are raucously painted and titled, and ridiculous-looking painted Korean girls—often very young—peer from the doors. Nothing is more silly-looking . . . than these girls in minny skirts *[sic]*. Several of them hooted at me as I walked by . . . but the most disconcerting of all was a middle-aged woman with two kids hanging on to her who, in the middle of the street, asked me to come and "hop on" in the chimdeh [bed]. . . . The town is crawling

> with mixed-blood children. They seemed fairly well cared for—certainly not beggars.... These kids are probably well cared for because the whole town is in the dregs, removed from the prejudices of wealthy Koreans from which the terrible treatment of mixed race kids results. There is no reason to shit on them—they'll bring in good money as whores or pimps when they're fourteen. Goofy-looking, stupid soldiers walk arm-in-arm with whores who are often only young girls—very very young girls.[47]

Although Cumings's observations are somewhat consistent with other depictions of the camptown from this era, his tone is highly moralistic, indicting both the "goofy-looking, stupid" GI clients and the "local parasitic population," but without implicating readers in the "filthy, backward, and shameful... whoring district" that he allows them to voyeuristically look at.[48]

Keller's novel *Fox Girl*, by contrast, shows the same world, yet it is a world that is thoroughly interimplicated with the ideals of America. Like Fenkl, Keller also looks at how colonization, war, and prostitution obscure family histories and create racial hierarchies among its ghosts. *Fox Girl* is set in an American town in Korea during the 1960s, a community made up of American GI's and the Koreans who serve them. It is a world that reflects the gaze of those who prefer to think of themselves on the outside—where biracial children are hated for being racially contaminated but envied if they are taken to the United States and where American goods are looked down on as "whore's rubbish" yet seductive enough to lure new generations of girls into the camptowns:

> Sometimes we'd open up a drawer and find strange things to eat, like Ho Hos. The first time I tried that chocolate roll, I spit out the cake with its too-sweet lining of sugar cream. I couldn't believe that Americans, who could have anything in the world, would eat that. I thought Sookie had played a joke on me, handing me that shiny-wrapped present and telling me it was *U.S.A.* so I would expect something delicious.... She and I ate our way through the box before I decided I liked it. I saved the wrappers from those Ho Hos for a long while after that day, pasting them on my bedroom wall with chewed up bits of rice.[49]

The story revolves around Hyun Jin (the narrator) and her ambiguously dark-skinned best friend, Sookie, two teenage girls who become second-generation yanggongjus, who are later revealed to be half sisters, and whose lives become more and more implicated in one another's as they are seduced by the pleasures and dangers of the camptown. In the landscape of *Fox Girl,* it is a transgenerational psychic bond to America that draws the girls into prostitution.

In one scene, the girls and their pimp, a seventeen-year-old boy fathered by a black soldier, are singing a song in English, even though they are uncertain of what the words mean. It is an army song they have heard American soldiers sing while marching. The boy-pimp may have learned this song from his Yankee father, although he cannot be sure because his memories of his father are as worn and faded as the letter from America that he carries in his pocket. They decipher the words, one by one. "Toad" is easy. *Toggobi.* But some of the words prove more challenging because there is no direct translation into Korean. "Fucked," one of the girls explains, "means . . . 'Your mama will die.' So don't ever say it." "Whore" is the second word that comes into question. This question is met with silence among the children, perhaps because the knowledge of this word is corporal: "We knew what whore meant. We knew whose mothers they were."[50]

> I found a whore by the side of the road.
> Knew right away she was dead as a toad.
> Her skin was all gone from her tummy to her head.
> But I fucked her, I fucked her even though she was dead.[51]

The children of yanggongjus, Keller suggests, carry the knowledge of their family histories in their bodies despite an absence of language to translate. One of the refrains of *Fox Girl* is "Blood will tell," referring to the future of the yanggongju's children. The suggestion, of course, is that there are generational continuities in military prostitution. "Blood" here can be regarded as genetic disposition, but it can also be read as a transgenerational haunting in which those who are more intimately tied to the violences of war and colonization are bound together.

***Yanggongju Seven* tells her daughter, "Don't be like me when you grow up," but she does not explain what that means. She tells her daughter to stay away from night-**

clubs and bars: "Stay away from men." She tells her daughter to ask no questions about what came before America. "Just go to school and be a good girl. Go to school and study hard, and you be anything you want to be, not like me." Yanggongju Seven does everything possible to change the course of her daughter's future so that history can be washed out of her blood.

As the story of *Fox Girl* unfolds, family lineages become more and more ambiguous as characters speculate about which of them "share the same whorish blood" and as memories of their American fathers fade away.[52] In their uncertainty, the young people in *Fox Girl* become increasingly entangled in the nightmare of the American dream. Hyun Jin, as the only teenage character who is clearly not black, escapes the camptown at the end of the novel but remains haunted by her past, embodied in the form of Sookie, who stays in Korea and in prostitution yet visits Hyun Jin nightly in her dreams. While Sookie is the shadowy figure in Hyun Jin's memory, it is Hyun Jin who is perhaps the clearest expression of a spectral agency in this text in that she seems to be everywhere at once. She is both the yanggongju and the diasporic subject whose unconscious remembers her. She is the GI bride who flees Korea to raise a child in America and the daughter transgenerationally haunted by her mother's secrets. She is the ghost and the dream.

One cannot help but wonder if this confusion of unconscious boundaries and the unraveling of an ambiguous family history born of U.S. military domination is also about the author's own sense of trauma. In an interview at AsianWeek.com, Keller is asked, "Do your characters haunt you?" She speaks to the ways in which she, too, became a part of the world she writes about: "I feel like I live a dual life. My waking life, which is my real life, is centered around my family. . . . Then there's my other life, my writing life, which usually takes place in the dark of night. . . . I had trouble shaking that darkness when I got up in the morning. . . . Towards the end of writing the book, I felt that parts of the characters were seeping into my own character."[53] Perhaps the effects of her writing were a kind of what Abraham and Torok call a "waking dream . . . [which] stages the parents' concealment of something."[54]

American GI feeding a blind and helpless girl.

Although we cannot be sure how much *Fox Girl* reflects Keller's own background as a biracial Korean American, the ghosts of U.S. militarism in Korea and of American–Korean intermarriage assert themselves in Keller's text, as well as in her own unconscious.

> **I dream of her still, but images of her do not appear like so many snapshots of our lives. I cannot say at what age she first worked in the GI clubs, for I did not witness her transformation into a yanggongju. Some nights when I dream of her, she is just an outline colored in by my confusion, or she is more amorphous still, an energy that moves through the empty spaces of memory. There is only one image that is in perfect focus, and I see it more clearly than my eyes are capable of.**
>
> **I am standing in shadows, and the city looks like the New York of an apocalyptic future in which all that remains are the blackened bodies of buildings. They, too, are dead. A voice speaks to me from the air and leads me away from the tall buildings until I am walking on**

dirt paths through a barren landscape. I keep walking, walking, until I come to a small wooden house. The voice leads me inside, into the kitchen, and my mother's sister is there, an old woman, as she is now. I enter the living room, where I encounter my mother chewing gum and watching television. She is much younger than I, almost still a child. There are other presences, too, shadowy figures whose faces are blurred and gray, faces once captured in photographs that burned up along with everything else, even his body. But my mother could never call him "dead." Only "disappeared."

I am no longer in a future New York, but in a former Gyeongsang province. It is 1960, and I am not yet born. But there I am, an adult woman with my teenage mother, watching television. On the screen is a little orphan girl wearing red lipstick, her hair curled, sitting in the lap of a white American soldier. He is trying to get her to smile for the cameras by bouncing her on his knee. She stares directly into the camera but refuses to smile. The show fast-forwards to a clip of a woman in a blue sweater disembarking from a ship in Seattle. Cameras flash, and American people bombard her with roses and affection, but the scene of arrival is then interrupted by an image of my mother. She is wearing a Western-style wedding dress and a dazzling smile, and her feet are wrapped in bandages. She looks just like the orphan girl grown up, the orphan girl who was fathered by American GIs and later went on to marry one. That is the end of the dream, but not of the story. There is also the story of what happens in the years between her postwar childhood and her arrival in America, and the story of what happens between arrival and assimilation.

The Unassimilable of Trauma

The psychic dynamics that are elaborated in Keller's ostensibly fictional work and in Fenkl's autobiography often disappear in narratives of Koreans as honorary whites, narratives that depend on the exclusion of a violent relationship, an exclusion that is in itself violent.[55] The intermarriages that are taken for granted as measures of assimilation also serve an allegorical function in the interrelated projects of U.S.–Korea relations and producing the fantasy of America. The marriage attests to interracial harmony and international cooperation, and it is within this frame that the yanggongju as GI bride is an exemplar of assimilation whose progeny become "honorary whites." And what if one is one of the "assimilated" and still has knowledge of the violent relationship that has been forgotten in public memory? What does it mean to be haunted by a history of division and destruction, then to migrate and become assimilated into a country that had an active role in creating and maintaining that division? What is the cost of honorary whiteness?[56] Contrary to sociological theories that view assimilation as progressive with each new generation, one of the unintended consequences of the project of assimilation is the passing down of ghosts.

The progress tales of assimilation and the American dream could not have existed without the woman in the shadows. Once here, the yanggongju helped earn Asian Americans the title of honorary whites because of the high incidence of her marriage to white Americans, her giving birth to biracial children who don't speak Korean, and her secrecy about her past life in Korea. But as much as she has been complicit with her own erasure, she also disturbs the dream. The transgenerational traumas that the yanggongju transmits to her presumed-to-be-assimilated children, as well as the new traumas induced by assimilation itself, sully honorary whiteness. As the work of Keller and Fenkl suggests, the traumatic effects of the Forgotten War cannot be fully assimilated into a story line about immigrant success. The ghosts of those who have been excluded from the American dream continue to haunt the memories of those who have come to the United States and have faded into sociological whiteness.

***Yanggongju Seven* passes every test of assimilation. She married a white man; gave birth to half-white, English-speaking children; sent them to college; and now lives in an affluent white suburb. She is well assimilated in the**

sense that her neighbors do not see her otherness, because they do not see her at all. She has stopped going around in circles, moving from place to place. In fact, she hardly moves at all. Yanggongju Seven wears the markings of her own erasure etched into her skin and bone, layers of unmaking and remaking, of covering over tracks, of fictionalizing a life that was ultimately deemed unfit to live anyway. But her *han* does not rest peacefully in her body.

The way in which the yanggongju has haunted the Korean diaspora complicates the narrative of honorary whiteness on two levels. On one level, the aspects of experience that have been erased from the official story line come back to haunt in the form of other narratives that bring the yanggongju back, such as the social work counternarrative and the creative works of biracial Koreans whose writing practices unconsciously remember the pasts from which they have been severed. The yanggongju as GI bride is a figure brought into being by an overinvestment in the American dream, a figure whose ability to assimilate rests on making her life history unintelligible. She is a traumatized figure, but the radical potential of trauma is that it is force independent of the will of the subject of trauma. Her haunting is distributed to all those who have tried to repress her and to those who have been complicit with or unaware of the erasures. But this is a matter not just of uncovering something that was previously unseen but of how the haunting produces something new that was not there before. On another level, the yanggongju opens up new sites of resistance that go beyond the counternarrative. This figure brings an inherent volatility to narrative because of the ways in which trauma often registers at the level of sensory perception but does not fully enter into consciousness.

The yanggongju's *han* is absorbed by both those who know about her but would rather forget and those who do not know but are afflicted by someone else's secret. It travels the paths along which yanggongjus have been banished or resurrected, and it creates new ones between disparate bodies and places. The ghosted secrets that have circulated with her have created gaps beneath the surface of narrative, rupturing "contemporary rhetorics of domination" by bringing the accumulated waste of injured and discarded bodies from the U.S. camptown back to the U.S. nation.[57] Eng and Kazanjian would argue that these ruptures are the "ghostly remains of an unrealized or idealized potential."[58] The ghostly remains of the yanggongju's *han* are the excesses that cannot be assimilated, either into a dominant narrative such as the story of Asian assimilation or honorary whiteness or into a counternarrative about the struggles of Korean military brides in America. The yanggongju's trauma disrupts the discourse of assimilation because trauma is precisely that which cannot be assimilated. Johnston says it is that which the "psychic apparatus can register but which cannot be integrated into an individual meaningful 'experience.'"[59] It is the unassimilable always hovering around the "honorary white" and made visible in flashes of memory that appear when the yanggongju is screened, thus creating an affective kinship between those for whom the fantasy of whiteness has been foreclosed and those for whom it is almost within reach but never quite accessible. But the unassimilable of trauma is also a protective space against the potentially dangerous consequences of assimilation, because to become fully assimilated, in this sense, means to assimilate that which is in excess of one's psychic apparatus. To become fully assimilated, then, is to risk madness and to render the fantasy fully incoherent.

5.
Diasporic Vision: Methods of Seeing Trauma

What gestures the unspeakable? In this other sociology, which is willy-nilly another politics, the ghost gesticulates, signals, and sometimes mimics the unspeakable as it shines for both the remembered and the forgotten. This other sociology stretches at the limit of our imagination and at the limit of what is representable in the time of the now, to us, as the social world we inhabit.

—Avery Gordon, *Ghostly Matters*

In the final pages of Toni Morrison's *The Bluest Eye,* the narrator tells us that "a little black girl yearns for the blue eyes of a little white girl, and the horror at the heart of her yearning is exceeded only by the evil of its fulfillment."[1] It is a story about a child's impossible wish, one that comes true alongside the character's destruction. Pecola Breedlove's mental breakdown at the end of the novel exemplifies the damaging effects of what W. E. B. Du Bois called "double-consciousness, this sense of always looking at one's self through the eyes of others, of measuring one's soul by the tape of a world that looks on in amused contempt and pity,"[2] or of what Ann Anlin Cheng describes as the "deep-seated, intangible, psychical complications for people living within a ruling episteme that privileges that which they can never be."[3] In Pecola's mind, she is granted not only the blue eyes of her dreams, but also a split self that is the result of incorporating her experiences of sexual abuse and racial violence:

> *It's all over now.*
> Yes.
> *That was horrible, wasn't it?*
> Yes.
> I don't like to talk about dirty things.
> *Me neither. Let's talk about something else.*
> What? What will we talk about?
> *Why, your eyes.*
> Oh, yes. My eyes. My blue eyes.[4]

Pecola believes that her blue eyes will protect her against further trauma because no one would dare hurt a child with pretty blue eyes, but the threat of an eye bluer than hers still lingers. The narrator reflects on Pecola's devastating outcome, concluding that she was all the waste and beauty in the world—other people's waste dumped onto her, other people's beauty made visible next to her ugliness. A seed buried in hostile soil. There were no flowers rising up from the ground that year, only a little girl who grew into pieces. Despite the tragic conclusion of *The Bluest Eye,* we are left to mull over the possibility that it is precisely the dislocation of Pecola's voice that gives expression to her traumatic memories. However, it is not such an easy task to know what exactly is being articulated here.

Until now, we have not seen this female figure except through the eyes of someone else, her story told by a narrator who has thus far shown her to us as an object of contempt and pity and a collection of psychic projections, a narrator who cannot know her experience but who is thoroughly implicated in her outcome. But through this story the narrator also raises ethical questions about the invisible girl whom people do not care for but whom they care about, in the sense that she provides a source from which they derive power. When the girl's state of incoherence becomes shockingly troublesome for the narration of her story, for the observer who must now see her but who can no longer make sense of her articulations, what becomes of those who are implicated in her outcome? What bodies make up the soil in which this seed has been planted? And how do we communicate the rest of the story?

While the narrator is still present in the end, there is also a gesture toward some other world in which she has become other to herself. Now we glimpse her through an inner dialogue about the shame of dirty things, the desire for whiteness, and psychotic imaginings about the symptoms of social disease. Thus, the ending makes a move toward performing something that the narrator cannot quite tell us. In the words of Jackie Orr, "The social becomes a piece of what the dis-eased body performs, in its symptomatic—sometimes tender and reparative—attempts to communicate."[5]

I return now to the figure of the yanggongju, the Korean woman who passes as almost white, transplanted to America, which does not see her or the ways in which its soil is hostile to her. Its composition is different from that which would not nurture black girls in 1941, but the questions I ask about consequences and implicated bodies and methods of telling the rest of the story are the same.

At the scene of writing this other sociology, I put Nicolas Abraham and Maria Torok's theory of transgenerational haunting to one last test. "It is a fact," they contend, that the "phantom . . . is nothing but" a "gap produced in us by the concealment of some part of a love object's life," a secret that takes the form of a ghost yet is capable of changing its disguise once more to appear as "individual or collective hallucinations."[6] The power of the secret to shift shape also affects the ways in which we look. I now shift my focus to the transmutation of the unspoken thing into a hallucination and to its capacity to decompose the usual interpretations of what we have come to know as madness and to challenge the limits of our perception.

As discussed in the last chapter, the writings of diasporic Koreans demonstrate how escape from the camptown and "making it" in America, as two sides of the same coin, are often fulfilled at the expense of the yanggongju's well-being, sometimes her very life. The GI bride's arrival in America is often met by psychic destruction as a result of the violence of a perpetually deferred assimilation and a traumatic history that is erased in the service of her assimilation. If some things cannot be assimilated into the subject's experience without damaging her perceptual apparatus, assimilation for the yanggongju propels her dangerously close to insanity.[7] In this chapter I address what happens when the wish for America gives way to the tragedy of the wish's fulfillment, along with the ways in which the outcome is not entirely tragic.

While it is important to recognize the real pain that comes with mental illness, such a concern does not exclude a critique of the ways in which the story of the yanggongju's descent into madness is part of a larger (Western) narrative of insanity that presumes that the state of hallucination is always and only dangerous.[8] Recent scholarship on the cultural construction of mental illness has taken the position that, in the words of Dwight Fee,

A Girl with a Tank. Copyright Injoo Whang/Still Present Pasts, 2005. Cloth, thread, sumi ink, ink. The image of a girl standing in front of a tank (based on the third photograph in this book; see chapter 1) was drawn on a piece of cloth; it was then cut up and reassembled with other materials. In the artist's words, "When something is broken apart and put back together it creates very different integrity but the newly created image still retains a history of the broken-apart parts."

"there is a pressing and often practical need for regarding mental disorder as entangled with social life and language, as well as a palpable, felt condition that damages mental functioning, interpersonal relationships, and other aspects of thought and behavior."[9] Ivan Leudar and Philip Thomas's work on verbal hallucination is similarly concerned with examining the cultural and political implications of "voice-hearing," which they argue is "caught between the rocks of mystification and pathologisation."[10] They note that the term *hallucination* comes from the language of contemporary psychology, which usually understands it as an "error in perception" and a symptom to be suppressed. Leudar and Thomas question the extent to which hearing voices is *only* something to be eliminated and instead consider the gamut of interpretations of the origins and functions of the hallucinatory voice: belated memory, ordinary inner speech, symptom of childhood sexual abuse, offspring of a "parent" memory, manifestation of grief, sign of divine power, confusion between past and present, "slightly altered repetitions of . . . past experiences," alien spirit, or "immaterial being."[11]

To the extent that the hallucinatory voice is any of these things, I want to propose that it is both an important source of information and a possible means for reading unacknowledged traumas carried into the diaspora. I am particularly interested in the ways in which *listening to the voice* allows us to *see trauma*, how seeing and speaking are mutually important parts in an assemblage of trauma. This capacity to see is a function of what Gilles Deleuze and Félix Guattari call "distributed perception," or what John Johnston calls "machinic vision," in which "what is perceived is not located at any single place and moment in time, and the act by which this perception occurs is not the result of a single or isolated agency but of several working in concert or parallel."[12] In searching for bodies through which to speak, the ghost is distributed across the time-space of the diaspora in order to create another type of body, an assemblaged body whose purpose is to see and speak the traumas that could not be seen and spoken by those who directly lived them. What happens in this process is that the power of the secret joins forces with media technologies that enable it to be seen in order to create alternate ways of reading both the silences surrounding an unspeakable trauma and the hallucinatory voices that speak.

This last chapter performs a phantomatic return, through a multiplicity of voices and *altered repetitions of past experiences,* that reaches toward a final destination. In chapter 1 I asked what methods can flesh out the ghost and what methods, in turn, are produced by haunting.[13] The displacements and crossings of the ghost as it travels from a guarded enclosure of secrecy to a flood of irrational speaking renders the voice into that which expands vision and thus leans towards a new kind of empiricism in which the senses are crossed. The project of seeing and speaking trauma requires new methodologies to facilitate forms of perception that register the unassimilable of trauma, as well as writing forms that register the nonnarrativizable. Performance is one such methodology that does so, both in its affinity with haunting and in its articulation of the "dis-eased body" as a symptom of the social. Playing off of Abraham and Torok's notion that "phantomogenic words" often become "staged words," that is, that secrets and taboo words carried in the unconscious are often acted out publicly by those who are haunted, I consciously "stage" the ghosts of the Korean diaspora's haunted history.[14] The hallucinatory voices in this text speak to a significant moment in Korean history, particularly the history of women's militarized sexual labor. September 1945 is the always present place to which we return, and the repeated speaking of "phantomogenic words" makes visible some of the unconscious traumas and bodies that have become tangled together.

This phantomatic return to the beginning is also a departure from the figure of the yanggongju toward a spectral agent whose potential is beyond the scope of any story that one can tell about the yanggongju. Still, it is a haunting that is facilitated by the figure of a woman whose roots were tenuously laid down in phosphorus-rich soil that nurtured her florid imagination. And in her crossing she kept some bound-up familial or geopolitical secret and caught in its bindings an excess of human waste that spilled beyond the designated dumping grounds, an overflow of grief spilling into the ocean.

Vision

> To awaken is thus to bear the imperative to survive . . .
> as the one who must tell *what it means*
> *to not see.*
>
> —Cathy Caruth, *Unclaimed Experience*

Forgive me for not knowing about our history, but even when I asked, you wouldn't tell me the truth about your life. Only once did I ask you why you had been born in the country that was not the one you called home. But you did not answer me with words. You were quiet and stared straight ahead as if there were something else in the room, something I could not yet see. You never talked about the circumstances of your birth, or of mine, or about any of the events that took place before I could witness them. And I took for granted that things were as you said they were, and even that the truth was available for you to tell. Maybe you were too young to remember what had happened before you began your life in Korea, and too broken to remember what had happened after. But you see, I began recording these events that you do not talk about long before either of us knew what would happen at 9:45. And then the steady repetition of that time activated my memory. And I listened carefully to your speaking, the gaps in between, and the patterns of noise and silence. Always at the same time every day, your voice sounding with the clock told me that something happened at that time, or that something was about to happen. It is only now that I have the capacity to read the information I've stored all these years. I am beginning to see these images of you sailing on the water, not knowing that you were moving toward a future that would silence you.

I Began Searching for a History

August 24, 1945, 5:20 p.m: A Japanese naval vessel carrying ten thousand Korean passengers sails through calm waters off the coast of Japan. There is an explosion from the front half of the ship, which becomes engulfed in flames. Pieces of ship and bodies of passengers are propelled into the ocean by the force of the explosion. A few bodies cling to the deck but eventually fall away into the water as the vessel splits in two, each half descending into the ocean. The passengers locked below panic as the lower decks of the ship fill with water. Two lovers search for each other even as their bodies are carried against their will by currents that are stronger than their desperation. Only after the split ship is fully submerged is there calm once more, the water flecked with dead bodies and debris. It is silent at first, but then there are sounds of life. A child's sobbing becomes audible. He is perched atop a floating fragment of the ship, and nearby a hand emerges from the water and reaches upward. It is the hand of the male lover, who had searched years for his beloved, from whom he had been separated after having been conscripted into the labor camps. He had finally found her aboard this ship, until they were separated once again by the disaster. The man and the little boy are the sole survivors of this tale, sometimes called "The Korean Titanic."[15]

The North Korean film *Soul's Protest* melodramatically reenacts the story of the first shipload of Korean slaves, which set sail for Korea from Japan on August 22, 1945. The film dramatizes the actual incident of August 24, 1945, when the *Ukishima Maru,* the Japanese naval vessel full of thousands of newly liberated Korean slaves, exploded off the coast of Maizuru, Japan, just nine days after the end of World War II. Weaving together memories of working in Japanese labor camps, celebratory scenes of returning home, and mundane occurrences of life on the ship as it sails toward Busan harbor, the film not only narrates the atrocities of Japanese slavery made even more tragic by the deaths of thousands of Koreans on board the ship but also expresses the Koreans' frustrated longing for freedom and their homeland. The film's depiction of a vessel that is split in two, rendering its passengers dead or separated from their loved ones, symbolizes the Koreans' return to a country already divided and occupied by external forces and soon to be decimated by war. The return home, however, is made impossible in the most literal sense.

It was the fate of those on board the *Ukishima Maru* to never arrive in Korea. It must also have been fate that decided that my mother would not be on that first ship. The Japanese officials would wait until September to put my mother and her mother on the second ship, or maybe it was the third.[16] But in any case, it was not the first. My mother would not die that day in 1945.

Much of *Soul's Protest* takes place over two days in August 1945 as the ship circles the waters between Korea and Japan while the Koreans on board grow restless anticipating the freedom that awaits them in Korea. The ship circles the waters, never reaching its purported destination, never returning the Koreans to their homeland. Instead, we learn that the ship's Japanese crew plans to blow up the vessel with the Koreans on board.[17] One Korean character does witness this scheme, but because his tongue had been cut out during his days as a slave, he is unable to speak at the very moment in which speaking becomes most urgent. He must inform the others without the use of his tongue, through wild bodily gestures, grunts, and panicked eyes that warn of danger. Through his movements and sounds, the passengers decipher that the ship is about to explode, but it is too late to prevent the tragedy. The ship full of Koreans goes nowhere and eventually explodes. There are survivors of this disaster, however, like the little boy who is too young to understand anything that has happened, who perhaps does not see anything yet returns to the site of the sinking ship years later to tell the story.

Besides being a heavy-handed tale about the cruelty of Japanese colonizers, *Soul's Protest* can also be read as a story of being left homeless by a history one can never know with certainty, a history that longs to be spoken nonetheless. Although the film expresses nostalgia for a homeland as it was prior to its division, whose unity could be measured against Japanese suppression of national identity, the final images of a return never completed suggest that Koreans remain in a state of permanent dislocation. Despite the political and geographic divisions between the two Koreas, the making of the film, in concert with the lawsuits brought against the Japanese government by a group of South Korean survivors of the incident, shows the ways in which both halves are similarly unsettled by an obscured and uncertain history. Both *Soul's Protest* and the actual events on which the film is based raise questions about seeing, speaking, and surviving for the displaced subject.

> I began searching for a history. My own history. Because I had known all along that the stories I had heard were not true, and parts had been left out. I remember having this feeling growing up that I was haunted by something, that I was living within a family full of ghosts. . . . There was this place that they knew about. I had never been there yet I had a memory for it. I could remember a time of great sadness before I was born. We had been moved. Uprooted. . . . She tells the story of what she does not remember.[18]

The *Ukishima Maru* tragedy had almost been forgotten in Korea and was practically unknown in other parts of the world, but a series of events would unfold to bring the 1945 sinking of the *Ukishima Maru* back to memory:

June 21, 2001: *Soul's Protest,* titled *Sara-itneun ryeonghondeul* (literally, "living souls") in Korean, makes its international debut at a film festival in Moscow.

June 27, 2001: *Soul's Protest* opens at the Hong Kong Film Festival and is purchased by a Hong Kong film import company for distribution.

August 23, 2001: A Japanese judge makes a ruling in a lawsuit against the Japanese government for failing to provide safe transport for Korean forced laborers on board the *Ukishima Maru.* The court rules in favor of some of the plaintiffs and orders that the government pay a total of US$375,000 to fifteen Korean survivors of the disaster. The claims of the other sixty-five plaintiffs are dismissed because they cannot prove that they had been on the ship.

August 24, 2001: It is the fifty-sixth anniversary of the *Ukishima Maru* incident. South Korean protesters hold a memorial service for the victims and "urge Japan to take full responsibility" for the sixty-five plaintiffs who were not awarded payment, to reopen the investigation into the cause of the explosion, and to give an official apology to the survivors and the victims' families.[19] Meanwhile, *Soul's Protest,* along with a Japanese film also commemorating the incident, is screened for the first time in Seoul.

August 24 and 25, 2001: Korean and Japanese newspapers report on the renewed controversy, casting doubt on official reports of what happened on August 24, 1945. According to Japanese government records, "There were 4,000 people on board. . . . Korean sources speak of 7,000, 7,500, or even 10,000 passengers. . . . The dead numbered 524 Koreans and 25 Japanese."[20] Korean groups claim that 5,000 Koreans had died, yet these victims do not exist in official Japanese records. According to Japanese numbers, close to 3,500 passengers should have survived, but only 80 Koreans have come forward as survivors in the lawsuit against the Japanese government. The cases of 65 of them were dismissed "because their presence aboard the ship could not be confirmed."[21] Their survival, their existence, did not appear in official documents. More controversial still are the discrepancies between Japan's official explanations of what had caused the explosion and survivors' memories. The *Korea Times* reports: "The Japanese government claims that the ship hit a mine planted in Maizaru Harbor by U.S. forces. However, survivors remembered seeing Japanese sailors fleeing the ship in boats before it sank, which raised their suspicions that the Japanese blew up the ship themselves to get rid of Koreans who were witnesses to the heinous deeds the Japanese committed during the war."[22] Another report claims: "Data and collected information on the incident indicate that the explosion was a plot concocted by the Japanese military leadership in an attempt to destroy its dark records on and atrocities against those Korean victims and survivors."[23] Kim Chun Song, the director of *Soul's Protest,* claims that the film is historically accurate and that "a number of north Korean historians and researchers cooperated with the scenario writer in his effort to further probe into the historical fact and collect all the relevant information available before this half-documentary film was completed."[24]

I knew all along that . . . parts had been left out. . . . I felt lost. Ungrounded. Like I was a ghost watching others live their lives without one of my own. . . .

She tells the story of what she does not remember, but remembers one thing: why she forgot to remember.

In mapping out the events of the *Ukishima Maru*'s return, what becomes apparent is a kind of haunting, as if the "living souls" in the title of the film might refer to the thousands of people on board the ship whom official records can claim as neither dead nor alive, or to those who testify to having survived the ship's sinking but are rendered nonexistent by their absence in government documents. The living souls haunt a history that is both perforated by attempts to erase it and left to die along with its witnesses. As the story goes in the Korean imagination, the Japanese wanted to ensure that there were no eyewitnesses to their atrocities, no trace of evidence. The ship itself was left on the ocean floor for nine years after the incident, as if the memory of the event could also be submerged. Accident or not, the first shipload of witnesses to the cruelties of Japanese slavery were eliminated, except for those eyewitnesses who describe scenes of Japanese soldiers fleeing the *Ukishima Maru* in rowboats prior to the explosion, who nevertheless have been banished from official memory.[25] The fact of the *Ukishima Maru*'s sinking remains unsettled, however. In what is legitimated as history there are gaps, which come to be lived as transgenerational haunting.

I Began Searching for a History—My Own History

There are things which have happened for which there have been no observers, except for the spirits of the dead.

While *Soul's Protest* focuses on the personal memories of survivors, as well as the unrecorded memories of the dead, the film not only resurrects these memories for viewers who lived during August 1945 but also creates new memories for those who were not eyewitnesses of the event, thus enacting a dispersal of traumatic memory into the diaspora. *Soul's Protest* offers an example of a distributed perception, because equally important to the telling of its story are both the man who sees but cannot speak and the child narrator who does not see the event but returns to tell the story years later. It is as if the mechanism for remembering were not an individual at the site of the tragedy but an assemblage of eyes, tongues, and other parts distributed through time.

This assemblage extends beyond the boundaries of the semi-fictional story to include the eyes of those watching the *Ukishima Maru* fifty-six years after its sinking. Johnston calls this type of seeing "machinic vision," one that is a function not merely of a passive sense organ, the eye, but of an assemblage of eyes distributed and working in concert with heterogeneous terms in an environment: "Within the social space of these assemblages (which amount to a new form of collective psychic apparatus), the viewing or absorption of images constitutes a general form of machinic vision."[26]

If, as Johnston suggests, machinic assemblages are a "a new form of collective psychic apparatus," we might consider transgenerational haunting an example of machinic vision and of distributed perception more generally. Like the transgenerational phantom who seeks other bodies through which to speak, the subject's inability to see the trauma that takes place before her very eyes causes her eyes to be distributed across bodies and generations. A diasporic machinic vision is perhaps the only means by which haunted histories can be "seen," through a distribution of the senses that at once resides in the film images of the *Ukishima Maru* exploding, in the eyes of the viewers of the film, in the silences of those who remember the incident but never speak about it, in the grief of survivors, in the bodies of those who absorbed their grief, in the skeletal remains found on the ship, and in the effects of the disaster itself. Diasporic vision is an assemblage of the body memory of transgenerational haunting and the haunted subjects' own cultural productions disseminated through technological apparatuses that make visible the trauma that one's own eyes could not see in time.

April 14, 2002: *Soul's Protest* is screened in New York City at what the organizers believe is the first-ever North Korean film festival in the United States. The screening room is packed, with standing room only. The mostly Korean American audience watches horrific scenes of forced laborers' being humiliated and beaten, body parts severed. The Korean body is subjected to direct control, to an exacting punishment that removes the disobedient tongue and dismembers the legs that try to run. At times, the viewers gasp in concert with the sounds of the tortured body on the screen. It is as if the viewing of this film draws the bodies of the living and the dead closer together until those in the audience are also suspended in the waters outside of Busan in 1945, moving toward an erased history. The "image renders present the failure of the voice," the absence of an intelligible discourse that can make sense of what we have just seen.[27] After the screening there is a discussion about how much of the film is historically accurate and the extent to which Korean Americans and Koreans living in the United States, as those who have been denied access to this history, can identify with the film. But after viewing *Soul's Protest,* "we, as spectators, inhabit this space, not through an identification with primary witnesses . . . but as our bodies enable us to being in place, a place where our conditions of perception themselves are challenged."[28]

"In transporting us into this world made strange by death," my identification and my being in this place arrive near the end when I am watching the child survivor, floating in the wreckage, and I am left thinking about fate, about "the 'strangeness' of death" that is now "a shared reality."[29] Like the little boy who survived the sinking of the ship, my mother also survived the sinking of the ship by virtue of being on the next one. But what does it mean to survive to the kind of life from which you want desperately to be relieved?

> In 1946, the year I turned 24, a ship came to take us back home. I didn't want to return, but I had to get on board as all Koreans had been ordered by the government to return home. The ship was filled with comfort women. I had no family, no relatives, and no home to go to. I thought it would be better to drown than to return to my country, but I didn't have the courage to throw myself overboard.
>
> —Yi Yongsuk, "I Will No Longer Harbour Resentment," in *True Stories of the Korean Comfort Women*

Do you consider throwing your body into the ocean so that you can be spared the fate of living? My mother was too young in 1945 to be tempted by such ideas or to know that she would wish for death later. She was four years old then, moving toward . . .

Voice

> The voice acquires a spectral autonomy, it never quite belongs to the body we see, so that even when we see a living person talking, there is always some degree of ventriloquism at work.
>
> —Slavoj Žižek, "I Hear You with My Eyes"

It murmurs inside. It murmurs. Inside is the pain of speech the pain to say. Larger still. Greater than is the pain not to say.[30]

She tells the story of what she does not remember . . . a beautiful woman who lost her mind.

When writing a history of the yanggongju, one is often "caught between the rocks of mystification and pathologisation," in the words of Leudar and Thomas.[31] She is mystified by the gaping holes in her history created by both an inability to remember and an enforced silence. She is pathologized by efforts to expose her suffering. In both the fiction and the film of diasporic Koreans and the social work literature on Korean sex workers and battered military brides, there is a narrative pattern that is now familiar in the yanggongju's life history. It begins in rural poverty and ends in psychosis. Take the story of Kyung Richards, for example.[32] As a young teenager in Korea she migrates to the city to look for employment and begins working as a prostitute near a U.S. military base. She marries one of her clients and moves to the United States with him and settles in a white community. They have two children together, but then her husband becomes abusive and she ends up alone with two children to support. She is imprisoned for the accidental death of one of her children (and this is perhaps the only aspect of her narrative that is unusual). Years later she is released from prison, but never regains custody of the surviving child. By the end of this story, we are told, she is homeless and schizophrenic and is "obliged to 'choose' between militarized prostitution and hunger, between domestic violence and homelessness, between police raids and violent clients, between mental illness and psychotropic drugs."[33]

Like Kyung Richards, the figure of trauma in the Korean diasporic imaginary is often the young woman whose body has been sexually violated—raped or coerced into sexual labor by some hegemonic force—whose voice is ultimately incapacitated. In *Soul's Protest,* there are two characters who literally cannot speak. One is the tongueless man who belatedly warns that the ship is about to explode. Despite the fact that his tongue has been removed, he nonetheless has the ability to translate his ideas into meaningful language and thus communicate crucial information. The other character in the film who has lost her voice is a young woman who had been enslaved as a comfort woman. She embodies the unspeakable word *wianbu,* but cannot speak the horror of being a wianbu. Ultimately, she cannot speak at all. Instead of speaking, she laughs while her body hangs limp, "an emptied-out body" as Chungmoo Choi would say, that must be moved along by the force of others.[34] At the precise moment when the word *wianbu* is uttered to explain her unusual condition, a hush falls over the other women in her company, who cast their eyes downward at the sound of "wianbu."

Does the character's inability to speak point to a "contested historiography," as Kyung Hyun Kim has argued about figures in "post-traumatic Korean cinema" who have lost both their language and their sanity? In his reading of *A Petal,* a film that depicts the 1980 Gwangju massacre, Kim posits the character of a mentally disturbed homeless teenage girl as the ghostly embodiment of Gwangju itself—"a specter that resides on street corners and in everyday life."[35] She endures the multiple traumas of witnessing the massacre of her family members, is left homeless and orphaned, and then is raped. Her inability to speak intelligibly of her own traumatic memories parallels the obscure and fragmented narratives of the Gwangju massacre as a larger historical event. Kim points out, "If language, according to Lacan, is the crucial means for the child to free him or herself from the preoedipal crisis, then the girl's identity will forever be impaired without the return of language. However, she remains hysterical: narration is ruptured, and her ability to recount history and to translate scattered images into verbal discourse is denied."[36]

Korean films such as *Soul's Protest* and *A Petal*, as well as writings about militarized sex work, depict a fragmented diasporic history through the woman who loses her mind and her place in the symbolic order. The wianbu and yanggongju are both placed on a trajectory toward madness. This is a madness that is marked not only by the silencing of one's own voice but by the hearing of other voices. According to Žižek, "The moment we enter the symbolic order, an unbridgeable gap separates forever a human body from 'its' voice. The voice acquires a spectral autonomy."[37] When one loses her place in the symbolic order, she is then bridging the gap between body and spectral voice, so ghost voices settle in the body. In the case of the woman who hears but cannot speak, her silence resonates with the voices of a haunted history.

> I began searching for a history. My own history. Because I had known all along that the stories I had heard were not true, and parts had been left out. . . . We had been moved. Uprooted.

1941: Born in Japan, under what exact circumstances I do not know. Born in Japan, of whose body I am uncertain. Of a woman conscripted for what purpose? Born to what father?

1945: Returned to Korea, shortly after liberation. "Returned," let us say, even though she had never been there before. The exact date of her return is undocumented. Maybe it was in September, shortly after liberation. "Liberation," let us say, even though she would find no freedom in her homeland, either. "Homeland," let us say, even though she had never lived there. Returned to her homeland in 1945, shortly after liberation, maybe in September. She was four years old then, moving toward . . .

June 25, 1950: A few days before her birthday, not quite nine years old. Years later, she would tell no stories to her children about what she did on that day or on the next thousand days. She would tell no stories about stepping over severed limbs and discarded babies or about eating the Americans' garbage full of napkins and toothpicks, or about watching bombs fall from the sky.

1971: Married an American, a high-ranking officer twenty-five years her senior. Maybe the other women reassured her that older men know how to take care of a woman. But I cannot be sure of this, either.

1975: Moved to America with her children and never returned.

Synesthesia: Seeing through the Other's Voice

> Her voices were really only slightly altered repetitions of her past experiences . . . attributed . . . to "parent events" in the past, the memories of which became dissociated from the rest of [her] person. . . . These delusions could become "parent events" of new hallucinations.
>
> —Ivan Leudar and Phillip Thomas, *Voices of Reason, Voices of Insanity*

And then the steady repetition of the time activated my memory. Always at the same time every day, your voice sounding with the clock told me that something happened at that time, or that something was about to happen. And so I was your witness. My eyes were already there when you were born into the labor camp. To labor in the same way as your mother, only for another country's army.

When the subject cannot speak her own history, when history is unintelligible or made unintelligible, who or what speaks for her? The thing that cannot directly be spoken becomes the phantom that "works like a ventriloquist, like a stranger within the subject's own mental topography."[38] As discussed in chapter 4, the phantom is passed down and across bodies, and the voice finds expression by distributing itself through different speakers. Alisa Lebow calls the phenomenon "memory once removed" when the memories of one generation are displaced onto another or when the memories of a time or place are projected into the future and take up residence in the seeming here and now of the everyday. One of the things produced by an unconscious pervaded by the voices of another generation is a writing form that Lebow refers to as "indirect" or "transitive autobiography," a story that the speaker tells neither of an original event nor of his or her own experience but of something new that bears the traces of past lives, in effect rendering the original fantasmatic.[39]

Both the theory of transgenerational haunting and theories about verbal hallucination suggest a kind of transitivity. If "voices are impulsive actions stemming from one's dissociated past experiences,"[40] as Pierre Janet theorizes, and being haunted transgenerationally is a condition of "the voices of one generation living in the unconscious of another," as Abraham and Torok believe, which past is the past of dissociated experience?[41] Are the voice-hearer's voices of her own past, or of the past of her past? And what of those who are haunted transgenerationally, who are listening to another's voices? As Abraham and Torok say, "The phantom which returns to haunt bears witness to the existence of the dead buried within the other"; thus, one is haunted by the ghost of the other's dead, or in some cases the ghosting is displaced further than one generation.[42] The notions of the transitive and the transgenerational open up the possibility of memory's being not just once removed but many times removed. One's mother's voices could be one's grandmother's memories. The yanggongju's dissociated past is not just her own but also that of the comfort woman.

I remember having this feeling growing up that I was haunted by something, that I was living within a family full of ghosts. . . . There was this place that they knew about. I had never been there yet I had a memory for it. I could remember a time of great sadness before I was born. . . . She tells the story of what she does not remember.

You went to great lengths to make this history inaccessible to me, but some secrets have already exposed themselves, as if my eyes were there in 1941 when you were

born into the labor camp. To labor in the same way as your mother. My eyes were already there when her body was forcibly moved from her home in Gyeongsang province to Osaka, where it was her duty to serve the Japanese Empire, where to speak Korean was to risk having one's tongue cut out. And so she learned to speak without the use of her tongue, to make language with the sounds of shuffling feet.[43]

A distributed perception of traumatic memory is synesthetic as well as transitive. The sensation belonging to one sense organ reverberates through the others, such as when the sound of the speaking voice fills in what the eye cannot see or when one generation's experiences are lived through another's. According to Žižek, "The reverberating sound itself provides the ground that renders *visible* the figure of *silence*.... Voice does not simply persist at a different level with regard to what we see, it rather points toward a gap in the field of the visible, toward the dimension of what eludes our gaze."[44] When seeing too much leads to an impairment of vision or when history is made invisible through erasure, one can look to the other's voice as that which gives body to the gap. What the voice enables us to see, however, is not a "direct representation of the parent event," as Leudar and Thomas put it,[45] but rather what Bennett calls an "image of the force of trauma" seen from the body.[46] The voice of the other, the voice that is the buried trauma in disguise, transmits an affective sense that *something* happened and thus allows us "to see from a series of compromised positions ... from the body of a mourner, from the body of one who shares space with the mourner, from the gap between these two."[47]

A Staging of Words: The Voice That Sees

It murmurs inside. It murmurs.... It festers inside. The wound, liquid, dust.

And I listened carefully to your speaking and the gaps in between and the patterns of noise and silence.

If the gap is the site of a wound or shameful secret, a breeding ground for ghosts, and a place from which we cannot see without compromise, why would we ever want to know what resides there? The voice that allows us to see is also, at times, a voice that *wants* us to see by moving unspeakable words from the psychic tomb to the stage of the social. This voice does not fully belong to the person who appears to be speaking, however. According to Abraham and Torok, "When people say 'I,' they might in fact be referring to something quite different from their own identity as recorded in their identification papers."[48] Instead, the "I" might be a spectral voice of the diasporic unconscious, a voice that has *seen* things that the hearer has not and that bears witness to the other's past and to the pasts she has inherited.

Your voice sounding with the clock told me that something happened at that time, or that something was about to happen. And so I was your witness. I am beginning to see these images of you sailing on the water, not knowing what future you were coming home to. You were four years old in September 1945 when the *migoon* soldiers arrived.

August 22, 1945: The *Ukishima Maru* set sail for Busan harbor, returning an estimated ten thousand Koreans to their homeland. It was the fate of those on board the first ship to never arrive in Korea, to never return. It also must have been fate that decided that my then four-year-old mother would not be on that first ship. The Japanese officials would wait until September to send my mother and her mother back to Korea. Before that, she must have been a subject of the Japanese Empire, though I do not know that for sure. I have seen no records to prove that she was ever Japanese. The only evidence is her own admission of guilt—that her birthplace was Osaka, that her first tongue was Japanese and not Korean. Documents later reconstructed her as a Korean national, daughter of a Korean mother and a Korean father.[49]

I had not yet been planted in your womb when it happened, but parts of me were already assembled and set

in motion. My eyes were already there when you dropped out of school to look for work in the city, and I saw how she wanted to keep you safe from the "*maengsu*" American soldiers. She wished she could give her own life so that yours might be different. She took the blame for your fall, as any Korean mother would have, but her blame also carried the weight of history. Had she not embodied an unspeakable word, you might have had the will to walk away. But you were also pulled by your desire for American men, by your desire for America.

September 1945: U.S. forces arrive in Korea just eighteen days after its liberation from Japan, installing an occupation government. In response to the Japanese colonial system of sexual slavery, the United States officially outlaws prostitution in Korea, but unofficially transfers the comfort stations from Japanese to U.S. control.

I have never heard the word *wianbu* spoken in my family. Nor have I heard *yanggongju.* These are the unspeakable words never spoken in my family. Words "wrapped in silence." Words that might be called "phantomogenic," "secreted . . . words giving sustenance to the phantom . . . the very words that rule an entire family's history."[50] Words mapped in blood. But I had no memory of them. Perhaps the sounds of these words never entered my consciousness and therefore could not be remembered, but traces of *wianbu* and *yanggongju* were folded into the "resonating vessel" of brain and skin and stored there.[51]

In an unconscious haunted by an unspeakable trauma, there is a constant tension between speaking and not speaking. In Abraham and Torok's theory, if a secreted word remains secret, it will be passed down through several generations, wreaking psychic havoc for its inheritors, but eventually the "phantom effect" will wear off. Speaking, on the other hand, or specifically a "staging of words," relieves the unconscious by "placing the effects of the phantom in the social realm."[52] The individual's unconscious attempts to speak secreted words do not make the ghosts disappear. Rather, "Shared or complementary phantoms find a way of being established as social practices along the lines of staged words."[53] The act of speaking secreted words sets the ghosts free, and the ones that have something in common find each other, like *wianbu* and *yanggongju*. These ghosts have an agency of their own in that silence shows itself to be inherently unstable as it becomes the background against which secreted words become audible, often to one who becomes a witness.

In Cathy Caruth's *Unclaimed Experience*, the ghost is a voice that speaks through the wound. It is the voice of the other to whom the listener is intimately tied but whose unfamiliar form renders its kinship unrecognizable. Caruth offers Tasso's *Gerusalemme Liberata* as an example of a voice speaking from the wound. The protagonist Tancred unknowingly kills his lover, Clorinda, then wounds her spirit a second time because he fails to recognize her: "He slashes with his sword at a tall tree; but blood streams from the cut and the voice of Clorinda, whose soul is imprisoned in the tree, is heard complaining that he has wounded his beloved once again."[54] In this scenario, the voice appears to be alien, but it is actually the voice of someone familiar, disembodied and transformed, "a voice that witnesses a truth that Tancred himself cannot fully know."[55] It is a voice that has *seen* and that demands to be listened to. According to Caruth, "We can also read the address of the voice here . . . as the story of the way in which one's own trauma is tied up in the trauma of another, the way in which trauma may lead, therefore, to the encounter with another, through the very possibility and surprise of listening to another's wound."[56] Together the listener and the voice speaking from the wound constitute a kind of storytelling machine, an assemblage of seeing, speaking, and listening components.

Schizophrenic Multiplicity: Madness as Memory

> She tells the story of what she does not remember, but remembers one thing: why she forgot to remember . . . a beautiful woman who lost her mind.

A voice came out of the oak tree. I don't know if this was the voice of a familiar whose spirit was imprisoned inside the trunk, if this voice was trying to tell her about something that she could not see or that her mother could not speak, if this was the voice of a silenced history. She encountered this voice from the tree and set it free into the world by speaking its secreted words. But the speaking of the words also multiplied the voices.

In Abraham and Torok's discussion of ghosts, there are two alternatives for relieving the familial unconscious from being haunted—to remain silent and allow the ghosts to wither away after several generations or to speak and set the ghosts free. But speaking the ghosts' secrets implies exposing them, not only to the world but to one another, and to allow them to find each other and multiply on their own to create new kinships. Abraham and Torok's prescription for exorcising ghosts yields not only and always a final burial of the other's dead but also sometimes the unpredictable effect of multiplication.

It murmurs inside. It murmurs. . . . She swallows once more. (Once more. One more time would do.) In preparation. To such a pitch. Endless drone, refueling itself. Autonomous. Self-generating.

How are we to understand this multiplicity of voices? Leudar and Thomas argue, "Hearing voices in itself does not indicate mental illness any more than do thinking, remembering, or any other ordinary psychological functions, even though *some* modes of thinking can indicate schizophrenia and *some* modes of memory imply trauma and abuse."[57] As a mode of memory, voice-hearing is one component of a diasporic vision that allows us to see the traumatic events of history that traumatized subjects themselves could not. Just as Lacanian psychoanalysis moved trauma out of the realm of the pathological and reconceived of it as the normal condition for human subjectivity, I want to suggest that schizophrenia is a normal mode of memory for a diasporic unconscious that is in constant displacement and that reverberates with the voices of haunted histories. The voices, too, are displaced, speaking from the pasts of pasts and casting origins in the shadows of uncertainty.

Even to the extent that voice-hearing is pathological, there are ways of developing productive methods of listening to the voices rather than only medicating or otherwise disappearing them. Psychosis, for example, is usually thought of in terms of lack, of what is missing from normalcy, but for Žižek (reading Lacan), psychosis is a result of excess: "Lacan pointed out that the consistency of our 'experience of reality' depends on the exclusion of what he calls the *objet petit a* from it: in order for us to have normal 'access to reality,' something must be excluded, 'primordially repressed.' In psychosis, this exclusion is undone . . . : the outcome of which, of course, is the disintegration of our 'sense of reality.'"[58]

In *Soul's Protest* there are two characters who literally cannot speak—the tongueless man and the wianbu. The wianbu's ability to create intelligible speech has broken down, but unlike in the case of the tongueless man, the breakdown has occurred because the Real is no longer being excluded, because of an excess rather than a lack. If trauma is that which exceeds one's frames of reference for understanding and is assimilated into the subject, her system becomes overloaded. But this excess also has the potential to create new methods of seeing, recording, and transmitting trauma.

There are things which have happened in the world while there were cameras watching, things that we have images for.

There are other things which have happened while there were no cameras watching which we restage in front of cameras to have images of.

There are things which have happened for which the only images that exist are in the minds of the observers present at the time.

There are things which have happened for which there have been no observers, except for the spirits of the dead.

A method of engaging the excess that escapes symbolization involves new forms of writing that are an assemblage of different media and temporalities that, according to Johnston, "constitute a heterogeneous and non-narrativizable realm reflecting the sudden and immense expansion of late 20th-century America's media storage capacities, and consequently the expansion of its realm of the dead."[59] This writing form makes a shift from a "molar narrative" to one that registers what Johnston describes as "gaseous, molecular, or fractal perceptions that are peripheral or only immanent to the narrative" or what Deleuze and Guattari call "microperceptions" or pure perception.[60] With various media for reading, storing, and transmitting trauma, including the capacities of the human body, the ghosts are multiplied, thus reminding us that the act of looking at something also changes it. These ghosts are not just figures of persons but also the ghosts of subindividual forces such as energies that change form from shame to hallucination. In a famous case, Pierre Janet's patient Marcelle, for example, experienced voices that were not linked to any kind of identifiable figure but were sensations. Janet then theorized different ways in which a voice makes its presence known to the senses. One can hear a voice speaking, see a voice writing, or feel a voice through a "muscular" or "kinesthetic image." The kinesthetic voice for Marcelle was usually her own voice speaking, which she could not hear but could feel as an external presence entering her body.

As another classic example of a schizophrenic multiplicity of voices that were largely kinesthetic, Judge Daniel Paul Schreber wrote in his memoirs about his self-described "nervous illness," as a result of which he not only heard voices but "shared his body" with them through the experience of "silent nerve language" and "sub-vocal speech" that was emitted by "divine rays" inserting themselves directly into his nerves. Schreber also reported hearing birds that emitted "rote phrases" that were for the most part not recognizable as human speech. Schreber categorized these perceptions as encounters with "souls" or "supernatural agencies."[61]

The small grove of trees surrounding the house quieted her grief and shaded her most private moments. Grief

was something she and the trees had come to share. Some of the older ones confided in her their most bitter memories: "I was tortured with electric shocks"[62] or "beaten because I spoke Korean, not Japanese."[63] "It was like a living death."[64] "When I recall my life, I feel an unspeakable anger rising in my throat."[65] But the trees did not have a throat, so she lent them hers. "My anger has become a kind of disease."[66] To purge themselves of this bitterness, sometimes they sang together: "The song . . . went something like . . . 'My body is like a rotting pumpkin left out in summer.'"[67]

Perhaps more important, the trees were her most trusted source of information because their vision went everywhere at all times: "There was a pregnant woman amongst us. . . . [She] gave birth to a daughter."[68] They could see into the dream her mother had dreamed the night before she was born, a dream of "a ghost in white with long, black hair and an ethereally beautiful face. . . . She appeared with the ghost of the Japanese Colonel, but they could not see each other."[69]

"Marcelle acted on her voices impulsively but she could also resist their commands."[70] "My daughters know nothing of my past," she said. "I don't think it is necessary to tell them."[71] And the trees did not insist, because they, too, were aware of the dangers of speaking. Therefore, they devised a nonverbal messaging system to prevent their secrets from leaking, and she learned it quickly. Indeed, she had always known how to communicate without the use of her tongue. This was also the way in which the trees communicated fragments of overheard conversations: "They would say 'These girls are obedient,' 'girls in such and such a place wouldn't listen to us,' and 'it is easy to work the girls from [Gyeongsang] provinces.'"[72] Sometimes the responsibility of knowing what they knew was too much to bear, so when Oak Tree dropped a clatter of acorns, she recognized the meaning of it instantly: "I went to the seashore, in-

tending to throw myself into the water. . . . I tiptoed back and never told anyone."[73] "But remember that Marcelle's voices were herself talking to herself automatically."[74] In her own words, "It is not a voice, I do not hear anything, I sense that I am spoken to."[75]

Contemporary psychology would describe experiences like these as "errors in perception," one such error being confusion between what is perceived and what is remembered. The distinction between perceived and remembered, however, discounts the possibility of transgenerational haunting, in which the past is in the present, or of affective memory, in which "pure perception" triggers memory that is stored in the body. Is the hallucination a state in which what is perceived is not real, and therefore dismissible, or does it indicate an overflow of the Real into the gap between the body and the voice, thus requiring its observers to open themselves to new forms of perception in order to make sense of it? This is particularly relevant when the traumatized subject cannot remember and recount her history in narrative form. When she cannot speak, who or what is implicated in not speaking? When her voice becomes incapacitated, who or what speaks for her? Who or what speaks to her? Her trauma is expressed in the form of voices from dissociated pasts, voices from the wounds of history.

There were voices that came out of the oak tree in front of the house, others that came out of images on television, newsprint, clocks.

They gave her directives: "Kill yourself tonight. Do it while your children are sleeping." But usually their orders were far more mundane: "Stop fermenting the *dwenjang*. It has been long enough." And "Get chocolate cake for mangnei's birthday."[76] Sometimes they spoke in verbal language to her, about her. At other times, their communication took the form of nonverbal, nonhuman sounds.

The pattering of acorns falling on the roof of her car signaled her involvement in government conspiracies.

The kitchen timer ringing meant that Ronald Reagan had set up surveillance equipment in her house. Eventually, many of the communicators stopped speaking from their original sources, so she always questioned whether or not to believe what she was hearing. The voice of technology often spoke as the oak tree, sometimes disguised as a small dog. The messengers even took the form of her own voice from time to time, speaking to her, through her. Every twelve hours at 9:45, the clock would borrow her voice to announce the time, but in the form of a date. September forty-five. Maybe it was a voice from another time speaking through the clockvoice speaking through her voice. But she could not hear the clockvoice when it spoke; otherwise she might have noticed that this date was significant for her, too. But maybe she was not old enough to remember what happened in September 1945. She was four years old then, moving toward . . . toward . . .

I began searching for a history.[77] My own history. Because I had known all along that the stories I had heard were not true, and parts had been left out. I remember having this feeling growing up that I was haunted by something, that I was living within a family full of ghosts. *It murmurs inside. It murmurs.* There was this place that they knew about. *Inside is the pain of speech the pain to say.* I had never been there *Larger still. Greater than is the pain not to say.* yet I had a memory for it. *[September forty-five.]* I could remember a time of great sadness before I was born. We had been moved. Uprooted. *It festers inside. [September forty-five.] The wound, liquid, dust.* She tells the story of what she does not remember. *She swallows once more. (Once more. One more time would do.) In preparation.* But remembers one thing: why she forgot to remember . . . *[September forty-five.] It murmurs. It augments. [It murmurs.] To such a pitch. Endless drone, refueling itself. Autonomous. Self-generating.* a beautiful woman who lost her mind. *Swallows with last efforts last wills against the pain that wishes it to speak.*

An Ethics of Entanglement

> A history of the modern subject as a history of implication. The subject is recognized by its inextricable ties to what cannot be experienced or subjectivized fully. And this unfinished becoming, surviving and being with others, is the form of being and its history. The subject in or of trauma is thus . . . culturally and politically a diasporic subject, en route toward subjectivity.
>
> —Petar Ramadanovic, "When 'To Die in Freedom' Is Written in English"

I have almost arrived at a final destination that we might call a conclusion. But I have not quite gotten there, so I pause here in this place, where I will reiterate findings and retrace methodological steps and comment on implications.

I Have Found Excess in the Place Where I First Perceived There to Be Nothing

Like Rea Tajiri, who created an image so that she could see what her mother could not remember, I began searching for a history that was both my own history and a history of the social. I cannot say for sure when or where this search began, but probably somewhere during the early 1990s when I was coming of age and feeling suffocated by the knot of emotional residue that Koreans call *han,* winding itself up and around the strange things my mother heard, a legacy of family secrets, and the seeming contradiction between hearing too much and not saying enough. Maybe my search began there, but it did not become apparent until much later.

Without a doubt, there were many beginnings, but one that I am certain of can be located in 2002, when I first began writing this project and experimenting with methods of the unconscious. I started under the assumption that seeing a ghost would require "radical new methods of looking," but I could not have imagined what new methods of seeing trauma this project would produce. It opened up a flood of dreams, no less than three or four every night, faithfully recorded and obsessively analyzed, to fill hundreds of diary pages, some of which have made their way into the pages of this book. In searching for things unspoken and some link between her hallucinations and my dreams, I traced this overflow of unconscious images backward into memory and forward into research and found evidence of a science that is always mixed up in the irrational.

And somewhere in the years between, I began to practice something akin to what Yoo Chul-In calls "sinse t'aryông (telling of the self)... to unleash [one's] knotted grudge, grief of frustration, or resentment." It is a rite performed to treat the "repetition of knotting... in the mind, in the body, and between human beings," but it is a self told through another voice or medium, such as a shaman:[78] "Because the patient is unable to tell her story with her own words, the shaman tells the story through her voice."[79] The medium is considered a healer "not only, or even primarily, of the sick, but also of societal dislocations."[80] I began to practice a "telling of the self" through the medium of speaking in someone else's voice, or in my own that was dislocated. On one hand, "to hear oneself speaking" is what gives us the experience of subjectivity. But on the other, to quote Žižek:

> Is, however, the voice not at the same time that which undermines most radically the subject's self-presence and self-transparence? I hear myself speaking but what I hear is never fully myself but a parasite, a foreign body in my very heart. As such the voice is neither dead nor alive: its primordial phenomenological status is rather that of the living dead, of a spectral apparition that survives its own death, that is, the eclipse of meaning.[81]

Like Rea Tajiri, I had heard stories that were not true, with parts that had been left out, and in the end I wrote new ones, slightly altered repetitions of past events, or full-blown hallucinations, countless stories that are neither true nor whole. In the end, the only story I can tell is an affective expression of memory that is not bound by a subject but lives in what we might call a diasporic unconscious.

The Ghost Decomposes in Analysis Its Methods; It Can Induce Vision but Cannot Be Seen

If it is true that the ghost is "nothing but" an objectified secret rising from *another's* psychic tomb to puncture holes in *my* psychic life, there remains the question of what kind of resolution might come of *my* staging *its* taboo words. When violent histories are subjected to secret burials, we can perhaps exhume the contents of the tomb, but the bodies we find are too disfigured to be positively identified. In fact, they have already turned into something else. Our findings are uncertain, and as Jacques Derrida has written, uncertainty has the curious power to "decompose in analysis this thing. . . . Nothing could be worse for the work of mourning than confusion or doubt: one *has to know* who is buried where—and *it is necessary* (to know—to make certain) that, in what remains of him, *he remains there.*"[82]

In the beginning, I set out to use autoethnographic vignettes "to give body to the uncertainty of diasporic memory," and I wrote my return to the place of this past, where mass graves failed to contain the grief of the dead. Even after the massacres of the Korean War have surfaced, the sparks from the ground still alight the grief of the living, who cannot find exactly where their families are buried. In the process of this search, I have uncovered some bodies, although I am not entirely sure who they belong to, and once again, uncertainty decomposes the body and the method of autoethnography. So it seems that the ghost deceived me and led me to stray from the methodological path I perceived myself to be on.

In looking for evidence of haunting, I found the imprints of rationally motivated erasures in hallucinations, dreams, documents, photographs, gaps between minds and bodies, and places in which I had no intention of ever looking. In following the movement of an erasure across boundaries, it became clear that this "thing" accumulated the affect of the unnameable and unquantifiable loss that permeated the spaces through which it moved. Thus, the ghost is not "nothing but" the secret objectified but rather a secret that exceeds the object to such an extent that it may appear to be nothing. The yanggongju may be a figure that haunts the Korean diaspora, but she is also more than that, for the ghost is an agency that cannot be conformed to a single shape, an agency that is everywhere but cannot be found.

While spectrality cannot be seen in any traditional sense, it can be sensed through a "schizophrenic multiplicity"—through the "kinesthetic image" in the body, through the medium of another's voice that is a witness, through a teletechnological circulation of the image of trauma, through "seeing feeling" in diasporic art and writing. Hallucination emerged as perhaps the best method by which to "see" haunting, because it accounts for the incompatibility between information and experience, thus creating a vision of that which is not available to direct experience. It is a vision that is fundamentally diasporic because it is the movement of haunting, along with its varied and multiplied effects, that allows spectrality to be perceived.

According to Johnston, the radical methodological shift toward "a schizophrenic multiplicity of views [is] implicitly suggestive of the limits of the human, and necessarily of the limits of human control."[83] Thus, this thing that can be neither found nor controlled also reconfigures the way we think about knowledge and knowledge production, for it compels researchers or readers to open ourselves to a different set of possibilities and questions about what might seep through our psychic and epistemological cracks. As Brian Massumi describes this shift, "The question is not, Is it true? But, Does it work? What new thoughts does it make possible to think? What new emotions does it make possible to feel? What new sensations and perceptions does it open in the body?"[84]

My relentless dreams during the course of this research were perhaps one manifestation of the "new" made possible. Taken with (or as) research, they induced a new vision of the violence that led to "our" now being in this place. And somewhere below, too deeply buried to rise to the dream's surface, was a body that could operate not quite as a figure but as a fugitive expression of the diaspora's trauma. But it took time—thousands of images dreamed, pages read and written, and instances of hearing my own voice speaking and mistaking it for another's—before I could see how trauma's scattered effects made connections to each other, as what Ramadanovic calls "an entanglement beyond all possibility of disengagement."[85]

"We" Are Bound by Gaps

And now there is no turning back, no return to a time before I was caught up in such a haunted social legacy. What I see now is that the ties that bind are not confined to those of family or nation but are formed by a kinship of trauma and its uncertainties. After all of this, I am certain of one thing: there are costs involved in unleashing some force that was previously (thought to be) contained. If conjuration is a "matter of neutralizing a hegemony or overturning some power," as Derrida sees it, and therefore a political project, it will always be met with opposition.[86] There are multiple hegemonic forces that have worked to keep things hidden about the Korean diaspora from the Korean diaspora. The kinship of uncertainty that has developed around the yanggongju, however, has the potential to change one's relationship to militarized violence, so proof of one's familial ties to the yanggongju becomes less relevant than recognizing one's implication in another's trauma. Although this project was explicitly laid out as an attempt to conjure ghosts of the Forgotten War, the Forgotten War is also a metaphor for a hegemony that depends on not seeing the violences that have created its ghosts.

But, according to Avery Gordon, "It is also true that ghosts are never innocent," nor are hallucinatory voices, whether ghosts in disguise or psychotic abnormalities, necessarily innocuous.[87] They can in fact be quite destructive, causing injury to those who perceive them, but, as Leudar and Thomas say, "Contrary to mass media wisdom . . . voices typically do not *impel* actions of voice hearers. . . . Hallucinatory voices influence the activities of their hearers very much the same way as people influence each other by talking."[88] Voices compel, but they do not control their hearers, especially when those hearers resist new perspectives and perceptions. And there are some who would prefer to avoid the risk of complication that might ensue when letting loose the pain of trauma, but this fear also presumes that pain is something bounded by the individual body and not something that already "surges beyond the boundaries of any given body," in Bennett's words.[89] Shoshana Felman and Dori Laub believe it is precisely the distribution of pain and the senses through which we perceive it that make it possible to "recognize, and meet, 'the gaping, vertiginous black hole' of the experience of trauma" without an irreparable sensory overload.[90]

My hope is that even in their ambiguity, ghosts will be relentlessly demanding of a society that relegates some bodies to nonexistence, whether motivated by shame, greed, or the delusion that

I can protect *my* self/family/nation from injury by being complicit with another's. "This is not to suggest," according to Bennett, "that the trauma of loss can be disembodied and given over to those who are not its primary subjects but rather the ability to see one's implication in another's trauma might also allow us to recognize the life that can be taken in every body."[91] Therefore, the pain that results from seeing another's trauma necessarily implies a distribution of both the injury and the responsibility for it. Indeed, such a recognition can create what Jacqueline Rose calls "a monstrous family of reluctant belonging."[92] But out of such monstrosity might also arise an ethics of entanglement.

I know that there are costs involved in releasing ghosts into the world, but although I do not know for sure, I will venture to guess that the costs of not recognizing the other that haunts the self are greater. According to Ramadanovic, an ethics of entanglement might now enable us to see the other, "so that the other is revealed and has come there where I was. It is . . . not you whom I become, nor do you suddenly change places with me, but it is the other (other to me, other to you)—the unnameable, the strange."[93] The other that "we" might now be able to see "allows another diasporic, entangled 'we'" to appear.[94] It is this vision that draws us into a future in which another entangled "we" can acknowledge the unknowable as that which subtends life and explore new possibilities for being in the spaces in between.

I have almost arrived at a final destination. Near the bridge that crosses into that other world made strange by death, a shadowy figure waits to make a reparative gesture—to perform the rite of unknotting our tightly wound *han,* unknotting it in a way that leaves us tied but loosens the bindings. And there at the edge, in the space that hovers over the gap, I can see her somewhere below—not where we thought we had secretly buried her, but in the texture of life, in the ground of possibility for the thing I call my self.

Bridge of Return. Copyright Yul-san Liem/Still Present Pasts, 2005. Wood, cloth, stone, ink. The different elements of the bridge include knotted cloth, stepping stones, wood planks, and cloth railing, representing wounds, division, shamanic healing rituals, reconciliation, and spiritual crossings into peace. This interactive piece encourages viewers to step onto the bridge and walk across.

Postscript
In Memoriam

I finished writing this on the eve of a departure. It was be my second return to Korea since my childhood, my second return to *gohyang,* a word that means "hometown" that Koreans use to refer to one's birthplace. I returned again to the place where I was born and that my mother called home, although I do not really consider any place in Korea my home, nor was my mother born there. The second time, I returned not to look for traces of an erased history but to be present in contemporary Korean politics as an activist who embodies the inextricable ties between the United States and Korea.

Even in the now of Korean society, the past is present as that which remains unresolved: anti-American groups are still protesting crimes committed against Korean women by American GIs; families are still grieving their permanent separation from siblings in the north; a dwindling group of grandmothers still gathers every Wednesday in front of the Japanese Embassy to demand reparations. There are new protestations against neoimperialism that saturate the current landscape of political struggle: rice farmers are up in arms about the loss of food sovereignty to the U.S.–South Korea free trade agreement, while other farmers are mourning the loss of their land and homes to the expansion of U.S. military bases. The effects of continued U.S. domination have called me to go to the peninsula in its contemporary state and to feel myself thoroughly engaged in both the place of my birth and the one in which I later arrived.

I opened this book with memory fragments of a childhood spent in my father's hometown, a town in which I felt perpetually estranged, more so the longer I lived there. In particular, the memory of my childhood dinner table foregrounded my father's presence, while my mother was somewhere in his shadow. The most salient examples were the dinners we shared each year on June 25. But no one in my family ever talked about the war, and perhaps I was the only one who found it curious that on June 25 the only thing we could remember was my father's birthday.

In the first chapter I tell a story about what I imagined my father's birthday to have been like on the day the Korean War broke out. I do this as a way of setting up a sense of being pulled into the future by an entanglement with trauma and also as a way of opening a path to tell another story about the significance of June 25, 1950, for the making of the yanggongju and the emergence of the Korean diaspora in the United States. I had initially thought that I would include other vignettes about my father, but in the end the spectral force that sometimes took the shape of my mother proved to overshadow the figure of my father. And ironically, as one of those few American men who *wanted* to claim responsibility for his Korean children, he ended up being absent from this text. In fact, he has been absent for most of my writing life, except in that felt sense in which the dead are always with us.

Perhaps my father's willingness to talk about his life meant that I did not inherit his secrets as ghosts, but this does not mean that my father's history has not also haunted me. This is the story my father used to tell me about himself, a story that is substantiated by the family photographs he left behind: He was born and raised in a farming community and grew up as a child of the Great Depression. Not only was he a poor child in an economically devastated country; he was a fatherless child during a time when single-parent families were rare. He had no memory of his father other than an image from a photograph taken shortly before his father disappeared. It is inscribed with the words "To my beloved wife and son." When my father was a young man, he became a farmer and took great pride in raising pigs, many of which won awards in state fairs. He wanted nothing other than to continue raising these animals, but he was poor, and then the war came. He joined the navy during Word War II, did his tour of duty, and went back to the farm. But as much as he loved his work, he could not make a living, so during the 1960s he became a merchant marine, traveled to all the major port cities in Asia, and enjoyed the privileges given to U.S. military personnel. This is how he met my mother.

South Korea was very much a Third World country in the 1960s when my parents met, and this fact served to draw my father further into the rescue fantasy he created about himself and my mother. She was a young woman working to support a family within a social context that foreclosed mobility for such women, as well as for their children. My father was invested in an image of his becoming the provider for a new generation, and his first wife had been unable to conceive a child, so his desire for my mother was also about wanting to be the father that he had not had, to provide financially for a struggling family, to fill in the hole of his own lack. My father's story is rooted in a trauma of a time and place very distinct from my mother's, yet their being drawn together is another test of the theory that disparate sites of trauma haunt one another. The story of my father's romance with my mother is also a story of love and domination, of the ways in which the intimate violence of the U.S.–Korea relationship plays itself out in the dynamic of a family.

And so I am affectively bound to both of my parents through transgenerational haunting. Although my father told me stories about himself, I am certain that there are plenty of unspeakable traumas I have psychically inherited from him but have not yet been able to access. The tangling together of my parents' histories surfaces sometimes in my unconscious, most remarkably in the form of recurring dreams. There is one in particular that speaks to how my father, even in his absence, still haunts the text of my unconscious.

There is nothing out of the ordinary at the start. This dream begins with a routine. The setting is my mother's suburban home on a sunny midsummer afternoon. I am preparing a meal for her, because this is something she can no longer do for herself. Then I realize that I must first butcher the meat, so I go out to the yard. I dread being responsible for taking the life of another, but because it is my obligation, I proceed almost mechanically. Blood-soaked, I am slaughtering my father's pigs, and then the animals I kill morph into the bodies of Korean women massacred by U.S. soldiers. I flee the scene and walk what

seems a very long distance. I walk to a place that was once fertile farmland but has turned barren and dry, burned by the sun or by chemical warfare. It is 1950 in some small farming community, in Gyeongsang province or in rural America. I have arrived at the home of my mother and my father.

I completed this book the day before my second return to Korea in August 2007. I had initially written this postscript in memory of my father, to acknowledge the way in which he is also enmeshed in the spectrality that haunts this text. A few weeks after I had begun graduate school with the intention of researching all the implications of my family history, my father had died. Since then I have often wondered what he would have said about my work if he had survived long enough to see it. In many ways, he was not the kind of American serviceman that the literature on GI brides describes, for he was interested in learning about Korean culture and attuned to the suffering caused by social injustice. At some level, he understood my need to conduct this research.

What I did not anticipate when I was finishing this book was that my mother would suddenly and mysteriously pass away shortly before its publication. Every time I saw her over the last few months of her life, she asked me for an update about the production of the book, and sometimes she offered suggestions as to how she thought it should be marketed. I was eager to share pieces of it with her, especially the parts that would allow me to communicate how deeply my life's work has been shaped by my love for her and my sincere wish for her vindication. When I received the cover design I was excited to show it to my mother, but she died two days later, before I had the chance to do so. Strangely, the deaths of my parents marked the beginning and end of this project.

Though there were many things that my mother never talked about, she was not a quiet woman. She was fiercely demanding and at the same time incredibly tender and loving, and this combination gave me a birthright to seek justice and compassion. My mother was a woman with tremendous potential, but she was eventually worn down by her circumstances. Because of her own misfortunes, she always impressed upon me the importance of cultivating my mind so that I would not have to work with my body. She did so with such zeal and urgency that it led me to my current life as a writer and scholar. But in fact she taught me to use my body as well as my mind, to insist with my entire being that some things really do exist no matter how many times they get covered up. In bearing witness to the unspeakable in my own family history, I have learned to see that beneath every act of destruction, beneath every horrible and violent situation, there is still a breath of life worth nurturing. This is the legacy my parents left to me.

My mother became the motivating force behind this book, but, as you can imagine, going public with family secrets cost me a lot. My staging of words created discontent and division in my family, but as this drama ensued, my mother came out as the sole supporter of my writing. This book never would have made it into print had she disapproved of it. In the end, my mother gave me the gift of relieving my unconscious by allowing me to speak the very words that I had wanted to vocalize for years. I was so happy to say to her, "Mama, there is nothing about you that I am ashamed of. You deserve to be recognized." *Haunting the Korean Diaspora* was written with the intention of keeping alive the memory of things that would otherwise become forgotten. I dedicate these words to my mother in the hope that they may finally bring her out of the shadows.

Notes

Introduction

1. Shaded portions of this text indicate an experimental writing voice that combines autoethnography and fiction. These vignettes are based sometimes on my family history and sometimes on the body of scholarly work I have researched for this project. They are often intended to show the mixing up of fact and fiction, of self and other, so neither a discrete narrator nor a clear story line is always present. These vignettes also typically refer back to the other portions of this text that are discussed in a more academic voice. All proper names in these vignettes have been changed, except where noted.

2. Nicolas Abraham and Maria Torok, *The Shell and the Kernel: Renewals of Psychoanalysis,* vol. 1, ed. and trans. Nicholas T. Rand (Chicago: University of Chicago Press, 1994), 176.

3. While I use the word *yanggongju* quite liberally throughout this text, I do not mean it pejoratively; rather, through exploring the different meanings accrued to it, I seek a radical resignification of the term away from either its stigmatic or its romantically tragic connotations.

4. Abraham and Torok, *The Shell and the Kernel,* 1: 176.

5. David Eng and David Kazanjian, eds., *Loss: The Politics of Mourning* (Berkeley: University of California Press, 2003), 2. Drawing on Benjamin's notion of animating the remains of history, Eng and Kazanjian take up the question of how loss can be productive. Rather than being merely a lack, the empty spaces left behind by loss can be thought of as "a field in which the past is brought to bear witness to the present—as a flash of emergence, an instant of emergency, and a moment of production" (5).

6. Ha Koon Ja is one of the surviving comfort women featured in Byun Young-Ju's documentary film *Sumgyeol—Najeun moksori* (My Own Breathing) (Seoul: Docu-factory, 1999).

7. Chungmoo Choi, "Introduction: The Comfort Women; Colonialism, War, and Sex," *positions: east asia cultures critique* 5, no. 1 (1997): v.

8. In March 2007, Japan's prime minister, Shinzo Abe, officially denied that the Japanese Imperial Army participated in any wrongdoing toward the former comfort women, claiming that there was no coercion on the part of the military and that the women were paid, voluntary prostitutes. Despite the assertion of Japanese historians and the testimonies of both victims and witnesses, Abe held onto his position of denial. After fifteen years of struggle toward a public acknowledgment and reconciliation of the past, this renewed controversy has opened up the psychic wounds caused by forced sexual labor.

9. Cho'e Myŏngsun, "Silent Suffering," in *True Stories of the Korean Comfort Women*, ed. Keith Howard (London: Cassell, 1995), 176.

10. Abraham and Torok, *The Shell and the Kernel*, 1: 175 (emphasis in the original).

11. Hyun Sook Kim, "Yanggongju as an Allegory of the Nation," in *Dangerous Women: Gender and Korean Nationalism*, ed. Elaine Kim and Chungmoo Choi (New York: Routledge, 1998), 175–202.

12. *Gijichon* translates as "military camptown," but I sometimes use the word as shorthand for the system of prostitution around military bases.

13. Much of what I have constructed as the story of my father's childhood and young adulthood I have come to know through his family photographs. There are a few that have impressed themselves most deeply on my memory—my father as a toddler, holding the reins of a plow horse; as a teenager, feeding his pigs; in his early twenties, sporting a U.S. naval uniform; and at the age of thirty, on the day his butcher shop opened. I have these memories of my father's memories through the photographs he passed on to me. My mother, on the other hand, had no photographic documentation capturing the history of her early life.

14. Even when I arrived in my father's hometown in the 1970s, few people I encountered knew where Korea was. They would ask, "Are you from China or Japan?" and respond with confusion when I answered "Korea."

15. This quote is from the collective art project based on Liem's oral histories, titled *Still Present Pasts: Korean Americans and the "Forgotten War,"* which first opened at the Cambridge Multicultural Arts Center in Cambridge, Massachusetts, in January 2005. For more information, see http://www.stillpresentpasts.org.

16. I use the term *articulate* in the same sense that Brent Hayes Edwards does in his study of the African diaspora. On one hand it refers to expression of an idea, but on the other it refers to the act of connecting different pieces. Brent Hayes Edwards, *The Practice of Diaspora* (Cambridge, Mass.: Harvard University Press, 2003).

17. Ji-Yeon Yuh notes that restrictions against Asian immigration applied to Korean war brides until 1952. Those who arrived prior to 1952 were allowed to immigrate under special circumstances. She also points out the way in which "the very term 'war bride' emphasizes the women's dependence on men and their link to war, conferring an identity on them as human war booty." Yuh, *Beyond the Shadow of Camptown: Korean Military Brides in America* (New York: New York University Press), 1.

18. Lisa Lowe, *Immigrant Acts: On Asian American Cultural Politics* (Durham, N.C.: Duke University Press, 1996), 16–17.

19. See, for example, Elaine Kim, "'Bad Women': Asian American Visual Artists Hanh Thi Pham, Hung Liu, and Yong Soon Min," *Feminist Studies* 22, no. 3 (Autumn 1996): 573–602.

20. Shoshana Felman and Dori Laub, *Testimony: Crises of Witnessing in Literature, Psychoanalysis and History* (New York: Routledge, 1992), 64–65 (emphasis in original).

21. This is a phrase used repeatedly in Alice Amsden, *Asia's Next Giant: South Korea and Late Industrialization* (New York: Oxford University Press, 1989), to describe the harsh conditions behind the many superlatives awarded to South Korea during its "economic miracle." In the 1980s, for example, South Korea held "the dubious honor" of having the longest workweek in the world, more than eighty hours per week. Most of those working under these conditions were young women, yet the labor of women during the economic miracle, like the labor of Korean military sex workers in the forging of geopolitical alliances between the United States and South Korea, was obscured by masculinist discourses of economic and sociopolitical development. This issue is discussed further in chapter 4.

22. Howard, *True Stories of Korean Comfort Women.* This concentration is suggested by the existing stories of Korean comfort women, but, given the stigmas associated with sexual labor of any kind (outside of marriage), this cannot be proven as fact when relatively few women have come forward as former comfort women. Similarly, it is impossible to confirm the exact location in which most civilians were massacred due to all the forces that have covered up such incidents.

23. Survivors of the Nogeun-ri massacre had been speaking out for almost fifty years to bring international attention to this war crime, but it was not until 1999, when an Associated Press reporter investigated the claims of the Korean witnesses, that their story was legitimated.

24. Lyndsey Stonebridge, "Bombs and Roses: The Writing of Anxiety in Henry Green's *Caught*," *Diacritics* 28, no. 4 (1998): 25–43.

25. On May 31, 2007, Ted Koppel reported on National Public Radio's *Morning Edition* that a senior military official in Iraq had spoken of the possibility that the United States could experience a long-term presence in Iraq. Koppel was particularly concerned that the official acknowledged that Iraq could become "like South Korea," indicating that a long-term U.S. military presence

could become permanent. Koppel also implied that the official used South Korea as an example of a successful intervention that was intended to give a positive spin to U.S. presence in Iraq. Since then, the Bush administration has made numerous references to implementing a "South Korea model" in Iraq.

26. Most of the popular information available in the United Stated about the Korean War come from Korean War veterans who have struggled to keep the memory of the war alive. Although the information provided by veterans' associations acknowledges the tragic consequences of the war for Korean civilians, these groups maintain the position that the killings of civilians and executions of prisoners of war were committed primarily by the North Korean army.

27. Theresa Hak Kyung Cha, *Dictée* (New York: Tanam, 1982), 81.

28. Valerie Walkerdine, "Video Replay: Families, Films, and Fantasy," in *The Media Reader,* ed. Manuel Alvarado and John O. Thompson (London: BFI, 1990), 187.

29. Cha, *Dictée,* 4.

30. For discussions of political investments in life and death, see Achilles Mbembe, "Necropolitics," *Public Culture* 15, no. 1 (2003): 11–40; João Biehl, "Vitae: Life in a Zone of Social Abandonment," *Social Text* 19, no. 3 (2001): 131–49; and Michel Foucault, *History of Sexuality,* vol. 1, *An Introduction* (New York: Vintage, 1978).

31. Mark Seltzer, *Bodies and Machines* (New York: Routledge, 1992).

32. Yuh, *Beyond the Shadow of Camptown.*

33. Gilles Deleuze and Félix Guattari, *Anti-Oedipus: Capitalism and Schizophrenia* (Minneapolis: University of Minnesota Press, 1983).

34. For an excellent example, see Eng and Kazanjian, *Loss.*

35. John Johnston, *Information Multiplicity: American Fiction in the Age of Media Saturation* (Baltimore, Md.: Johns Hopkins University Press, 1998).

36. Judith Butler, "After Loss, What Then?" in *Loss,* ed. Eng and Kazanjian.

37. Patricia Clough, ed., with Jean Halley, *The Affective Turn: Theorizing the Social* (Durham, N.C.: Duke University Press, 2007), 3.

38. Gilles Deleuze and Claire Parnet, *Dialogues* (New York: Columbia University Press, 1987), 84.

1. Fleshing Out the Ghost

1. Jacques Derrida, *Specters of Marx: The State of the Debt, the Work of Mourning, and the New International,* trans. Peggy Kamuf (New York: Routledge, 1994), 11.

2. Avery Gordon, *Ghostly Matters: Haunting and the Sociological Imagination* (Minneapolis: University of Minnesota Press, 1997), 8.

3. Ibid., 19.

4. Ibid.

5. Nicolas Abraham and Maria Torok, *The Shell and the Kernel: Renewals of Psychoanalysis,* vol. 1, ed. and trans. Nicholas T. Rand (Chicago: University of Chicago Press, 1994), 169.

6. For a discussion of transgenerational haunting among Japanese Americans, see David Eng and Shinhee Han, "A Dialogue on Racial Melancholia," *Psychoanalytic Dialogues* 10, no. 4 (2000): 667–700.

7. Jacqueline Rose, *States of Fantasy* (Oxford, England: Oxford University Press. 1996), 31 (emphasis in the original).

8. Abraham and Torok, *The Shell and the Kernel,* 1: 168.

9. Gordon, *Ghostly Matters,* 8.

10. Karen Barad, "Getting Real: Technoscientific Practices and the Materialization of the Real," *Differences: A Journal of Feminist Cultural Studies* 10, no. 1 (1998): 87–128.

11. Judith Butler, "After Loss, What Then?" in *Loss: The Politics of Mourning,* ed. David Eng and David Kazanjian (Berkeley: University of California Press, 2003), 469.

12. Abraham and Torok, *The Shell and the Kernel,* 1: 176.

13. Eve Kosofsky Sedgwick, *Touching Feeling: Affect, Pedagogy, Performativity* (Durham, N.C.: Duke University Press, 2003), 140.

14. Mark Seltzer, *Bodies and Machines* (New York: Routledge, 1992), 96; Valerie Walkerdine, "Video Replay: Families, Films, and Fantasy," in *The Media Reader,* ed. Manuel Alvarado and John O. Thompson (London: BFI, 1990), 190.

15. Gordon, *Ghostly Matters,* 16.

16. Ibid., 27. Gordon goes on to point out the irony that a discipline so concerned with haunting could also produce its own ghosts. This becomes particularly apparent when examining the founding fathers' desire to legitimate psychoanalysis as a science. The ghost that haunts the second chapter of her text is Sabina Spielrein, a student of psychoanalysis and a contemporary of Freud and Jung, who is absent from photographic documents of the psychoanalytic field. She is documented in a popular narrative account about the field, however, but only as a patient of Jung who falls madly in love with him. This account "does not mention that Spielrein wrote about the death drive ten years before Freud published his seminal work on the death instinct" (34).

17. Ibid., 22.

18. Bruce Cumings, "Silent but Deadly: Sexual Subordination in the U.S.–Korean Relationship," in *Let the Good Times Roll: Prostitution and the U.S. Military in Asia,* ed. Saundra Sturdevant and Brenda Stoltzfus (New York: New Press, 1992), 170.

19. Ibid.

20. J. T. Takagi and Hye Jung Park, *The Women Outside: Korean Women and the U.S. Military* (New York: Third World News Reel, 1996); Ji-Yeon Yuh, *Beyond the Shadow of Camptown: Korean Military Brides in America* (New York: New York University Press, 2002).

21. Eng and Kazanjian, *Loss,* 8–9.

22. Abraham and Torok, *The Shell and the Kernel,* 1: 176.

23. Ibid., 188.

24. Ibid., 167.

25. Ibid., 189.

26. See, for example, Chungmoo Choi, "Nationalism and Construction of Gender in Korea," in *Dangerous Women: Gender and Korean Nationalism,* ed. Elaine Kim and Chungmoo Choi (New York: Routledge, 1998), 9–31; Cumings, "Silent But Deadly," 169–75; Hyun Sook Kim, "Yanggongju as an Allegory of the Nation," in *Dangerous Women: Gender and Korean Nationalism,* ed. Elaine Kim and Chungmoo Choi (New York: Routledge, 1998) 175–202; Diana S. Lee and Grace Lee, directors, *Camp Arirang* (New York: Third World News Reel, 1996); John Lie, "The Transformation of Sexual Work in 20th-Century Korea," *Gender & Society* 9, no. 3 (1995): 310–27; Katharine H. S. Moon, *Sex among Allies: Military Prostitution in U.S.–Korea Relations* (New York: Columbia University Press, 1997).

27. Gordon, *Ghostly Matters,* 22.

28. See, for example, Wendy Chapkis, *Live Sex Acts: Women Performing Erotic Labor* (New York: Routledge, 1997), and Kamala Kempadoo and Jo Doezema, eds. *Global Sex Workers: Rights, Resistance, and Redefinition* (New York: Routledge, 1998).

29. Rose, *States of Fantasy,* 5.

30. Brent Hayes Edwards, *The Practice of Diaspora* (Cambridge, Mass.: Harvard University Press, 2003), 11.

31. Ibid., 13.

32. Rose, *States of Fantasy,* 31.

33. Patricia Ticineto Clough, *Autoaffection: Unconscious Thought in the Age of Teletechnology* (Minneapolis: University of Minnesota Press, 2000), 17.

34. Ibid.

35. Ibid., 69.

36. Jill Bennett, *Empathic Vision: Affect, Trauma, and Contemporary Art* (Stanford, Calif.: Stanford University Press, 2005).

37. David Eng, *Racial Castration: Managing Masculinity in America* (Durham, N.C.: Duke University Press, 2001), 37. Similarly, anthropologist Michael Fischer also proposes that the social sciences take up the study of the unconscious and suggests a method of remembering, "a modern version of the Pythagorean arts of memory: retrospection to gain a vision for the future. In so becoming, the searches also turn out to be powerful critiques of several contemporary rhetorics of domination." See Michael M. J. Fischer, "Ethnicity and the Post-Modern Arts of Memory," in *Writing Culture: The Poetics and Politics of Ethnography,* ed. James Clifford and George E. Marcus. (Berkeley: University of California Press, 1986), 198.

38. Gordon, *Ghostly Matters,* 41 (emphasis in the original).

39. Trinh T. Min-ha, *Framer Framed* (New York: Routledge, 1992).

40. See, for example, Barad, "Getting Real"; Patricia Ticineto Clough, *The End(s) of Ethnography: From Realism to Social Criticism* (Newbury Park, Calif.: Sage, 1992); Elena Tajima Creef, "Discovering My Mother as the Other in the *Saturday Evening Post,*" *Qualitative Inquiry* 6, no. 4 (2000): 443–55; Donna Haraway, Modest_Witness@Second_Millennium.FemaleMan©_Meets_OncoMouse™

(New York: Routledge, 1997); Karin Knorr Cetina, "Sociality with Objects: Social Relations in Postsocial Knowledge Societies," *Theory, Culture & Society* 14, no. 4 (1997): 1–30; Jackie Orr, "Performing Methods: History, Hysteria, and the New Science of Psychiatry," in *Pathology and the Postmodern: Mental Illness as Discourse and Experience,* ed. Dwight Fee (London: Sage, 2000), 49–73.

41. Gordon, *Ghostly Matters,* 10.

42. Walkerdine, "Video Replay," 186.

43. Gordon, *Ghostly Matters,* 26.

44. For more on this distinction, see Susannah Radstone, *Memory and Methodology* (Oxford, England: Berg, 2000).

45. Clough, *End(s) of Ethnography,* 114.

46. Jennifer C. Hunt, *Psychoanalytic Aspects of Fieldwork* (Newbury Park, Calif.: Sage, 1989).

47. Orr, "Performing Methods," 68.

48. Saidiya Hartman, *Scenes of Subjection: Terror, Slavery and Self-Making in Nineteenth-Century America* (New York: Oxford University Press, 1997), 12.

49. Marianne Hirsch, quoted in Alisa Lebow, "Memory Once Removed: Indirect Memory and Transitive Autobiography in Chantal Akerman's *D'Est,*" *Camera Obscura* 52, no. 18 (2003): 47.

50. Clough, *Autoaffection,* 16. It is important to mention here that not all deployments of autoethnography are critical. This method can often reproduce the same logic it seeks to unsettle—that there is a true story to be revealed, and for some autoethnographers, it is just a matter of replacing a dominant narrative with a revisionist one. Clough, however, is quite aware of the problems associated with what Derrida calls "autoaffection," or the desire for one's own voice "that gives the natural grounds to the subject privileged in the western modern discourse of Man" and therefore proposes an autoethnography that seeks to bring unconscious thought to bear on the writing of the self (17).

51. Ann Anlin Cheng, *The Melancholy of Race* (New York: Oxford University Press, 2001), 147.

52. Ibid.

53. See Joseph Roach, *Cities of the Dead: Circum-Atlantic Performance* (New York: Columbia University Press, 1996), and Richard Schechner, *Between Theater and Anthropology* (Philadelphia: University of Pennsylvania Press, 1985).

54. Diana Taylor, "'You are Here:' The DNA of Performance," *Drama Review* 46, no. 1 (2002): 149–69.

55. See Brian Massumi, *Parables for the Virtual: Movement, Affect, Sensation* (Durham, N.C.: Duke University Press, 2002), and Gilles Deleuze, *The Fold: Leibniz and the Baroque* (Minneapolis: University of Minnesota Press, 1992).

56. Jill Bennett, *Empathic Vision: Affect, Trauma, and Contemporary Art* (Stanford, Calif.: Stanford University Press, 2005), 56 (emphasis in the original).

57. John Johnston, *Information Multiplicity: American Fiction in the Age of Media Saturation* (Baltimore, Md.: Johns Hopkins University Press, 1998), 1998 (emphasis in the original).

58. Jackie Orr, *Panic Diaries: A Genealogy of Panic Disorder* (Durham, N.C.: Duke University Press, 2006), 21.

59. For a discussion of borrowed voices in Cha's work, see chapter 6 of Lisa Lowe, *Immigrant Acts: On Asian American Cultural Politics* (Durham, N.C.: Duke University Press, 1996).

60. The voices heard in the book appear as quotations within the text and quotations set off from the text. Some—the autoethnographic vignettes described in note 1 to the introduction—are indicated by shading, others later in the book by boldface type and shading. And some overlapping voices are presented by means of quotes within passages.

61. Cheng, *Melancholy of Race,* 149.

62. Gordon, *Ghostly Matters,* 8.

63. Butler, "After Loss, What Then?" 467.

64. Clough, *Autoaffection,* 20.

2. A Genealogy of Trauma

1. To read more about Daniels's life history, see Ramsay Liem, "So I've Gone around in Circles . . .": Living the Korean War, *Amerasia Journal* 31 (2005): 155–77, and Ramsay Liem, "Crossing Over: One Woman's Account of a Forgotten War—Interview with Helen Kyungsook Daniels," *Boston College Magazine* (winter 2004), available at http://www.bc.edu/publications/bcm/winter_2004/11_koreanwar.html (accessed May 12, 2004). Daniels had just finished junior high school at the time that the war broke out. As a resident of Pyeongyang, which was the target of the most intense air strikes during the war, her story of displacement and survival is perhaps one of the most dramatic personal histories documented in the United States.

2. Bruce Cumings, "The Division of Korea," in *Two Koreas*—One Future? ed. John Sullivan and Roberta Foss (Lanham, Md.: University Press of America, 1987), 13.

3. Sheldon Harris, *Factories of Death: Japanese Biological Warfare, 1932–45, and the American Cover-up* (London: Routledge, 1994).

4. Ramsay Liem, "History, Trauma, and Identity: The Legacy of the Korean War for Korean Americans," *Amerasia Journal* 29, no. 3 (2003/4): 114.

5. Sahr Conway-Lanz, "Beyond No Gun Ri: Refugees and the United States Military in the Korean War," *Diplomatic History* 29, no. 1 (January 2005): 49. Conway-Lanz goes on to note that the work of Bruce Cumings is exceptional in focusing on the war's impact on civilians.

6. For an evocative pictorial account, see Patrick Dowdy, *Living through the Forgotten War: Portrait of Korea* (Middletown, Conn.: Mansfield Freeman Center for East Asian Studies at Wesleyan University and the Korea Society, 2003).

7. Saidiya Hartman, *Scenes of Subjection: Terror, Slavery and Self-Making in Nineteenth-Century America* (New York: Oxford University Press, 1997), 12.

8. Jill Bennett, *Empathic Vision: Affect, Trauma, and Contemporary Art* (Stanford, Calif.: Stanford University Press, 2005), 42.

9. While many of the vignettes are written in the voice of a fictional piece of writing, the ones that I imagine to be about my family's experiences are more self-consciously fictionalized as a means of expressing the ambiguity about the kinds of traumatic histories that are passed down through transgenerational haunting.

10. Patricia Ticineto Clough, *Autoaffection: Unconscious Thought in the Age of Teletechnology* (Minneapolis: University of Minnesota Press, 2000), 69.

11. Wolcott Wheeler asserts: "Enlisting the aid of the U.S. [the South Korean government], made Cheju-do America's first military intervention in postwar Asia, our first Vietnam." The impact on civilians, according to Wheeler, was that at least thirty thousand (10 percent of the island's population) were killed, another forty thousand fled to Japan, and over half the island's villages were destroyed through scorched-earth tactics during the course of a year of fighting. See Wolcott Wheeler, "The 1948 Cheju-do Civil War," http://www.kimsoft.com/1997/43wh.htm (accessed April 19, 2001). For information on the treatment of women during this incident, see Oh Gun Sook, "Violation of Women's Rights and the Cheju April 3rd Massacre," http://www.kimsoft.com/1997/43women1.htm (accessed April 19, 2001).

12. Bruce Cumings, *Korea's Place in the Sun: A Modern History* (New York: Norton, 1997); Wheeler, "The 1948 Cheju-do Civil War"; Yang Han Kwan, "The Truth about the Cheju April 3rd Insurrection," http://www.kimsoft.com/1997/43hist.htm (accessed April 19, 2001).

13. Don Oberdorfer, *The Two Koreas: A Contemporary History*, rev. ed. (1997; repr. New York: Basic Books, 2001).

14. Cumings, *Korea's Place in the Sun.*

15. I. F. Stone, *The Hidden History of the Korean War*, 2nd paperback ed. (1952; repr. New York: Monthly Review Press, 1971).

16. Cumings, *Korea's Place in the Sun*, 238.

17. Stone, *Hidden History*, viii.

18. David K. Song, "Dark Days of the Korean War: Mass Murder at Nogunri," http://www.hardboiled.org/3–2/nogunri.html (accessed October 15, 2002).

19. Korean Central News Agency of the Democratic People's Republic of Korea (DPRK), "GIs' Mass Killings," http://www.lai-aib.org/lai/article_lai.phtml?section=A3ABBSBD&object_id=7030 (accessed October 14, 2002).

20. Park Sung Yong, "Rethinking the Nogun-ri Massacre on the 50th Anniversary of the Outbreak of the Korean War," http://www.kimsoft.com/1997/nogun13.htm (accessed October 15, 2002).

21. Green Korea, "U.S. Bombs Korean Village: Puerto Rico Has Vieques; Korea Has Maehyang-ri," *Earth Island Institute: Earth Island Journal* (Winter 2000–2001), available at http://www.earthisland.org/eijournal/new_articles.cfm?articleID=49&journalID=43 (accessed October 14, 2002).

22. International Action Center, "Solidarity between Puerto Rico and Korea," http://www.iacenter.org/pr_korea.htm (accessed October 14, 2002).

On April 18, 2004, U.S. military officials decided to close down the Kun-ni bombing range to U.S. bombing practice and transfer the control of Kun-ni from the U.S. Air Force to Seoul. This decision came shortly after fourteen plaintiffs from Maehyang-ri won a lawsuit for injury and physical damage to homes and property. The Kun-ni range has since closed, and the residents of Maehyang-ri will build a peace museum in its place.

23. Jacqueline Rose, *States of Fantasy* (Oxford, England: Oxford University Press, 1996), 31 (emphasis in the original).

24. Brian Massumi, *Parables for the Virtual: Movement, Affect, Sensation* (Durham, N.C.: Duke University Press, 2002). Massumi notes that the time between the registration of perception in the body and the subject's cognition of it is half a second. The "missing half second" is a space between what one knows and feels, the content of which is inaccessible to human knowledge even by means of the most rigorous of scientific methods, yet this is also a space of possibility. What is folded in during the missing half second is unpredictable in that it is unknowable yet can become activated at any moment, independent of the will of the subject.

25. In addition to the irony that these orphans were likely to have lost their parents during military offensives by the United States is the fact that many of the children were literally fathered by American soldiers and then abandoned by their mothers because of the stigma of having a mixed-race child. In some instances, orphanages themselves were bombed during the war. For examples of artistic works that deal with the issue of Americans' relationship to Korean war orphans, see the work of Borshay Liem and Hosu Kim at http://www.stillpresentpasts.org.

26. Park, "Rethinking the Nogun-ri Massacre."

27. David Eng, *Racial Castration: Managing Masculinity in America* (Durham, N.C.: Duke University Press 2001), 37.

28. Bennett, *Empathic Vision,* 41.

29. As I was reading *The Bridge at No Gun Ri,* the haunting memories that belonged to the survivors of the incident began to permeate my own memory. Because of the way in which this story resonated with a broader sense of being haunted, many of the vignettes I have written for this chapter are inspired by the work of the AP reporters who wrote the story, and I have kept the names of actual survivors of the massacre. I have also retained the spellings of their names as they appear in the book.

30. After the AP story broke, the Pentagon conducted an official investigation into the incident. Their report concluded that the killings had been accidental and that the American soldiers must have misinterpreted or misunderstood a more general policy on containing the movement of refugees. The American veterans testified, however, that they had been given direct orders to shoot the refugees at Nogeun-ri. The Pentagon's denial suggests that all the eyewitnesses must have hallucinated the event in that they perceived something that did not really happen. The denial has also functioned to keep the memory alive and to

provoke more investigation into the incident and, more broadly, into the killing of civilians during the Korean War. As Sahr Conway-Lanz points out, the Pentagon's explanation of the events helped to reveal the fact that lethal force was authorized to contain the movement of refugees not just on this occasion but as a general policy that was subject to misinterpretation. These were practices that were in explicit violation of the Geneva Conventions. See Conway-Lanz, "Beyond No Gun Ri."

31. Charles J. Hanley, Sang-Hun Choe, and Martha Mendoza, *The Bridge at No Gun Ri: A Hidden Nightmare from the Korean War* (New York: Henry Holt and Company, 2001), 127.

32. Ibid., 126.

33. Kim Soo-hye and Lee Kil-song, "Nogeun-ri Survivors Reconcile with Soldier," *Digital Chosun Ilbo*, November 4, 1999, http://www.chosun.com/w21data/html/news/199911040402l.html (accessed May 15, 2004).

34. Rose, *States of Fantasy*, 31.

35. Hanley, Choe, and Mendoza, *Bridge at No Gun Ri*, 139.

36. Ibid., 138.

37. Cathy Caruth, *Unclaimed Experience: Trauma, Narrative, and History* (Baltimore, Md.: Johns Hopkins University Press, 1996), 92.

38. Marc Nichanian and David Kazanjian, "Between Genocide and Catastrophe," in *Loss: The Politics of Mourning*, ed. David Eng and David Kazanjian (Berkeley: University of California Press, 2003), 133.

39. Ibid., 113.

40. According to Bruce Cumings, the beginning of armed conflict and "organized guerrilla warfare on the Korean mainland dates from November 1948. . . . In early 1949 the CIA estimated that the total number of guerrillas in the South was somewhere between 3,500 and 6,000, not counting several thousand more on Cheju Island" (*Korea's Place in the Sun*, 243). Cumings also asserts that during the time between the withdrawal of U.S. troops in July 1949 and the beginning of the war in June 1950, Americans never actually left Korea, because they were "the principal source of external involvement in the guerrilla war" (245).

41. Conway-Lanz, "Beyond No Gun Ri," 55.

42. Hanley, Choe, and Mendoza, *Bridge at No Gun Ri*, 181.

43. Ibid., 102.

44. As documented by Roy Appleman, an officially employed military historian, some of the worst atrocities were committed by the North Korean army. One of these incidents was the Tajeon massacre, in which five to ten thousand people were killed and buried in mass graves. According to Jon Halliday and Bruce Cumings, "What actually happened in the Taejon atrocity is not at all clear"; a London newspaper suggested that the Tajeon massacre was committed by "South Korean police, under the supervision of American advisers" (*Korea: The Unknown War* [New York: Pantheon Books, 1988], 90). In *Korea's Place in the Sun*, Cumings contends that "all sides in the war were guilty of atrocities," but

"captured North Korean documents continued to show that high-level officials warned against executing people" (272–73). While it is well documented that the North Korean military was brutal, the point is that official histories in the United States have deleted all information about similar atrocities committed by Americans.

45. From the oral history of Chun Suntae, who was a high school student at the time that the war officially broke out. In his interview, he recalled that North Korean soldiers gave him survival tips to protect himself against "indiscriminate" American bomber planes. Chun Suntae, quoted in the collective art project *Still Present Pasts: Korean Americans and the "Forgotten War."* For more information, see http://www.stillpresentpasts.org.

46. People's Korea, "GIs' Mass Killings and U.S. Germ Warfare in Korea: Joint White Paper," http://www.korea-np.co.jp/pk/181st_issue/2002061503.htm (accessed October 14, 2002).

47. Hanley, Choe, and Mendoza, *Bridge at No Gun Ri,* 188.

48. Roy Appleman, *South to the Naktong, North to the Yalu: June–November 1950* (Washington, D.C.: Office of the Chief of Military History, Department of the Army, 1961), 251. This is from a five-volume series that calls itself "the narrative of the Korean War."

49. Conway-Lanz, "Beyond No Gun Ri," 65.

50. George Barrett, "U.N. Losing Favor by Korean Damage," *New York Times,* March 3, 1951, 2.

51. Colonel Turner C. Rogers, "Memo: Policy on Strafing Civilian Refugees," July 25, 1950, declassified June 6, 2000, U.S. National Archives, College Park, Maryland.

52. Jackie Orr, *Panic Diaries: A Genealogy of Panic Disorder* (Durham, N.C.: Duke University Press, 2006), 6–7.

53. Rogers, "Policy on Strafing."

54. Hanley, Choe, and Mendoza, *Bridge at No Gun Ri,* 164.

55. "Korea Aid Pledges Worry U.N. Agent," *New York Times,* August 9, 1951, 2.

56. Stone, *Hidden History,* 256–58.

57. GlobalSecurity.org, "Napalm," http://www.globalsecurity.org/military/systems/munitions/napalm.htm (accessed June 22, 2007).

58. Cumings, *Korea's Place in the Sun,* 290.

59. Halliday and Cumings, *Unknown War,* 123.

60. The caption of a 1951 Department of Defense, Department of the Air Force, photograph reads: "Napalm Carrier. . . . One hundred and fifty gallons of flaming death . . . speeds on its way towards enemy lines in Korea." U.S. National Archives and Records Administration, Washington, D.C.

61. *This is Korea!* directed by John Ford, videorecording (Uncle Sam Movies, 1951). The scene depicts the use of napalm against Korean civilians as John Wayne narrates.

62. Reginald Thompson, *Cry Korea* (London: MacDonald, 1951), 143, as quoted in Cumings, *Korea's Place in the Sun*, 271.

63. Cumings, *Korea's Place in the Sun*, 271.

64. Halliday and Cumings, *Unknown War*, 92.

65. Barrett, "U.N. Losing Favor by Korean Damage."

66. Lieutenant Colonel Dave Grossman, *On Killing: The Psychological Cost of Learning to Kill in War and Society* (Boston: Little, Brown, 1995), 137.

67. Hanley, Choe, and Mendoza, *Bridge at No Gun Ri*, 224. From Thomas Anderson's novel *Your Own Beloved Sons*, in which, after having executed two North Korean prisoners, the protagonist shrugs off the killing by asking, "What's a couple of gooks? A couple of goddamn gooks?"

68. GlobalSecurity.org, "Napalm."

69. Gilbert Dreyfus, "Classification of Napalm Burns," expert testimony presented at the Vietnam War Crimes Tribunal, session 2, Roskilde, Denmark, 1967, available at http://www.911review.org/Wget/www.homeusers.prestel.co.uk/littleton/v1201dre.htm (accessed May 4, 2004).

70. Harry Truman, "Statement by the President," June 27, 1950, available at http://www.trumanlibrary.org/whistlestop/study_collections/korea/large/week1/kw_27_1.jpg (retrieved May 4, 2004).

71. Oberdorfer, *Two Koreas*, 8–9.

72. Hanley, Choe, and Mendoza, *Bridge at No Gun Ri*, 225.

73. People's Korea, "GIs' Mass Killings."

74. Stone, *Hidden History*, 258.

75. People's Korea, "DPRK Foreign Ministry Memorandum on GI Mass Killings," http://www.korea-np.co.jp/pk/135th_issue/2000032902.htm (accessed October 15, 2002).

76. Conway-Lanz, "Beyond No Gun Ri," 78–79.

77. "100 Children Reported Killed," *New York Times*, March 30, 1951, 5.

78. As I. F. Stone pointed out in *The Hidden History of the Korean War*, the U.S. military's operational summaries reported "excellent results" regardless of how devastating their operations were to civilian life. He even suggested that the scale of destruction was the measure by which the success of operations was judged.

79. Dreyfus, "Classification of Napalm Burns."

80. Ibid.

81. Conway-Lanz, "Beyond No Gun Ri," 70, 79.

82. "Korea Aid Pledges Worry U.N. Agent."

83. Hanley, Choe, and Mendoza, *Bridge at No Gun Ri*, 180.

84. From the oral history of Chun Suntae in *Still Present Pasts*.

85. Halliday and Cumings, *Unknown War*, 144.

86. Ibid., 172.

87. Judith Butler, *Antigone's Claim: Kinship between Life and Death* (New York: Columbia University Press, 2000), 64.

88. Hanley, Choe, and Mendoza, *Bridge at No Gun Ri,* 189.

89. Ibid., 191.

90. Ibid., 192.

91. Ibid., 244.

92. Massumi, *Parables for the Virtual,* 28–29.

93. Catherine Lutz and J .L. Collins, *Reading National Geographic* (Chicago: University of Chicago Press, 1993), 35.

94. During my analysis of the National Archives' photographic documents of U.S. involvement in the Korean War, I looked at about a thousand photographs taken during 1950–54. I found several hundred depicting Americans visiting orphanages, distributing relief goods to refugees, handing out candy to crowds of children, teaching Korean boys how to play American sports, enjoying the entertainment provided by young (typically female) singers and dancers, and participating in a generally convivial relationship with South Koreans. While it was common to find photographs of refugee groups or of the bodies of dead and living North Korean and Chinese POWs, I found only four photographs that depicted collateral damage that was a direct result of U.S. or U.N. bombings and two others that showed wounded civilians without naming the sources of their wounding. Three of these six photographs were stamped "Restricted for Security Purposes" or "For Official Use Only." Additionally, I found several photographs from a U.N. civil assistance series that depicted families whose homes had been damaged or destroyed, as well as "women in squalor," but without making an explicit link between the U.N.'s complicity in the destruction that had caused these people to live "in squalor." The paucity of photographs showing damage to civilian life, in relation to the surplus of photographs showing Americans aiding Koreans, demonstrates Avery Gordon's notion of finding photographic evidence of an absence. See Gordon, *Ghostly Matters: Haunting and the Sociological Imagination* (Minneapolis: University of Minnesota Press, 1997), 35.

95. Kang Sŏk-kyŏng, "Days and Dreams," in *Words of Farewell: Stories by Korean Women Writers,* ed. and trans. Bruce Fulton and Ju-chan Fulton (Seattle: Seal Press, 1989), 17–18.

96. Bruce Cumings, *The Origins of the Korean War: Liberation and the Emergence of Separate Regimes, 1945–1947* (Princeton, N.J.: Princeton University Press, 1981), xix.

97. One Korean War survivor commented on the inequitable distribution of resources among Koreans and Americans during the Korean War, noting particularly that property that had once belonged to Koreans was appropriated by the U.S. military: "Americans in Korea live with big equipment, big car, big house. Even M&M's and Snickers are huge. And they take big buildings everywhere. We just live in the street. The small elementary school, middle school, high school is their camp. We cannot go inside the school, even though it was our school before the war, we just stayed outside the wall" (quoted in *Still Present Pasts*).

98. Katharine Moon argues that Koreans living near camptowns were almost completely dependent on the U.S. military for their livelihoods during the 1960s and 1970s; 60 percent of the population of Uijeongbu in the 1960s and 80 percent of the population of Songtan in the 1970s catered to American servicemen in one way or another. See Katharine H. S. Moon, *Sex among Allies: Military Prostitution in U.S.–Korea Relations* (New York: Columbia University Press, 1997), 28.

99. Hosu Kim, "The Parched Tongue," in *The Affective Turn: Theorizing the Social,* ed. Patricia Clough with Jean Halley (Durham, N.C.: Duke University Press, 2007), 40. These words were familiar to any Korean, as Kim suggests, because of a popular wartime song about begging Americans for their leftovers. It roughly translates as "Hello, hello, please give me chocolate. I'll even take the one you're eating."

100. Chungmoo Choi, "Nationalism and Construction of Gender in Korea," 15. This word appears again in chapter 4, where it is transliterated in Park Wan-so's short story as "saxi."

101. *Still Present Pasts.*

102. It is interesting to note the superlatives that were commonly used by high-ranking officials in their statements about the harm inflicted on the Korean people. Donald Kingsley, the agent general of the U.N. Korean Reconstruction Agency, said that refugees in South Korean camps were "in the worst condition I've ever seen, and that includes Greece in 1947" ("Korea Aid Pledges Worry U.N. Agent"). Similarly, Charles R. Joy, head of an international relief organization, wrote in a 1952 summary of the devastation caused by the war, "In twelve successive years of relief work in different parts of the world I have never seen such destitution and widespread misery as I have seen here" (as quoted in Conway-Lanz, "Beyond No Gun Ri," 80).

103. Halliday and Cumings, *Korea: The Unknown War,* 118.

3. Tracing the Disappearance of the Yanggongju

1. Theresa Hak Kyung Cha, *Dictée* (New York: Tanam, 1982), 49.

2. Brent Hayes Edwards, *The Practice of Diaspora* (Cambridge, Mass.: Harvard University Press, 2003), 7.

3. Ibid., 15.

4. In looking at the African diaspora and black internationalism, Edwards also notes the ways in which the city represents a kind of movement, "even for populations that did not travel" (ibid., 4). Similarly, the division of the peninsula and the unresolved status of the war psychically stand for movement, for both the Korean populations that have traveled and those that have not.

5. Hyun-Yi Kang, "Re-Membering Home," in *Dangerous Women: Gender and Korean Nationalism,* ed. Elaine Kim and Chungmoo Choi (New York: Routledge, 1998), 250.

6. Kang, "Re-Membering Home," 250.

7. South Korea, because of its subordinate status to the U.S., was not a signatory.

8. David Eng and David Kazanjian, eds., *Loss: The Politics of Mourning* (Berkeley: University of California Press, 2003), 2.

9. Bruce Cumings, "Silent but Deadly: Sexual Subordination in the U.S.–Korean Relationship," in *Let the Good Times Roll: Prostitution and the U.S. Military in Asia,* ed. Saundra Sturdevant and Brenda Stoltzfus (New York: New Press, 1992), 174.

10. Yoshimi Yoshiaki, *Comfort Women: Sexual Slavery in the Japanese Military during World War II* (New York: Columbia University Press, 2000), 180.

11. Keith Howard, *True Stories of the Korean Comfort Women* (London: Cassell, 1995).

12. Chunghee Sarah Soh, "Women's Sexual Labor and State in Korean History," *Journal of Women's History* 15, no. 4 (2004): 171. Chungmoo Choi also discusses the stigmas associated with the *hwanhyangnyeo* and their effects on returning comfort women in "Nationalism and the Construction of Gender in Korea," in *Dangerous Women: Gender and Korean Nationalism,* ed. Elaine Kim and Chungmoo Choi (New York: Routledge, 1998), 9–31.

13. Elaine Kim, "Teumsae-eso: Korean American Women between Feminism and Nationalism," in *Violence and the Body: Race, Gender, and the State,* ed. Arturo Aldama and Alfred Arteaga (Bloomington: Indiana University Press, 2003), 311.

14. Cha, *Dictée,* 57.

15. Elaine Kim, "'Bad Women': Asian American Visual Artists Hanh Thi Pham, Hung Liu, and Yong Soon Min," *Feminist Studies* 22, no. 3 (Autumn 1996): 575.

16. These numbers are from Joan Nagel, *Race, Ethnicity, and Sexuality: Intimate Intersections, Forbidden Frontiers* (New York: Oxford University Press, 2003), 178. However, in 2004 the Bush administration announced a plan for global troop redeployment that would reduce the number of troops stationed in Korea (37,000 in 2004) by one-third over the course of four years, and thirty-six bases are scheduled to be returned to Korea by 2011. These changes have really resulted not in a reduction of U.S. troop power in South Korea but rather in a consolidation of power and an expansion of Camp Humphreys into a megabase that has displaced residents in the farming region of Pyeongtaek. A series of clashes between farmers and the military ensued in 2006. This is one of the most recent sites of anti-American protest in South Korea.

17. In addition to the political and economic forces that have sent Southeast Asian and Russian sex workers to Korea in recent years, the closings of military bases have also caused transnational flows of labor. Anti-American protest in the Philippines, for example, led to the closings of U.S. bases there. These closings were followed by an influx of Filipina workers into the camptowns in Korea. See Gwyn Kirk and Carolyn Bowen Francis, "Redefining Security: Women Challenge U.S. Military Policy and Practice in East Asia," *Berkeley Journal of Law*

15 (2000): 229–72. For a discussion of the impact of base closings on women's lives, particularly in the absence of a larger feminist critique of militarism, see Cynthia Enloe, *Bananas, Beaches, and Bases: Making Feminist Sense of International Politics* (Berkeley: University of California Press, 1989).

18. Jungmin Seo, "Korean Chinese Migrant Workers and the Politics of Korean Nationalism," paper presented at the annual meeting of the International Studies Association, Hilton Hawaiian Village, Honolulu, Hawaii, March 5, 2005.

19. J. T. Takagi and Hye Jung Park, *The Women Outside: Korean Women and the U.S. Military* (New York: Third World News Reel, 1996).

20. Katharine H. S. Moon, *Sex among Allies: Military Prostitution in U.S.–Korea Relations* (New York: Columbia University Press, 1997), 155.

21. The translator's note states: "A Pasque-flower is called in Korean an 'old woman flower,' because it has very little attraction of any kind. The name of the flower, therefore, is often used as a simile for old women who have lost all attraction as women." Park Wan-so, "A Pasque Flower on That Bleak Day," in *The Rainy Spell and Other Korean Stories,* trans. J. Suh (New York: M. E. Sharpe/UNESCO Publishing, 1998), 204.

22. Park, "A Pasque Flower," 206–7.

23. Ibid., 212.

24. Ibid., 209, 212.

25. Charles J. Hanley, Sang-Hun Choe, and Martha Mendoza, *The Bridge at No Gun Ri: A Hidden Nightmare from the Korean War* (New York: Henry Holt and Company, 2001).

26. Yun Jeong-mo, as quoted and translated by Yoo Chul-In in "Life Histories of Two Korean Women Who Marry American GIs," Ph.D. diss., University of Illinois at Urbana-Champaign 1993, 27. Yoo also notes that Yun confesses in her postscript that the story was based on her younger sister and that writing it allowed her "to liberate myself fully from my 'blood' history, and to relieve myself from the swamp of my past" (12).

27. Chang Soam, as quoted in the collective art project *Still Present Pasts: Korean Americans and the "Forgotten War."* For more information, see http://www.stillpresentpasts.org.

28. Moon, *Sex among Allies,* 8; Ji-Yeon Yuh, *Beyond the Shadow of Camptown: Korean Military Brides in America* (New York: New York University Press, 2002), 34.

29. Takagi and Park, *The Women Outside.*

30. Ibid.

31. Jacqueline Rose, *States of Fantasy* (Oxford, England: Oxford University Press, 1996), 5.

32. Nagel, *Race, Ethnicity, and Sexuality,* 179.

33. John Lie, "The Transformation of Sexual Work in 20th-Century Korea," *Gender & Society* 9, no. 3 (1995): 316.

34. Ibid.

35. Moon, *Sex among Allies,* 46.

36. Hanley, Choe, and Mendoza, *Bridge at No Gun Ri;* Kang Sŏk-kyŏng, "Days and Dreams," in *Words of Farewell: Stories by Korean Women Writers,* ed. and trans. Bruce Fulton and Ju-chan Fulton (Seattle: Seal Press, 1989); Hosu Kim, "The Parched Tongue," in *Affective Turn: Theorizing the Social,* ed. Patricia Clough with Jean Halley (Durham, N.C.: Duke University Press, 2007), 34–46.

37. Hyun Sook Kim, "Yanggongju as an Allegory of the Nation," in *Dangerous Women: Gender and Korean Nationalism,* ed. Elaine Kim and Chungmoo Choi (New York: Routledge, 1998), 175–202.

38. Nagel, *Race, Ethnicity, and Sexuality,* 141.

39. Hong Sung-nam, *A Flower in Hell: Fascinating Inferno of Desire,* http://www.piff.org/eng/program/shin_5_1.asp (accessed October 6, 2002).

40. Park, "A Pasque Flower," 212.

41. According to Moon, in *Sex among Allies,* a series of prohibitions against prostitution were enacted during the U.S. occupation of South Korea from 1945 to 1948. There were conflicting regulations and loopholes that prevented the enforcement of these laws against the U.S. military, and by the 1948 transfer of power to Koreans, "GI prostitution [was] already in full swing" (47).

42. Soh, "Women's Sexual Labor and State in Korean History," 174. Soh includes income generated from commercial sex establishments catering to both Japanese businessmen and American servicemen. Both forms of prostitution have been supported by the South Korean state and are historically located within a context of postcolonial and neocolonial relations with the countries in question.

43. Young-Ju Hoang, "The Political Power of Mythology: A Feminist Critique of Modern State Practices in Korea," *Social Alternatives* 24, no. 2 (2005): 68.

44. Ibid. In particular, Hoang offers a reading of the folktale of Shimchong as an allegory of the idea that women's labor is included in nationalist discourses only when their work involves a personal sacrifice to save their fathers or the nation. In the folktale, the eleven-year-old Shimch'ong must earn three hundred bags of rice to save her father's eyesight. She sacrifices her virginity to the sea god in exchange for the rice, saves her father and herself, and is thus exalted to the status of an empress. Hoang argues that military sexual laborers were modern-day versions of Shimchong who "had to sell their bodies . . . to save their fathers and the state. But the reward these women received was rather different than the one Shimchong was given in the fairy tale. There was no glorification, no happy end" (68).

45. Moon, *Sex among Allies,* 158.

46. Ibid., 154.

47. Hoang, "Political Power of Mythology," 68.

48. Ibid. As reported in Yoo Chul-In's dissertation, "Life Histories of Two Korean Women," both women featured said that supporting their brothers' educations had been one of the biggest factors in their decisions to seek work at a camptown.

49. For a good overview of this issue, see Enloe, *Bananas, Beaches, and Bases.*

50. Seungsook Moon, *Militarized Modernity and Gendered Citizenship in South Korea* (Durham, N.C.: Duke University Press, 2005), 75–76.

51. Ibid., 75.

52. Choi Jang Jip, "Political Cleaveages in South Korea," in *State and Society in Contemporary Korea,* ed. Hagen Koo (Ithaca, N.Y.: Cornell University Press, 1993). According to Choi, the years 1967–76 saw the largest migration of people (20 percent of the entire population) from rural areas into the cities than did any other period during South Korea's history, including the period during the Korean War. By the mid-1970s, "the bulk of the population had migrated to the cities and the farming population had declined by half" (28).

53. Moon, *Sex among Allies,* 3.

54. Yuh, *Beyond the Shadow of Camptown,* 238.

55. Moon, *Sex among Allies;* Saundra Sturdevant and Brenda Stoltzfus, eds., *Let the Good Times Roll: Prostitution and the U.S. Military in Asia* (New York: New Press, 1992).

56. Wendy Chapkis, *Live Sex Acts: Women Performing Erotic Labor* (New York: Routledge, 1997), 166 (emphasis in the original).

57. Sturdevant and Stoltzfus, *Let the Good Times Roll,* 211.

58. Moon, *Sex among Allies,* 39.

59. For a discussion of the imperfect discipline of social identities, see Rafael de la Dehesa, *Sexual Modernities: Queering the Public Sphere in Latin America* (Durham, N.C. Duke University Press, forthcoming).

60. Moon, *Sex among Allies,* 153.

61. Besides being under constant surveillance, camptown prostitutes are also typically debt-bound, according to Moon and the women she has interviewed. A worker in the clubs accrues large debts before she ever sees her first client, and because she does not typically earn enough money to cover her expenses, the debt accumulates, motivating her to take on more and more clients. But it is unlikely that a woman will be able to pay off her debts by herself. This places her in a position in which her choices are to continue working this way until she ages out and is let go, to look for a benevolent American client who will settle her account, or to escape. If a *gijichon* worker attempts to leave before she has paid, a "slicky boy" is sent out to "rough up the girls who [don't] pay [their club debts]" (*Sex among Allies,* 21).

62. Yoshiaki, *Comfort Women,* 180.

63. Moon, *Sex among Allies,* 153.

64. Sturdevant and Stoltzfus, *Let the Good Times Roll,* 213–14.

65. Giorgio Agamben, *Homo Sacer: Sovereign Power and Bare Life* (Stanford, Calif.: Stanford University Press, 1998), 168–69.

66. Ibid., 171.

67. Ibid., 170–71.

68. People's Action for Reform of the Unjust ROK–US SOFA (Status of Forces Agreement), unpublished educational materials. People's Action is one of many *ban-mi,* or antibase activist groups in Korea. They have taken up concerns

of environmental damage caused by U.S. forces in Korea and were instrumental in the closing of the bombing range at Maehyang-ri.

69. While official statistics in Korea document hundreds, sometimes thousands, of crimes perpetrated by U.S. servicemen against Koreans each year, the SOFA prohibits the Korean government from exercising jurisdiction over U.S. military personnel. In essence, the SOFA provides protections to U.S. servicemen who are accused of crimes, but not to Koreans who are crime victims. What these statistics do not accurately portray is the extent to which the victims are sex workers, because most of these crimes are committed in the camptowns.

70. Kim, "Yanggongju as an Allegory," 189.

71. Choi, "Political Cleavages," 24.

72. Kim, "Yanggongju as an Allegory," 191.

73. The first major event of the *minjung* movement took place in May of 1980, when the people of the city of Gwangju spontaneously organized en masse to protest the imposition of martial law. Subsequently, hundreds, perhaps thousands, of protesters were massacred by the military police and the use of lethal force was authorized by a U.S. military commander. The second significant event of the 1980s was "The Great June Struggle" or "The June Uprising" of 1987, which involved ongoing nationwide protests by students and workers demanding constitutional reform and direct presidential elections.

74. Cheong Seon-hoe, *21 Segi yeoksa i–agi* (Telling the story of 21st-century history) (Seoul: Korea Media, 2005), 59. The translation was provided by Hosu Kim.

75. Ibid.

76. Kimsoft, "U.S. Military Personnel Commit More Than 600 Crimes a Year in Korea: None of the Crimes Committed 'While on Duty' Has Been Prosecuted in Korean Courts," http://www.kimsoft.com/2002/us–sofa.htm (accessed November 15, 2005).

77. Go Yoo-gyeong, "Present and Past of Crimes Committed by the U.S. Forces in South Korea," *Afghan Tribunal*, 2002, http://afghan-tribunal.3005.net/english/presentandpastofcrimescommitedbytheusforcesinsk.htm (accessed November 17, 2005).

78. See also "The National Campaign for the Eradication of Crimes by U.S. Troops in Korea," available at the Web site for the National Campaign for the Eradication of Crimes by U.S. Forces in Korea (USKF), http://usacrime.or.kr/ENG/introduction–main.htm (accessed November 17, 2005), and K. N. Kim, "Rising U.S. Army Crimes," *Asian Human Rights Commission*—Human Rights Solidarity, 1994, available at http://hrsolidarity.net/mainfile.php/1994vol01no01/1937/ (accessed November 17, 2005).

79. Kim, "Rising U.S. Army Crimes."

80. Cheong, *21 Segi yeoksa i–agi*, 60.

81. Rose, *States of Fantasy*, 24. Here Rose discusses the idea that an object can become so overinvested with feeling that it becomes the disputed subject of

a political battle. Borrowing the concept of "land pornography" from Palestinian writer and lawyer Raja Shehadeh, Rose describes how transgenerational haunting materializes—in "the way exile and loss transmute themselves into the most fervent forms of nationalist possession" (24).

82. Rolando Tolentino, "Mattering National Bodies and Sexualities: Corporeal Contest in Marcos and Brocka," in *Violence and the Body*, ed. Arturo J. Aldama and Alfred Arteaga (Bloomington: Indiana University Press, 2003). In his discussion of violence and nationalism in the Philippines, Tolentino argues that "the mattering of national bodies involves the politicization of bodies for hegemonic use" (121). The primary means through which this mattering is achieved is the use of spectacle, which Tolentino says is a mechanism for demarcating privileged from marginalized bodies, privileged from marginalized positions in national and transnational politics. He cites the creation of bodies for strategic purposes and the disappearance of these same bodies when they are no longer useful for the politics of nation.

83. Kim, "Teumsae-eso," 317.

84. Kim, "Yanggongju as an Allegory," 190.

85. Ibid.

86. Min-Jung Kim describes the major concern of dissident nationalism as "rewriting the official history through the reinscription of subaltern experience," but says that, as an activity often carried out by intellectuals, such rewriting "may deploy the idea of the minjung so that the masses will provide an opening for their own entry into politics." Kim, "Moments of Danger in the (Dis)continuous Relation of Korean Nationalism and Korean American Nationalism," *positions: east asia cultures critique* 5, no. 2 (1997): 365.

87. Inderpal Grewal, "On the New Global Feminism and the Family of Nations: Dilemmas of Transnational Feminist Practice, in *Talking Visions: Multicultural Feminism in a Transnational Age*, ed. Ella Shohat (Cambridge, Mass.: MIT Press/New Museum, 1998), 503.

88. Sara Ahmed, "Affective Economies," *Social Text* 22, no. 2 (2004): 117.

89. Ibid.

90. Cha, *Dictée*, 4.

91. Ch'oe Myŏngsun, "Silent Suffering," in *True Stories of the Korean Comfort Women*, ed. Keith Howard (London: Cassell, 1995), 176.

92. Katharine Moon, "South Korean Movements against Militarized Sexual Labor," *Asian Survey* 39, no. 2 (1998): 310–25.

93. Ibid., 316.

94. Ibid., 313.

95. The question of choice versus force continues to be a contentious issue among women's rights advocates and sex worker activists who are concerned about the fact that anti-trafficking laws provide protection only to workers who can prove that they were forced to work against their will, not to those who entered the sex industry as a means of making a living or for any reason other

than deception or force. A current example of this debate has played out in sex workers' protests against Korea's Sex Trade Prevention Act, which would provide protection and services only to "victims" of the sex industry and would penalize anyone who is deemed to have entered such employment willingly. For more information on these debates, see Sealing Cheng, "Korean Sex Trade 'Victims' Strike for Rights," *Asia Times Online,* December 22, 2004, http://www.atimes.com/atimes/Korea/FL22Dg01.html (accessed July 5, 2007); Kim Moonhee, "A Declaration," trans. Kim Young Mi, *Inter-Asia Cultural Studies* 7, no. 2 (2006): 338–40; and Ko Gaphee, "Sex Work in Asia and Voices from the Spot: Sex Trade/Sex Work in Korea and Asia," *Inter-Asia Cultural Studies* 7, no. 2 (2006): 319–21. For a more general discussion of trafficking discourse, see Melissa Ditmore, "In Calcutta, Sex Workers are Organizing," in *Affective Turn: Theorizing the Social,* ed. Patricia Clough with Jean Halley (Durham, N.C.: Duke University Press, 2007), 170–86, and Melissa Hope Ditmore, "Feminism," in *Encyclopedia of Prostitution and Sex Work,* ed. Melissa Hope Ditmore (Westport, Conn.: Greenwood, 2006), 154–60.

96. Soh, "Women's Sexual Labor and State in Korean History," 170.

97. Kim, "Bad Women," 574.

98. I was in Korea during the time of the girls' deaths, but the incident was not picked up by the media right away because the country was consumed by World Cup fever. Because of my limited Korean, I gravitated toward English-language television stations, one of which was the USFK channel. It issued warnings to American military personnel about "mobs of angry Koreans." No matter how long I watched the USFK channel, I could not identify the cause for such anger in the midst of national elation over "the Reds'" stunning victories. I learned of the travesty in Uijeongbu belatedly, after I returned to the United States.

99. See the photo gallery of the crime scene and investigation at http://voiceofpeople.org/new/photo/index.htm, among other sites.

100. Hosu Kim, personal communication, 2005.

101. Ann Anlin Cheng, *The Melancholy of Race* (New York: Oxford University Press, 2001), 145.

102. Edwards, *Practice of Diaspora,* 12.

103. "The Dream of the Audience" was the title of a retrospective exhibit of Theresa Hak Kyung Cha's life and work organized by the University of California–Berkeley Art Museum, on tour from 2001 to 2003. The quotations in this passage are from Cha's *Dictée.*

104. In the fall of 2002, I participated in Bill Stimson's dream group, which used Monte Ullman's process of collective dream interpretation. I had this dream shortly after my first trip back to Korea as an adult and shortly before I began working on this project. It was one of my first engagements with a method of examining the collective unconscious, one that propelled me into writing about haunted histories.

4. The Fantasy of Honorary Whiteness

1. Katharine H. S. Moon, *Sex among Allies: Military Prostitution in U.S.–Korea Relations* (New York: Columbia University Press, 1997); Kang Sŏk-kyŏng, "Days and Dreams," in *Words of Farewell: Stories by Korean Women Writers,* ed. and trans. Bruce Fulton and Ju-chan Fulton (Seattle: Seal Press, 1989), 22.

2. Alexandra Suh, "From 'A Short Time' to 'A Way Out': Race, Militarism, and Korean Sex Workers in New York," *Colorlines* 2, no. 1 (Spring 1999): 30.

3. "A War Bride Named 'Blue' Comes Home: Johnie Morgan Returns to the U.S. with a Korean Wife Who Once Walked 200 Miles to Be with Him," *Life Magazine* 31, no. 19 (November 5, 1951): 41.

4. Ibid.

5. Yoo Chul-In, "Life Histories of Two Korean Women Who Marry American GIs," Ph.D. diss., University of Illinois at Urbana-Champaign 1993, 33. Yoo's interpretation of the name "Western princess" is that it reveals how "Korean society imagines her as 'Cinderella' becoming a western princess is an escape from poverty and the Korean morals of virginity and chastity" (33).

6. Yoo, "Life Histories of Two Korean Women," 142.

7. Kang, "Days and Dreams," 23.

8. Ibid., 24.

9. Ibid., 27.

10. Ibid.

11. Unlike in much of the social science and social work research on Korean military sex workers, we see in Kang's work a portrayal of a yanggongju who takes a certain kind of pleasure in her work, even if she is jaded. I have been asked about the extent to which desire plays a role in women's decisions to enter camptown prostitution. Although I am reluctant to answer this question without first deconstructing the notion of "choice," the sources of data available about camptown prostitution say that most women are drawn into the work by economic necessity rather than coercion, on one hand, or sexual desire, on the other. However, the stigma against prostitution, particularly military prostitution, is so great that few women would actually admit that sexual desire was one of their motivations. As I suggest in this chapter, a collective desire for America is a motivating force that trumps individualized sexual desire.

12. Hyun Sook Kim, "Yanggongju as an Allegory of the Nation," in *Dangerous Women: Gender and Korean Nationalism,* ed. Elaine Kim and Chungmoo Choi (New York: Routledge, 1998).

13. Yoo, "Life Histories of Two Korean Women," 33.

14. David Eng and David Kazanjian, eds., *Loss: The Politics of Mourning* (Berkeley: University of California Press, 2003), ix.

15. The following vignettes about Yanggongjus One through Seven are based on Ramsay Liem's oral history work with Korean War survivors as presented in the collective art project *Still Present Pasts: Korean Americans and the "Forgotten War"* (see http://www.stillpresentpasts.org) and as published in "History,

Trauma, and Identity: The Legacy of the Korean War for Korean Americans," *Amerasia Journal* 29, no. 3 (2003/4): 111–29; Ji-Yeon Yuh's oral history work with military brides as depicted in *Beyond the Shadow of Camptown;* Yoo Chul-In's dissertation, "The Life Histories of Two Korean Women Who Married American GIs"; the women featured in J. T. Takagi and Hye Jung Park's documentary film *The Women Outside: Korean Women and the U.S. Military* (New York: Third World News Reel, 1996); social work literature about battered Korean immigrant women; media interviews with biracial Korean Americans; accounts of high-profile yanggongjus such as Yun Geum-i and Chong Sun France, a Korean military bride who was convicted of murdering her child; personal communications with Korean military brides and their children; and my childhood memories of growing up in a mixed-race household and among other children whose Korean mothers were married to U.S. military personnel.

16. *Still Present Pasts.*

17. Jong Yeon Brewer, "Language Loss in Korean–American Biracial/Bicultural Military Families," Ph.D. diss., University of Arizona, Tucson, 2003, 13.

18. Yoo, "Life Histories of Two Korean Women," 110.

19. Kim, "Bad Women," 577.

20. Although the school recently changed its name to Cross-Cultural School, I have chosen to use the name that was used when Yang Hyang Kim was featured in the film in 1996. For most of the school's history, from 1971 until 2000, this service was called "Bride School" and catered to Korean women who were married or engaged to U.S. servicemen. Besides the name change, there has been an effort to recruit couples rather than just brides-to-be, but, as Yvonne Park, the school's director points out, most American servicemen are not interested in learning about the cultures of their spouses and fiancées: "Their idea is: 'We are not going to live in Korea. . . . Just teach my wife." See Jacob Adelman, "Bride School Prepares Korean Women for Challenges of Married Life Stateside," 1999, http://jacobadelman.com/clips/kh/brd.html (accessed March 2, 2004).

21. Michael Baker, "The Perfect American Wife, Korean-Style," *Christian Science Monitor,* November 17, 1998, http://search.csmonitor.com/durable/1998/11/17/p1s4.htm (accessed March 2, 2004).

22. Yuh, *Beyond the Shadow of Camptown,* 12.

23. Robert E. Park and E. Burgess, *Introduction to the Science of Sociology* (1921; repr. Chicago: University of Chicago Press, 1969); Herbert Gans, "Symbolic Ethnicity: The Future of Ethnic Groups and Cultures in America," *Ethnic and Racial Studies* 2 (1979): 1–20.

24. Ann Anlin Cheng, *The Melancholy of Race* (New York: Oxford University Press, 2001), 28.

25. A particularly significant challenge from within the field came from Mia Tuan, *Forever Foreigners or Honorary Whites? The Asian Ethnic Experience Today* (New Brunswick, N.J.: Rutgers University Press, 1998).

26. A. Williams, "Sisters Think Parents Did O.K.," *New York Times,* Style, October 16, 2005, 1.

27. Richard Alba and Victor Nee, "Rethinking Assimilation Theory for a New Era of Immigration," *International Migration Review* 31, no. 4 (1997): 839.

28. Pyong Gap Min, ed., *Asian Americans: Contemporary Trends and Issues* (Thousand Oaks, Calif.: Sage, 1995).

29. Foner gave her talk about one week after September 11. In the talk, she did not make distinctions among Asian groups, treating South Asians and East Asians alike as "honorary whites." During the question-and-answer period, I asked how she understood the wave of violence against South Asians and people "who appeared to be Arab" during the aftermath of September 11 if all Asians were indeed "honorary whites." I suggested that the events following 9/11 showed evidence that Asian Americans were not as close to being white as sociologists of immigration once thought and that the moment in which we were living provided an opportunity for sociologists to revise the story line about Asian assimilation in the United States. At this point, the seminar coordinator went to the next question rather than giving Foner time to respond to my concerns. A few questions later, another Asian American scholar said, "I would like to repeat the question Grace asked since it was not answered," but the question was glossed over again. Perhaps the revision of the story about Asians in the United States is also a rupturing of a sociological fantasy in which sociologists have as much investment as do those who are called "honorary whites."

30. Cheng, *Melancholy of Race;* David Eng, *Racial Castration: Managing Masculinity in America* (Durham, N.C.: Duke University Press 2001); David Eng and Shinhee Han, "A Dialogue on Racial Melancholia," *Psychoanalytic Dialogues* 10, no. 4 (2000): 667–700; Lisa Lowe, *Immigrant Acts: On Asian American Cultural Politics* (Durham, N.C.: Duke University Press, 1996); Jasbir Puar and Amit Rai, "The Remaking of a Model Minority: Perverse Projectiles under the Specter of (Counter)Terrorism," *Social Text* 22, no. 3 (2004): 75–104.

31. Lowe, *Immigrant Acts,* 17.

32. Alba and Nee, "Rethinking Assimilation Theory;" Pyong Gap Min and Rose Kim, eds., *Struggle for Ethnic Identity: Narratives by Asian American Professionals* (Walnut Creek, Calif.: AltaMira, 1999).

33. Min, *Asian Americans,* 219–20.

34. Ibid., 220.

35. Brewer, "Language Loss in Korean–American Families," 10.

36. Yoo, "Life Histories of Two Korean Women," 132.

37. Eng, *Racial Castration,* 37.

38. Cheng, *Melancholy of Race,* 10.

39. Ibid., 7.

40. Takagi and Park, *Women Outside.*

41. Lowe, *Immigrant Acts,* 33.

42. Nicolas Abraham and Maria Torok, *The Shell and the Kernel: Renewals of Psychoanalysis,* vol. 1, ed. and trans. Nicholas T. Rand (Chicago: University of Chicago Press, 1994), 176.

43. Ishle Park, *The Temperature of This Water* (New York: Kaya, 2003).

44. Heinz Insu Fenkl, *Memories of My Ghost Brother* (New York: Dutton, 1996), 267.

45. For an analysis of how this investment produces Korean birth mothers and overseas adoptees as bodies of national development, see Hosu Kim, "Mothers without Mothering: The Emergent Figure of the Birthmother in South Korea," in *International Korean Adoption: A 50-Year History of Policy and Practice,* ed. Kathleen Ja Sook Bergquist, E. Vonk, and Dongsoo Kim (Binghamton, N.Y.: Haworth, 2007).

46. Fenkl, *Ghost Brother,* 229.

47. Bruce Cumings, "Silent but Deadly: Sexual Subordination in the U.S.–Korean Relationship," in *Let the Good Times Roll: Prostitution and the U.S. Military in Asia,* ed. Saundra Sturdevant and Brenda Stoltzfus (New York: New Press, 1992)," 171.

48. In the spirit of self-reflexivity, Cumings acknowledges the "superior" tone of his 1968 diary, yet felt compelled to share this depiction with his audience in 1992.

49. Nora Okja Keller, *Fox Girl* (New York: Penguin, 2002), 11.

50. Ibid., 81.

51. Ibid.

52. Ibid., 111. In terms of the issue of missing American fathers in the lives of biracial children in Korea, Keller's work resonates with that of the biracial Vietnamese choreographer Maura Nguyen Donahue, whose work looks at the impact of U.S. militarism on Vietnamese children fathered by U.S. soldiers during the Vietnam War. One of the statistics presented in Donahue's dance piece "SKINning the SurFACE" is that only one in a hundred Amerasian children ever meets his or her biological father. Taken together, these works speak not only to the transgenerational impact of U.S. wars in Asia but also to an unequal historical relationship between the United States and the Asian countries it has invaded in which American soldiers are not held accountable as fathers. This is not simply a fact of war or of U.S. military presence: built into the SOFA governing U.S. troops in Germany, for example, is a requirement that U.S. military officials cooperate with German women who are trying to identify and locate the fathers of their children; the SOFA between the United States and South Korea includes no such provision.

53. Terry Hong, "The Dual Lives of Nora Okja Keller," *Asianweek.com,* April 5, 2002, http://www.asianweek.com/2002_04_05/keller.htm (accessed May 23, 2002). In other interviews, Keller has spoken of being the biracial child of a Korean mother and an American father, but to my knowledge, she has not revealed any details about how her parents met. Perhaps, like other biracial Korean Americans, she may never have been told explicitly about her family history, or, like the haunted subjects of Abraham and Torok's work, she may have felt the tension between her own need to express the traumatic secret and to maintain loyalty to her mother. I have had a number of personal communications with other biracial Korean American scholars and writers who did not want to

"come out" about their own family histories but who remarked that they did indeed feel "haunted" by what their parents would not reveal.

54. Abraham and Torok, *The Shell and the Kernel,* 1: 182.

55. As I have been suggesting, there is not a clear delineation between fact and fiction, particularly when one takes into account both the force of the unconscious and the stigma of prostitution. Even in empirically driven social research there is an element of fictionalization both in the stories that interviewees tell about themselves and in the way the interview data is put into a coherent sociological narrative.

56. Not only are there psychic consequences of investing in honorary whiteness, but there are political costs as well. As Puar and Rai point out, certain Asian bodies have become "ambivalent tests of the model minority construct." For more discussion, see their "Remaking of a Model Minority." Just as the South Asian has slid from model minority to potential terrorist in post-9/11 America, the specter of the axis of evil and North Korean communism have also troubled honorary whiteness in that the scrutiny of Korean American and South Korean activists in the United States has intensified since 9/11. The New York–based Korean community organization Nodutdol, for example, held an antiwar event that was shut down by the Korean Consulate and the Korean CIA for fear that Korean Americans would appear to be "anti–U.S." Those who still aspire to be "honorary whites" must play the role of "good" and "grateful" Koreans by constantly demonstrating loyalty to the United States and disavowing sympathy with North Korea, thereby underscoring that critique is much more dangerous for the nonwhite than for the white, and even for the "honorary white."

57. Michael M. J. Fischer, "Ethnicity and the Postmodern Arts of Memory," in *Writing Culture: The Poetics and Politics of Ethnography,* ed. James Clifford and George E. Marcus. (Berkeley: University of California Press, 1986), 198.

58. Eng and Kazanjian, *Loss,* 13.

59. John Johnston, *Information Multiplicity: American Fiction in the Age of Media Saturation* (Baltimore, Md.: Johns Hopkins University Press, 1998), 45.

5. Diasporic Vision

1. Toni Morrison, *The Bluest Eye* (New York: Plume, 1970), 204.

2. W. E. B. Dubois, *The Souls of Black Folk* (New York: Bantam Books, 1903), 2.

3. Ann Anlin Cheng, *The Melancholy of Race* (New York: Oxford University Press, 2001), 7.

4. Morrison, *Bluest Eye,* 201 (emphasis in the original).

5. Jackie Orr, *Panic Diaries: A Genealogy of Panic Disorder* (Durham, N.C.: Duke University Press, 2006), 18.

6. Nicolas Abraham and Maria Torok, *The Shell and the Kernel: Renewals of Psychoanalysis,* vol. 1, ed. and trans. Nicholas T. Rand (Chicago: University of Chicago Press, 1994), 171.

7. The collaborative work of literary critic David Eng and clinical psychoanalyst Shinhee Han offers an example showing that transgenerational haunting is a symptom of assimilation. They develop a theory of racial melancholia in which the Asian American subjects of their research, patients seeking therapy as well as the subjects of semiautobiographical works of fiction and film, have inherited the unconscious desires and unspoken traumas of their parents. Moving beyond the psychotherapeutic paradigm of "cultural difference," Eng and Han call for a politicization of Asian American therapeutic interventions to recognize that inherited traumas are often linked to collective traumas such as economic and racial injustice. The most dramatic example they give is the internment of Japanese Americans. In the face of legacies of trauma, the notion of Asian American assimilation becomes problematic, if not psychotic. The implication for clinical work is that a psychic haunting can be resolved only transgenerationally and that "an incipient healing process" often involves returning to the site of the other's trauma. Eng and Han, "A Dialogue on Racial Melancholia," *Psychoanalytic Dialogues* 10, no. 4 (2000): 354.

8. My questioning of constructions of mental illness is in no way intended to discount or discourage the efforts of social service providers who work with Korean military brides and sex workers who suffer from psychic pain.

9. Dwight Fee, ed., *Pathology and the Postmodern: Mental Illness as Discourse and Experience* (London: Sage, 2000), 3.

10. Ivan Leudar and Phillip Thomas, *Voices of Reason, Voices of Insanity: Studies of Verbal Hallucinations* (London: Routledge, 2000), 6.

11. Ibid., 83, 13. Leudar and Thomas go on to say, "Most psychiatrists see the 'voices' as symptoms to be suppressed—like coughs, aches, and measles spots—and many users of psychiatric services do indeed want to be rid of voices. Other voice hearers, however, may want to talk about their exceptional experiences in public" (52–53). This suggests that destigmatization is just as important a goal for voice hearers as the medication of their condition.

12. Johnston, "Machinic Vision," Critical Inquiry 26, no. 1 (1999): 44. See also Gilles Deleuze and Félix Guattari, *Anti-Oedipus: Capitalism and Schizophrenia* (Minneapolis: University of Minnesota Press, 1983).

13. This chapter is also an adaptation of a performance text. Portions of it have been performed as "Dreaming in Tongues" (with Hosu Kim), which debuted in *Performing Bodies: Human and Beyond,* Martin Segal Theater, City University of New York, December 13, 2002, and as "6.25: History beneath the Skin" (with Hosu Kim and Hyun Lee, directed by Carolina McNeeley), which debuted as part of the art exhibit *Still Present Pasts: Korean Americans and the "Forgotten War,"* Cambridge Multicultural Arts Center, January 29, 2005. In the live performance, I use sound recordings so that audiences can hear the multiplicity of voices that speak about diasporic trauma.

14. Abraham and Torok, *The Shell and the Kernel,* 1: 176.

15. In the semifictional film version of the *Ukishima Maru* incident, we see only two survivors. At least eighty people have come forward as survivors of the actual incident, however.

16. The *Ukishima Maru* was the first of a series of Japanese naval ships that would return the conscripted Koreans, many of whom were comfort women, to Korea.

17. While the historical accuracy of *Soul's Protest* is debatable, the story is based on the survivors' eyewitness accounts of the *Ukishima Maru* incident, in which they testified that some of the Japanese crew members evacuated the ship shortly before the explosion.

18. Rea Tajiri, *History and Memory*, videorecording (New York: Women Make Movies, 1991). In this chapter, all quotes shaded and set in this type are from the voice-over of *History and Memory*, in which the narrator recounts her mother's experiences in a Japanese American internment camp during World War II. These are experiences that the mother never speaks of and perhaps cannot even remember, yet the daughter inherits the memories through dreams, screen images, and affects of feeling haunted.

19. Hwang Jang-jin, "South Koreans Urge Japan to Take Full Responsibility for 1945 Ship Blast," *Korea Herald*, August 25, 2001, http://www.koreaherald.co.kr/servlet/kherald.article.view?id=200108250034 (accessed June 6, 2002).

20. Richard Lloyd Parry, "Korea Rallies round Kim Jong Il's 'Titanic' Tale of Slave Ship," *Asia Times*, August 24, 2001, http://www.archk.net/news/mainfile.php/ahrnews_200108/1818 (accessed June 6, 2002).

21. "Japan/Korea: 15 South Koreans Awarded 45 Million Yen over Ship Blast," *Japan Times*, August 24, 2001, http://www.archk.net/news/mainfile.php/ahrnews_200108/1818 (accessed June 6, 2002).

22. Chung Hye-Jean, "Two Films Shed Light on 1945 Ship Tragedy," *Korea Times*, September 17, 2001, http://www.koreatimes.co.kr/kt_culture/200109/t2001091717180846110.htm (accessed June 6, 2002).

23. "Korean 'Titanic' Amazes Moscow and Hong Kong Audience; To Be Exported to West," *People's Korea*, July 25, 2001, http://www.korea-np.co.jp/pk/165th_issue/2001072515.htm (accessed June 6, 2002).

24. Ibid.

25. Paintings by former comfort women and Japanese women artists bear witness to that which is omitted from historical documents. Their images show a world in which the story of the *Ukishima Maru* is not only likely to be accurate but also unremarkable, particularly when the drowned bodies were those of comfort women. See *positions: east asia cultures critique* 5, no. 1 (1997) for reproductions of Tomiyama Taeko's *Memory of the Sea*, which depicts a shaman's encounter with a sunken navy ship and its human remains on the ocean floor while performing a ritual to recover the souls of lost comfort women who had disappeared during their crossings of the Pacific, as well as Kang Tŏk-kyŏng's *Drowned Woman*, which "commemorates numberless comfort women whom the Japanese military drowned in order to eliminate the evidence of atrocity" (276).

26. Johnston, "Machinic Vision," 46.

27. Slavoj Žižek, "'I Hear You with My Eyes,' or The Invisible Master," in *Gaze and Voice as Love Objects*, ed. Renate Salecl and Slavoj Žižek (Durham, N.C.: Duke University Press, 1996), 93.

28. Jill Bennett, *Empathic Vision: Affect, Trauma, and Contemporary Art* (Stanford, Calif.: Stanford University Press, 2005), 68.

29. Ibid.

30. In this chapter, all quotes unshaded and set in this type are from Theresa Hak Kyung Cha, *Dictée* (New York: Tanam, 1982).

31. Leudar and Thomas, *Voices of Reason, Voices of Insanity,* 6.

32. As told by Alexandra Seung Hye Suh in "Military Prostitution in Asia and the United States," in *States of Confinement: Policing, Detention, and Prisons,* ed. Joy James (New York: Palgrave, 2000).

33. Ibid., 157.

34. See Chungmoo Choi's introduction to *the comfort women: colonialism, war, and sex,* special issue, *positions: east asia cultures critique* 5, no. 1 (1997), for a discussion of the psychological effects of forced sexual labor on surviving comfort women.

35. Kyung Hyun Kim, "Post-Trauma and Historical Remembrance in Recent South Korean Cinema: Reading Park Kwang-su's *A Single Spark* (1995) and Chang Son-u's *A Petal* (1996)," *Cinema Journal* 41, no. 4 (2002): 109. In the various accounts of the Gwangju uprising or massacre, an incident that is sometimes called "Korea's Tiananmen Square," the numbers of protesters killed by the Korean military police range from two hundred to two thousand. The contested historiography that Kim refers to encompasses both the discrepancies in the body count and the varying interpretations of the extent of U.S. involvement in the massacre. Many believe that the Korean authorities fired under direct orders from the U.S. military, while the most lenient interpretation points out that the South Korean military, because of its subordinate status to the United States, cannot mobilize its forces to the extent that it did in Gwangju without prior authorization from the United States.

36. Kim, "Post-Trauma and Historical Remembrance," 109.

37. Žižek, "I Hear You with My Eyes," 92.

38. Abraham and Torok, *The Shell and the Kernel,* 1: 173.

39. Alisa Lebow, "Memory Once Removed: Indirect Memory and Transitive Autobiography in Chantal Akerman's *D'Est,*" *Camera Obscura* 52, no. 18 (2003): 37.

40. Leudar and Thomas, *Voices of Reason, Voices of Insanity,* 2.

41. Abraham and Torok, *The Shell and the Kernel,* 1: 166.

42. Ibid., 175.

43. See Howard, *True Stories of the Korean Comfort Women,* for testimonies of former comfort women in which the women describe nonverbal communication systems they had developed in order to secretly communicate with one another.

44. Žižek, "I Hear You with My Eyes," 93 (my emphasis).

45. Leudar and Thomas, *Voices of Reason, Voices of Insanity,* 82.

46. Bennett, *Empathic Vision,* 69.

47. Ibid.

48. Abraham and Torok, *The Shell and the Kernel,* 1: 179.

49. For an interesting discussion of the making of the captive subject, see Hortense Spillers, "Mama's Baby, Papa's Maybe: An American Grammar Book,"

Diacritics 17 (Summer 1987): 65–81. For Spillers, the image of a sailing ship packed with slaves suggests a suspension in the "oceanic," a feeling reminiscent of a preoedipal state in which the baby does not sense its separation from the mother, the breast, and the milk. This oneness of the infant with its surroundings, followed by the development of an individuated identity, is assumed to be universal in a Freudian narrative of oedipalization. Spillers, however, looks at the paradoxical situation in which enslaved Africans were subjected to the oedipal fiction as a tool of normalization even in the absence of the conditions for making that normalization possible. Slavery separated children from their mothers, obscured bloodlines so that one's parentage was always in question, and therefore laid the ground for nonoedipal psychobiographies, perhaps ones that Western psychology would call fractured. Furthermore, in the context of the slave vessel, the oceanic feeling associated with a oneness with the universe or mother is displaced by an oceanic of "undifferentiated identity removed from indigenous land and culture." These captives were "culturally unmade" beings whose destinies were "exposed . . . to an unknown course" (72). Unlike the slave vessel in Spillers' text, however, the *Ukishima Maru* was not transporting slaves to an unknown land, but rather returning them to a home that was once known but existed only fantasmatically for the returnees.

50. Abraham and Torok, *The Shell and the Kernel,* 1: 176.

51. Brian Massumi, *Parables for the Virtual: Movement, Affect, Sensation* (Durham, N.C.: Duke University Press, 2002).

52. Abraham and Torok, *The Shell and the Kernel,* 1: 176.

53. Ibid., 176.

54. Sigmund Freud, *Beyond the Pleasure Principle,* quoted in Cathy Caruth, *Unclaimed Experience: Trauma, Narrative, and History* (Baltimore, Md.: Johns Hopkins University Press, 1996), 2.

55. Caruth, *Unclaimed Experience,* 3.

56. Ibid., 8.

57. Leudar and Thomas, *Voices of Reason, Voices of Insanity,* 209 (emphasis in the original).

58. Žižek, "I Hear You with My Eyes," 91.

59. Johnston, *Information Multiplicity,* 224.

60. Ibid., 230.

61. Daniel Paul Schreber, *Memoirs of My Nervous Illness* (London: W. Dawson, 1955; repr. New York: New York Review of Books, 2000).

62. Yi Yŏngsu, "Return My Youth to Me," in *True Stories of the Korean Comfort Women,* ed. Keith Howard (London: Cassell, 1995), 91.

63. Cho'e Myŏngsun, "Silent Suffering," in True Stories of the Korean Comfort Women, ed. Keith Howard (London: Cassell, 1995), 173.

64. Yi Yŏngsuk, "I Will No Longer Harbour Resentment," in True Stories of the Korean Comfort Women, ed. Keith Howard (London: Cassell, 1995), 54.

65. Yi Okpun, "Taken Away at Twelve," in *True Stories of the Korean Comfort Women,* ed. Keith Howard (London: Cassell, 1995), 101.

66. Yi Sangok, "I Came Home, but Lost My Family," in *True Stories of the Korean Comfort Women,* ed. Keith Howard (London: Cassell, 1995), 133.

67. Yi Okpun, "Taken Away at Twelve," 101.

68. Yi Sunok, "It Makes Me Sad That I Can't Have Children," in *True Stories of the Korean Comfort Women,* ed. Keith Howard (London: Cassell, 1995), 120.

69. Heinz Insu Fenkl, *Memories of My Ghost Brother* (New York: Dutton, 1996), 35.

70. Leudar and Thomas, *Voices of Reason, Voices of Insanity,* 89.

71. Kim T'aeson, "Death and Life Crises," in *True Stories of the Korean Comfort Women,* ed. Keith Howard (London: Cassell, 1995), 157.

72. Yi Sunok, "It Makes Me Sad That I Can't Have Children," 120.

73. Yi Okpun, "Taken Away at Twelve," 101.

74. Leudar and Thomas, *Voices of Reason, Voices of Insanity,* 89.

75. Ibid., 77.

76. *Mangnei* is a colloquial Korean expression referring to the youngest child in a family.

77. This section renders into text the audio component of a performance piece in which the audience hears a number of overlapping voices. The voices include recordings of my voice reading the texts of Rea Tajiri (in roman type) and Theresa Hak Kyung Cha (in italics). My own words are in brackets.

78. Chul-In Yoo, "Life Histories of Two Korean Women Who Married American GIs," Ph.D. diss., University of Illinois at Urbana-Champaign, 1993, 9.

79. Ibid., 10.

80. Ibid., 12.

81. Žižek, "I Hear You with My Eyes," 103.

82. Jacques Derrida, *Specters of Marx: The State of the Debt, the Work of Mourning, and the New International,* trans. Peggy Karnuf (New York: Routledge, 1994), 9 (emphasis in the original).

83. Johnston, *Information Multiplicity,* 230.

84. Brian Massumi, *A User's Guide to Capitalism and Schizophrenia: Deviations from Deleuze and Guattari* (Cambridge, Mass.: MIT Press, 1992), 8.

85. Petar Ramadanovic, "When 'To Die in Freedom' Is Written in English," *Diacritics* 28, no. 4 (1998): 54–67, quote on 62.

86. Derrida, *Specters of Marx,* 47.

87. Avery Gordon, *Ghostly Matters: Haunting and the Sociological Imagination* (Minneapolis: University of Minnesota Press, 1997), 22.

88. Leudar and Thomas, *Voices of Reason, Voices of Insanity,* 53 (emphasis in the original).

89. Bennett, *Empathic Vision,* 50.

90. Shoshana Felman and Dori Laub, *Testimony: Crises of Witnessing in Literature, Psychoanalysis and History* (New York: Routledge, 1992), 64. For another discussion of the paradox of seeing the black hole, see Jacqueline Rose's work on Melanie Klein. Klein uses the metaphor of the black hole in space as that which tests the limits of human knowledge. If one is too far away, the black hole cannot

be observed because it appears to not be there. Getting too close, on the other hand, runs the risk of destroying the observer. The challenge, then, is that in order to meet another's trauma, one must come as close as possible without getting too close, without getting sucked in. Rose, *Why War? Psychoanalysis, Politics, and the Return of Melanie Klein* (Cambridge, Mass.: Blackwell, 1993).

91. Bennett, *Empathic Vision,* 50.

92. Jacqueline Rose, *States of Fantasy* (Oxford: Oxford University Press, 1996), 31.

93. Ramadanovic, "When 'To Die in Freedom' Is Written in English," 63.

94. Ibid., 58.

Index

Grace M. Cho is assistant professor of sociology, anthropology, and women's studies at the City University of New York, College of Staten Island. She is a contributing performance artist for the art collective *Still Present Pasts: Korean Americans and the Forgotten War.*